IMAGINING LAND

Anthropological Studies of Creativity and Perception

Series Editor: Tim Ingold, University of Aberdeen, UK

The books in this series explore the relations, in human social and cultural life, between perception, creativity and skill. Their common aim is to move beyond established approaches in anthropology and material culture studies that treat the inhabited world as a repository of complete objects, already present and available for analysis. Instead these works focus on the creative processes that continually bring these objects into being, along with the persons in whose lives they are entangled.

All creative activities entail movement or gesture, and the books in this series are particularly concerned to understand the relations between these creative movements and the inscriptions they yield. Likewise in considering the histories of artefacts, these studies foreground the skills of their makers-cum-users, and the transformations that ensue, rather than tracking their incorporation as finished objects within networks of interpersonal relations.

The books in this series will be interdisciplinary in orientation, their concern being always with the practice of interdisciplinarity: on ways of doing anthropology *with* other disciplines, rather than doing an anthropology *of* these subjects. Through this anthropology *with*, they aim to achieve an understanding that is at once holistic and processual, dedicated not so much to the achievement of a final synthesis as to opening up lines of inquiry.

Other titles in the series:

Redrawing Anthropology
Materials, Movements, Lines
Edited by Tim Ingold

Conversations With Landscape
Edited by Karl Benediktsson and Katrín Anna Lund

Ways of Walking
Ethnography and Practice on Foot
Edited by Tim Ingold and Jo Lee Vergunst

Imagining Landscapes
Past, Present and Future

Edited by

MONICA JANOWSKI
University of London, UK

TIM INGOLD
University of Aberdeen, UK

LONDON AND NEW YORK

First published 2012 by Ashgate Publishing

Published 2016 by Routledge
2 Park Square, Milton Park, Abingdon, Oxfordshire OX14 4RN
711 Third Avenue, New York, NY 10017, USA

First issued in paperback 2016

Routledge is an imprint of the Taylor & Francis Group, an informa business

British Library Cataloguing in Publication Data
Imagining landscapes : past, present and future. --
  (Anthropological studies of creativity and perception)
  1. Geographical perception. 2. Environmental psychology.
  3. Human ecology.
  I. Series II. Janowski, Monica. III. Ingold, Tim, 1948-
  304.2-dc23

Library of Congress Cataloging-in-Publication Data
Imagining landscapes : past, present and future / by Monica Janowski and Tim Ingold,
[editors].
    p. cm.
  Includes bibliographical references and index.
  ISBN 978-1-4094-2971-5 (hardback) -- ISBN 978-1-4094-2972-2 (ebook)
1. Landscape assessment. 2. Landscape changes. 3. Geographical perception.
I. Janowski, Monica. II. Ingold, Tim, 1948-
  GF90.I56 2012
  712--dc23

2012019359

ISBN 13: 978-1-138-24477-1 (pbk)
ISBN 13: 978-1-4094-2971-5 (hbk)

Contents

List of Figures   *vii*
List of Tables   *ix*
Notes on Contributors   *xi*
Preface and Acknowledgements   *xiii*

1   Introduction   1
    Tim Ingold

2   Seeing Ruins: Imagined and Visible Landscapes
    in North-East Scotland   19
    Jo Vergunst

3   Scottish Blackhouses: Archaeological Imaginings   39
    Tessa Poller

4   OrkneyLab: An Archipelago Experiment in Futures   59
    Laura Watts

5   Imagining Aridity: Human–Environment Interactions
    in the Acacus Mountains, South-West Libya   77
    Stefano Biagetti and Jasper Morgan Chalcraft

6   Meaningful Resources and Resource-full Meanings:
    Spatial and Political Imaginaries in Southern Belize   97
    Sophie Haines

7   Imagining and Consuming the Coast: Anthropology, Archaeology,
    'Heritage' and 'Conservation' on the Gower in South Wales   121
    Kaori O'Connor

8   Imagining the Forces of Life and the Cosmos
    in the Kelabit Highlands, Sarawak   143
    Monica Janowski

Index   *165*

List of Figures

2.1 Bennachie in Aberdeenshire, north-east Scotland 22
2.2 An area in the forest to be surveyed 25
2.3 Drawing together 26
2.4 'Middle Square' – one of the drawings photographed
    at the end of a day's work 27
2.5 A detail from the finished result 30
2.6 A new path being made up the hill 34

3.1 Reconstruction of No. 42 Arnol blackhouse in 2004 43
3.2 The dark interior of No. 42 Arnol blackhouse 44
3.3 Collage of images of people and places from
    the NALS survey report 46
3.4 NALS surveyor with dGPS enroute between sites in
    the townships of Ness 48
3.5 An example of a modified and reused house
    and outbuilding in Ness 49
3.6 The remains of another blackhouse in Ness that
    has a complex history of adaptation and change 50

4.1 Ferry MV Hamnavoe and the town of Stromness, Orkney 62
4.2 Ring of Brodgar stone circle, Orkney 64
4.3 Anaerobic digester built by Heat & Power Limited,
    Westray, Orkney 70

5.1 The area licensed to The Italian Libyan Archaeological Mission
    in the Acacus and Messak (central Sahara) 78
5.2 The Tadrart Acacus 79
5.3 Wadi Teshuinat and the Kel Tadrart campsite TES_07/1 83
5.4 The Kel Tadrart campsites, the gueltas, and the wells placed
    upon the geomorphological map by Marcolongo (1987) 87

6.1 Structure at the site of Lubaantun 102
6.2 Walking in the *milpa* 106
6.3 Village view showing thatch, zinc, timber and
    cement building materials 111

7.1   Eloquent food: Laver from the Gower Peninsula in
      Welsh language packaging which reads 'Cooked seaweed.
      Fresh, pure and ready to eat'   128
7.2   Persistent people and persistent places: Ashley Jones,
      member of a family associated with Welsh seafood for
      generations, picking seaweed in the Burry Estuary, Gower   131
7.3   Gorse and golden sands: Three Cliffs Bay, Gower Peninsula   134

8.1   The longhouse community of Pa' Dalih, with, in the distance,
      a mountain ridge said to be a longhouse turned to stone
      (*ruma batu*)   144
8.2   The twin stone peaks of Batu Lawi mountain,
      said to be male and female   149
8.3   Melkey, Roger and Lian of Pa' Dalih at the megalithic cemetery
      at Long Diit   150
8.4   Baye Ribuh of Pa' Dalih by the giant 'sharpening stone' of
      the culture hero Tukad Rini   151
8.5   A 'footprint' said to have been made by the culture hero
      Tukad Rini on a stone in the Kelapang river   152
8.6   A collection of hard objects from the forest collected by
      Telona Bala of Pa' Dalih   153
8.7   A 'thunderstone' (*batu pera'it*), once kept in a rice barn
      in Pa' Dalih   153
8.8   A carved stone (*batu narit*) near the abandoned Kelabit
      settlement of Pa' Bengar, said to have been made at an
      irau feast in the past   155

List of Tables

5.1	The Kel Tadrart campsites and their inhabitants	85
5.2	Distance between the Kel Tadrart campsites and the well in the Acacus Mountains	88
5.3	Mobility	89

Notes on Contributors

Stefano Biagetti is Research Fellow at the Dipartimento di Scienze dell'Antichità, Sapienza Università di Roma. His interests include ethnoarchaeology, pastoralism, and arid lands archaeology. His research focuses on the development of human–environment interactions in the central Sahara throughout the last 10,000 years. Currently, he is involved in the ethnoarchaeological and historical study of pastoralism in South-West Libya.

Jasper Morgan Chalcraft is Research Fellow in the Department of Sociology at the University of Sussex, UK. His research interests and publications focus on the ethnography of World Heritage rock art sites in the Sahara, Tanzania and Italy, as well as covering cultural cosmopolitanism, festivals, heritage discourse and memory institutions.

Sophie Haines received the 2010 Firth Award from the Royal Anthropological Institute/Association of Social Anthropologists for her doctoral research, which involved fieldwork in southern Belize and was funded by the Economic and Social Research Council and Firth Centenary Fund. Her research interests include the anthropology of environmental change, infrastructure development, borders and political processes. She is currently working as a parliamentary researcher.

Tim Ingold is Professor of Social Anthropology at the University of Aberdeen. He has carried out ethnographic fieldwork in Lapland, and has written on environment, technology and social organisation in the circumpolar North, on evolutionary theory in anthropology, biology and history, on the role of animals in human society, on language and tool use, and on environmental perception and skilled practice. He is currently exploring issues on the interface between anthropology, archaeology, art and architecture. His latest book, *Being Alive*, was published by Routledge in 2011.

Monica Janowski is Research Associate and Senior Teaching Fellow at the School of Oriental and African Studies, University of London. Her research interests include South-East Asian cosmologies, human–environment relations and food. She has co-produced nine radio series with the BBC, has made museum collections for the British Museum and Sarawak Museum and has developed online and computer-based materials. Her monograph *The Forest, Source of Life: The Kelabit of Sarawak* was published by the British Museum in 2003. In 2011 she co-edited *Why Cultivate? Anthropological and Archaeological Approaches to*

Foraging-Farming Transitions in SE Asia with Graeme Barker, published by the McDonald Institute.

Kaori O'Connor is Senior Research Fellow in the Department of Anthropology at University College London, where she specialises in new materials, material culture, marine resources and the anthropology of food. She won the Sophie Coe Prize for Food History 2009 for her study of the Hawaiian luau. Her book *The English Breakfast: The Cultural Biography of a National Meal* was published by Kegan Paul in 2007, her most recent book *Lycra: How a Fiber Shaped America* was published by Routledge in 2011 and she is currently working on a history of feasts and feasting.

Tessa Poller is an archaeologist with a PhD in the later prehistory of Scotland; however, her archaeological interests span many time periods. She has been involved in a wide range of projects throughout Scotland, focusing on both the distant and not-so-distant past. She currently works in the School of Humanities at the University of Glasgow as Research Support Officer for Archaeology.

Jo Vergunst is Lecturer in the Department of Anthropology at the University of Aberdeen. His research interests are in rural society and landscapes in Scotland and Europe, focusing particularly on environmental governance and outdoor access, and in creativity and environmental art. Amongst his publications are *Rural Transformations and Rural Policies in the UK and US*, co-edited with Mark Shucksmith, David Brown, Sally Shortall and Mildred Warner, *Comparing Rural Development*, co-edited with Arnar Árnason and Mark Shucksmith, and *Ways of Walking*, co-edited with Tim Ingold.

Laura Watts is an ethnographer and Assistant Professor at the IT University of Copenhagen. Her research is concerned with the effect of landscape and location on how futures are imagined and made; how different landscapes make different futures. She has worked with people and places in the Orkney Islands, the mobile telecoms industry, the renewable energy industry, and the public transport sector. She is co-editor of the prose and poetry collection *Orkney Futures: A Handbook* (published by Brae Editions). Much of her work is published on her website at <www.sand14.com>.

Preface and Acknowledgements

This collection originated in a panel convened by Tim Ingold and Monica Janowski at the ASA conference held at the University of Bristol in the UK between 13–16 April 2009, on the theme of *Archaeological and Anthropological Imaginings: Past, Present and Future*. The title of our panel was *Imagining Past and Present Landscapes*, and this is echoed in the title of the book. The papers presented there fitted well with the conference theme, including a focus on the future as well as on the past and the present.

In keeping with the interdisciplinary theme of the conference, the panellists included both anthropologists and archaeologists, and this book likewise brings together contributions from both disciplines. It is a combination that resonates for both of us in relation to our own work.

We would like to thank all the participants in the panel. Besides those who have contributed to this book, they also included Chris Gosden, Marisa Lazzari and Christian Park.

We would also like to thank the Department of Archaeology and Anthropology at the University of Bristol, which hosted the conference, and in particular the organiser of the conference, David Shankland.

Tim Ingold and Monica Janowski
Aberdeen and London, May 2012

Chapter 1

Introduction

Tim Ingold

Perception and Imagination

In 1933, the Belgian surrealist artist, René Magritte, composed a painting which he entitled *La Condition humaine*. The painting depicts a window, curtained on either side, as seen from the inside of a room. In front of the window, and taking up about half of its area, is placed an easel upon which is mounted a completed painting. The painting (within the painting) is of a landscape including a tree, verdant hills, and a blue sky with scattered clouds. Through the remainder of the window aperture not obscured by the painting, one sees what appears to be a continuation of the same scene. The viewer is consequently led to believe that the painting represents, with canny realism, precisely what would be seen through the area of the window pane that it occludes, were it to be removed. The tree in the painting, for example, hides a tree that – if the painting were not standing in the way – could actually be seen through the window, and which would look exactly the same. Thus the tree is at once inside the room, in the painting, and outside it, in the actual landscape. Five years later, Magritte referred to this picture, in a lecture entitled 'Lifeline' (*La Ligne de vie*), presented at the Museum of Fine Art in Antwerp. Its purpose, he explained, was to reveal something fundamental about the way in which human beings see the world. 'We see it', he said, 'as being outside ourselves, even though it is only a mental representation of what we experience on the inside' (cited in Schama 1995: 12).

The human condition, in Magritte's hands, is that of a being who can know the world, recognise its forms and appreciate their beauty only through their having been cast as interior images from the material of sensory experience. We think we see an outside world with our eyes, but that – for Magritte – is an illusion. In fact we see an inner world with our mind's eye. Since what this mind's eye sees is a picture of the world, the world as seen and its pictorial representation are continuous with one another, and only the faintest rectangular outline of the canvas and the presence of the easel allow us to tell where one ends and the other begins. Percept and image are all but indistinguishable. Do we seek the real tree behind its painterly representation? It too, as it turns out, would be part of a picture – one that Magritte might have painted of the same room, had he first removed the easel, with its canvas, from its position before the window. And the tree in this second picture would be identical to that in the first. Right now I am writing at a table in front of a window, not unlike the one that Magritte depicts. Outside the window I see the lawn of my garden, bushes and trees, the outer walls and roofs of houses on the street next to ours, and a generally cloudy sky which is just beginning to clear after yesterday's rain. I do not think I am imagining these things – they truly exist for me. Yet if I were Magritte, I would have to admit that what I claim to see is really but a picture that my mind has painted for me.

All seeing, in this view, is imagining. To perceive a landscape is therefore to imagine it. This is the premise on which the historian Simon Schama bases his magnum opus, *Landscape and Memory*. 'Before it can ever be a repose for the senses', Schama contends, 'landscape is the work of the mind. Its scenery is built up as much from strata of memory as from layers of rock' (Schama 1995: 6–7). Literally, landscape means 'land shaped', and the unification of land and shape for Schama is one of physical substance and ideal form. The world as it exists beyond the pale of human sensibility is formless and inchoate, comprised of matter in the raw – layers of rock deposited though geological processes. It is our 'shaping perception', Schama asserts, that converts this raw material into the kind of vista that we recognise as a landscape (ibid.: 10). And it does so by imposing a design whose source lies in the sedimentations of memory, ratified by convention and transmitted in culture, upon the otherwise chaotic flux of bodily sensation. 'What lies beyond the windowpane of our apprehension', writes Schama, referring back to Magritte's depiction of the human condition, 'needs a design before we can properly discern its form, let alone derive pleasure from its perception. And it is culture, convention and cognition that makes that design; that invests a retinal impression with the quality we experience as beauty' (ibid.: 12).

For the psychologist of perception James Gibson, however, this conclusion could not be more wrong. It is simply fallacious, Gibson argues, to suppose that vision entails the mental enhancement of impressions stamped upon the surface of the retina. For the retina is not an eye: it may be in receipt of sensory stimuli, but it is not an organ of perception. The eye is a perceptual organ, or rather part of the dual organ comprised of our two eyes, set in a head that can turn, in a body that moves from place to place (Gibson 1979: 53). When we see, Gibson insists, this entire eyes-head-body system is at work. Thus visual perception is the achievement of the whole organism as it moves around in its environment; not that of a mind confined within the interiority of a body and bound to the interpretation of patterns projected onto the back of the retina. As we move around, the array of light reaching our eyes, reflected from surfaces in our surroundings, undergoes continuous modulation. Underlying these modulations, however, are parametric constants, or so-called 'invariants', that specify the properties and qualities of the things we encounter. To see these things is to extract their invariants from modulations of the optic array. Thus it is not the mind that gives shape to what we perceive. It does not shape the land, or its features. For these shapes are already there in the world, awaiting discovery by any creature (human or non-human) whose perceptual system is so attuned as to attend to them – or more precisely, to pick up the invariants by which they are specified.

It follows that the real word and the perceived world do not lie on opposite sides of an impermeable division between 'outside' and 'inside'. For Gibson the perceived world *is* the real world, as it is given in relation to a being with certain capabilities of action and perceptual attunements – or in short, as an *environment*. In this perceived reality, however, there is no place for the imagination. Perceiving and imagining, far from being more or less the same, are poles apart. Gibson (1979: 256–8) proposes a series of tests that enable us to distinguish the reality of the perceived world from its imagistic representation. They boil down to the point that no more can be gleaned from an image than what has already been put there in making it. Suppose that you have before you, either on canvas or in your mind's eye, an image of a tree, painted with the exquisite realism of a Magritte. Taking a magnifying glass to the leaves will not reveal the intricacies of their veins, nor will microscopic examination reveal their cellular structure. But with a real tree, there is always more to be discovered. The key test, in Gibson's words, 'is whether you can discover new features and details by the act of scrutiny' (1979: 257). The real world is inexhaustible; the image contains only such information as the mind has already contributed to it. No amount of scrutiny will reveal what is not there. True, one might find in an image meanings of which one had not at first been aware, but this is to add to it by way of interpretation, not to discover more of what there is. Perceiving is to imagining, then, as discovery to interpretation.

It seems, in short, that Gibson's ecological approach to perception has contrived to close the gap between the reality of the world and our perception of it, only by opening up a chasm between perception and imagination. But are we forced to choose between these alternatives? Must we side either with those who would attribute a decisive role to the imagination in giving shape to the landscapes of our perception, or with those for whom it plays no more than an ancillary or retrospective role, in the interpretation of landscapes already perceived? Our aim in this volume is to find a way beyond these alternatives: a way that would reunite perception and imagination while yet acknowledging the human condition, *contra* both Magritte and Schama, to be that of a being whose knowledge of the world, far from being shaped by the operations of mind upon the deliverances of the senses, grows from the very soil of an existential involvement *in* the sensible world. To achieve this aim, we will need to reconsider the significance of imagination: to think of it not just as a capacity to construct images, or as the power of mental representation, but more fundamentally as a way of living creatively in a world that is itself crescent, always in formation. To imagine, we suggest, is not so much to conjure up images of a reality 'out there', whether virtual or actual, true or false, as to participate from within, through perception and action, in the very becoming of things. What follows is an amplification of this suggestion.

Truth and Illusion

According to one commonly accepted meaning of the term, 'to imagine' means to conjure up, in the mind, or perhaps in words and images, things or happenings that are not actually present to the senses. One definition of *imagination*, gleaned from several in the *Oxford English Dictionary*, may serve as an example: 'that faculty of mind by which we conceive the absent as if it were present'. Thus the archaeologist or environmental historian might imagine how a landscape could have looked in the past, and a landscape architect or designer might imagine how it could look in the future. The novelist might imagine a landscape that could conceivably have existed but which is nevertheless of his own invention; the surrealist painter might imagine one that could not conceivably exist at all. We could, if we were so inclined, distinguish landscapes of memory, of design, of fiction and of fantasy. But we could, just as well, adduce all sorts of reasons why these distinctions cannot be watertight. What work of fiction, for example, is not informed by its author's memories and anticipations? And when have these memories and anticipations not been infused by – and in turn infused – our dreams and fantasies? It is not my intention to address these questions here. However a more general problem has to be tackled. How is it possible to square the ontological division between domains of reality and the imagination, with the division between absence and presence? Despite their radical differences, this is a problem that both the approaches introduced above have had to confront.

Let us consider first the view that in the shaping of landscape, the mind brings its own conceptions, culturally acquired and sedimented in memory, to the interpretation of retinal impressions. If what we believe we see 'out there' is, as Magritte would have it, but the projection of an internal image, then must we conclude that some images are imaginary and others real? Picture yourself in the room of Magritte's *La Condition humaine.* The painted landscape includes a tree. You want to know whether there really is a tree outside, beyond the window. So you remove the painting from the easel and take a look. No tree. Did the painter, then, just imagine it? Did he paint an imaginary reality, so as to produce an image of the imaginary? Or alternatively: the tree is indeed there. So did the painter paint a real reality, so as to produce an image of the real? An image of the imaginary is, of course, what is more commonly known as an *illusion*, and it comes as no surprise that among both historians of art and psychologists of vision who have adopted this approach to perception, the study of illusions and of what gives rise to them has become something of an obsession. The problem, in essence, is this: if we can have no direct access to the world – if it cannot reveal to us what is there and what is not – and if, to the contrary, we can know the world only by bringing our own mental representations, bequeathed by culture and convention, to bear on the evidence of the senses, then how can we possibly distinguish truth from illusion?

The answer is that we cannot. The most we can do is to regard perception as a kind of guesswork. 'There seems to be no sudden break between *perceiving* an object and *guessing* an object', writes visual psychologist Richard Gregory. 'If all perceiving of objects requires some guessing, we may think of sensory stimulation as providing *data* for *hypotheses* concerning the state of the external world' (Gregory 1973: 61–2, original emphases). Thus every perception is a hypothesis, or a conjecture about what might be there. Illusions, then, are failed hypotheses (ibid.: 74). But we can never know, a priori, whether a perception is illusory or not. A hypothesis thought to be false may, on further testing against the data of experience, turn out to be true, and vice versa. For Gregory, the creative power of the human imagination lies precisely in its capacity to come up with hunches, conjectures, even visions of other worlds, which deviate from accepted truth. Though most will fail the test of experience, some may not, and in an ever changing world it is the latter that open the way to invention and discovery (ibid.: 94). In this, Gregory appeals to the model of progress in the history of science originally proposed by the philosopher Karl Popper (1950). Scientific knowledge, Popper had argued, advances through a perpetual process of conjecture and refutation. But an identical case can be made for the history of art, as Ernst Gombrich showed in his celebrated work on *Art and Illusion.* As science proceeds by hypothesis, test and revision, so in art, according to Gombrich, there is an endless process of 'making, matching and remaking' (Gombrich 1960: 272). At any moment in this process, however, the artist can only paint (project onto canvas) what is in his mind, not copy what is in the world. So too, according to Gregory, it is on the basis of our conjectures of the world, not of the data of experience, that we act (Gregory 1973: 89). The direction of formal projection is univocally from mind to world, not from world to mind.

Turning now to the alternative, ecological approach to perception, the problem of presence and absence appears in quite another guise. It is no longer a question of separating truth from illusion. Most people, most of the time, are not fooled by what they see, precisely because what they see is *not* a picture of the world. Take yourself back for a moment to the room of Magritte's painting. Would you really be tricked into confusing the painting on the easel with the view through the window? Of course not, for one simple reason that Gibson is at pains to stress. The painting on the easel is two things at once: it is a representation of a scene, and it is an artefact with a textured surface and edges. 'A picture', as Gibson explains, 'is always a treated surface, and it is always seen in a context of other, non-pictorial surfaces' (Gibson 1979: 281). In this sense, the picture has just the same artefactual status as (say) the curtains flanking the windowpane. The treated canvas of the painting is just as real – just as present – as the woven fabric of the curtains, and indeed as the bark or foliage of the tree you see outside. All may be subjected to the same test for reality: they can be inexhaustibly scrutinised by the moving observer. That is why the conceit of the *trompe l'oeil* painters, to have fooled us into mistaking their depictions for reality, rings hollow (Gombrich 1960: 172–3, Gibson 1979: 281). The eye of the observer is fooled only if artificial constraints are placed on the viewing situation that prevent him from being able to pick up the invariants that specify what he is looking at. Such constraints, often built into the design of experiments on vision informed by retinal image optics, have no counterpart in the world outside the laboratory.

But if we can access, by direct perception, what is really there, what are we to make of our awareness of things that do not currently exist, or that cannot be discovered through the processes of information pickup that Gibson describes? This awareness, as Gibson acknowledges, can take many forms, including reminiscence, expectation, imagination, fantasy, and dreaming. Yet he is convinced that they have no essential role to play in perception itself: rather, 'they are kinds of visual awareness other than perceptual' (1979: 254–5). How, then, are we to account for these kinds of 'non-perceptual awareness'? How is it possible, for example, to imagine a landscape other than that in which we find ourselves? Gibson's answer is tentative and far from clear. Of one thing, however, he is certain, namely that imagining cannot be understood as an operation of the mind, nor should it be supposed to result in the production of mental imagery. Perceiving and imagining may be quite different, but they have in common that they do not begin with a stimulus input and end with an image. Rather, they *carry on*. Starting from this premise, Gibson's best guess is that imagining is the activity of a perceptual system, but one that is temporarily relieved of its routine business of information pickup. It is what happens when a system already attuned to the extraction of particular invariants from the stimulus flux is disengaged from that flux and enters what we might call a 'free-wheeling' or auto-generative mode. In this sense, imagination is as much an achievement of the whole organism in its environment as is perception. It is, in Gibson's words, 'an activity of the system, not an appearance in the theatre of consciousness' (ibid.: 256). But it is an activity of a system decoupled from its usual engagement with the world, and that has, as it were, turned in upon itself.

Past, Present and Future

What do our contributors have to say about this? Jo Vergunst (Chapter 2) has joined with a local community group in excavating and surveying a cluster of cottages – a former crofting settlement – long ago deserted and now ruined, at the foot of the hill of Bennachie in north-east Scotland. In the on-site gestures of digging, shovelling and trowelling, as well as in the manual gestures of drawing which trace on paper the lines of stone walls as they are unearthed, measured and recorded, Vergunst finds himself reliving a visceral engagement with the landscape that brings into the vivid present the past lives of the original inhabitants. These were real people, who were once at home in the buildings over and around which he and his fellow excavators now clamber in unearthing the stones. 'We draw out their presence', he writes, 'not as guests in our work, but as hosts in their own houses'. In what remains of the wall of one cottage, a gap indicates where there had once been a doorway. It is easy to cross from one side of the wall to the other simply by straddling the stones. Alternatively, you can pass through the gap. But this latter move, Vergunst finds, yields a quite different experience, namely one of 'entry'. Hunching your shoulders and bending your head a little as you pass, as if through a low and narrow door, you find yourself 'inside'. Although the present ruin is open to the elements, the very movement of entry yields a sense of the house as the interior space that it once was for its erstwhile inhabitants. The point is that a home exists for those who live there not as a plan or elevation, or as a three-dimensional structure, but as an ensemble of familiar movements and gestures. While the people are long gone, and the structure is a ruin, the re-enactment of these movements can, at least to some degree, bring the dwelling back to life.

To enter *as if* through a doorway; to stand and look around *as if* in the interior of a dwelling: these are surely acts of imagination. This is not to say, however, that they are purely cognitive, 'inside the head' operations, intended to reconstruct the image of a lost past – one that might then be projected onto paper as an 'artist's impression' of what it might have looked like indoors. Imagination is not the work of mind alone but of one's entire being. So far, this is not incompatible with Gibson's view of the matter. But Vergunst's account of his encounters with the landscape of Bennachie takes us one step further. For it is quite evident that in acts of imagination, the perceptual systems of the observer, far from being decoupled from immediate involvement with the environment, as Gibson would have us believe, are more closely engaged than ever. Perceiving, here, *is* imagining – not, however, because the percept is an image, but because the world that is perceived is continually brought forth in the very act of imagination. Gibson's mistake, it appears, was to assume that while perception is always going on, always casting about, the world as perceived is pre-cast in fixed and final forms, as a structure of invariants. But what if the world, too, carries on? What if it is always in the casting?

We could take our cue here from the celebrated *Creative Credo* of the artist Paul Klee. 'Art', Klee declared, 'does not reproduce the visible but makes visible' (Klee 1961: 76). Thus the painter does not project onto canvas forms that already exist as representations inside his head, but rather brings these forms into existence – or 'grows' them, as the gardener might grow a plant from its seed – in his very activity of mark-making, so that they are there to be seen. This is exactly how Vergunst describes the process of archaeological drawing, as a *drawing-out*, a way of making visible rather than reproducing the visible. Perception is imaginative, then, in so far as it is generative of a world that is continually coming into being with and around the perceiver, in and through his or her own practices of movement, gesture and inscription.

In another example, archaeologist Tessa Poller (Chapter 3) is recording the remains of traditional 'blackhouses' on the Hebridean island of Lewis. During the early decades of the twentieth century, these buildings were progressively abandoned in favour of the more comfortable and well-appointed 'whitehouses' of today. Only a few blackhouses still stand intact, now preserved as museums. Yet the remains of the original dwellings are everywhere, often incorporated into newer structures, or put to use as barns or for storage, or simply visible as grass-covered humps in the ground. Poller describes how on one occasion, as she was in the backyard of a croft trying to locate the traces of a blackhouse that was marked on an old map, the present owner – in the midst of hanging out her laundry on the line – tapped her foot on the ground beneath the line. That, she said, was where the house of her grandfather was.

In this little encounter, and by contrast to the case described by Vergunst, the interests and perspectives of local residents and of archaeological researchers, far from harmonising with one another, come across as discordant. For residents, the remains of the ancestral past are fully integrated into the quotidian landscape of the present. They are simply *there*, part of a taken-for-granted backdrop for mundane activity. In such a commonplace, domestic task as hanging out the laundry, life goes on upon the foundations that grandfather laid. But one does not have to imagine grandfather's house as it was then, when he was alive, rather than as it is now, in order to keep the household going. What matters is its continuation. For residents, the past of grandfather's day figured as a bygone era, and while they were quite happy to talk and tell stories about it, they had no particular interest in bringing it back to life through constructive re-enactment. Nostalgia, or romantic yearnings for a lost past, is for outsiders, or perhaps for the returning grandchildren of emigrants.

As an archaeologist, however, Poller found that her relationship with the landscape was of a very different kind. She calls it a *materialising* relationship, one that was performed in her activities of observing, moving around, recording and measuring the remains of old buildings. But this relationship, too, differs from the kind of relationship that Vergunst describes from his Bennachie fieldwork. It accords, perhaps, more strictly with the professional conventions of archaeological science. What matters in this relationship are not the activities themselves but the representations they yield – drawings, photographs, images on computer screens – which can then be classified and compared. The significance of the tasks of observing, measuring and recording is not that they re-enact an engagement with the environment as intimate and intensive as that of its erstwhile inhabitants, but that they yield the data from which to construct a picture of the 'material culture' of past times. In relation to this material culture, the people – to return to Vergunst's metaphor – are not hosts but guests: witnesses to a past that has been converted for their benefit into an educational resource.

We may distinguish, then, at least three ways of imagining the past in the landscape. There is the *materialising* mode, which turns the past into an object of memory, to be displayed and consumed as heritage; there is the *gestural* mode, in which memories are forged in the very process of redrawing the lines and pathways of ancestral activity, and there is the *quotidian* mode in which what remains of the past provides a basis for carrying on. Each, moreover, entails a different sense of the present. In the present of the materialising mode, the past appears as another culture: a 'foreign country', in the celebrated opening words of L.P. Hartley's novel *The Go-Between*, where they do things differently (Lowenthal 1985, see Hartley 1953). The gestural present is a generative movement that remembers the past even as it presses forward, since to go forth along a line of life is simultaneously to retrace the paths of predecessors (Ingold 2000: 148). In the quotidian mode, by contrast, the very immediacy of the present eclipses the past as the latter sinks into the inconspicuous and unremarked ground of the everyday. What, then, of the future? Are there as many ways of imagining the future in the landscape?

In Chapter 4, Laura Watts addresses this question through a vivid account of the arrival of an unusual visitor to the Orkney Islands, an archipelago located just to the north of the Scottish mainland. The visitor, Alec, is a venture capitalist from California's Silicon Valley. He has come to assess the prospects for large-scale investment in Orkney's burgeoning renewable energy sector. In the course of a single day, and guided around the islands by Watts, he visits an ancient stone circle (the world-famous Ring of Brodgar), observes a marine test site for tidal power, and visits a farm where cattle slurry is being converted by a novel chemical process into biogas fuel.

The Ring of Brodgar is carefully preserved as an ancient monument, as if those who made it imagined the future just as contemporary visitors to the site are enjoined to imagine the past, namely as a fixed and final form, the materialisation of a concept of awesome scope – no less than an entire cosmology – in the bedrock and stone of the physical world. The original architects of the Ring, according to a well-rehearsed narrative, thought big, and the fact that the structure still survives, many thousand years after its construction, is testimony to the power of their ideas. As a venture capitalist on the lookout for big ideas, which might be realised in equally monumental solutions, this narrative should have appealed to Alec. Indeed it did. Had he been around in prehistory he might well have backed the enterprise of the Ring-builders, as a solid investment for the future. But although much taken by the story that Orkney was a world-class centre of invention *then*, it held no guarantee for him that it was still so today.

By contrast to the Ring, in the tidal turbine Alec saw a future that was being imagined in the very process of testing it out, in the engagement of living metal with surging waters. This was a future brought forth and drawn out in the skilled practices – of observation, movement and gesture – of mariners, engineers, marine biologists, divers, ornithologists, and countless others. And in the anaerobic digester, turning slurry to fuel, he saw a future already underway as old pipes and rusty containers, junk from the previous generation of agricultural machinery, had been incorporated into a structure that would hopefully allow it – and other farms on the island – to carry on. In that one day, in short, our visitor was shown the future in its materialising mode (embodied in the stone circle), in its gestural mode (embodied in the tidal turbine) and in its quotidian mode (embodied in the anaerobic digester). Yet at the end of the day, he remained unconvinced. His vision was of a future that could be exported around the globe. What he had seen, however, were possible futures whose very promise and potential resilience lay in the way they were grown from the soil of Orkney itself, and from its surrounding waters. These futures were not for export. As Watts observes, they remain tethered to the Orcadian landscape. They are not products of disembodied, intelligent design

– or of 'blue-skies' thinking, in a currently popular jargon – divorced from any engagement with the world. They rather emerge from laborious, environmentally emplaced activity. In a sense, it is not so much the people of Orkney who are imagining the landscape as the landscape of the islands that is imagining and re-imagining itself, by way of the ingenuity, resourcefulness and sheer hard work of its people.

Up Close and Distant

It has long been the conceit of planners and policy-makers, or of those entrusted with projects of 'development', to suppose that to imagine the future is to predict: that is, to conjecture a novel state of affairs, as yet unrealised, and to specify in advance the steps that need to be taken in order to get there. Governments and other agencies demand what they call scenarios: images of what the world will look like, say, 20, 50 or 100 years from now. What we have learned from the foregoing, however, is that the work of imagination lies not, as Gregory for example would have it, in 'continually inventing a fictional future' (Gregory 1973: 94), but rather in bringing forth a present that, following dance philosopher Erin Manning, is ever emergent as the future's past (Manning 2009: 69). To imagine a landscape is to live upon the cusp of this emergence. The imagination, we often say, 'roams', and in so doing, opens up paths in and through the world, rather than fixing end-points in advance. It consists not in the power of prediction but in the gift of prophecy or foresight. Seeking not to speculate *about* the future but to see *into* it, to exercise this gift is to run ahead of things, to improvise a passage, rather than to innovate with representations of the unprecedented (Ingold and Hallam 2007). It is to tell how things will go, in a world where everything is 'not preordained but incipient, forever on the verge of the actual' (Ingold 2011: 69). In this world, indeed, there are no objects to represent, only materials; no fixed and final forms, only potentials for things to grow and transform. To foresee, then, is to 'join forces' with materials in the anticipation of what might emerge. It is to bear witness, as the philosopher Maurice Merleau-Ponty put it, to how 'things become things, how the world becomes a world' (Merleau-Ponty 1964: 181).

An imagined landscape, then, is a landscape not of being but of becoming: a composition not of objects and surfaces but of movements and stillness, not there to be surveyed but cast in the current of time. It is, in this regard, closer to music than painting. The Estonian-born naturalist, Jakob von Uexküll, a pioneer in the study of the perceived worlds of animals and humans, compared the landscape of our imagination to polyphonic music (von Uexküll 1982[1940]: 62–3). Philosopher Gilles Deleuze and psychoanalyst Félix Guattari speak, in similar vein, of *melodic landscapes*. The melodic landscape, they explain, is not a landscape associated with a melody: it is not as though the melody stands for the landscape, like a placard or poster. Rather, 'the melody itself is a sonorous landscape'. It is landscape resounding. Consider the songbird, an inhabitant of this landscape. Does it sing simply to announce the boundaries of its territory, in a world already laid out? Or does it sing in counterpoint to the currents of life that flow around it? The latter, say Deleuze and Guattari, is the mark of the 'musician bird'. To describe the bird as a musician is to indulge not in anthropomorphism but in geomorphism (Deleuze and Guattari 2004: 351). It is to say that the bird, in its singing, resonates with the song of the earth.

And so it is, too, with the human. Picture a composer, at work on a symphony. The music flies ahead in his imagination like a bird on the wing. It is all he can do to catch it and get it down before it is lost beyond the horizon of his recollection. With so many staves, each for an instrument of the orchestra, it can take many hours of painstaking work to notate a passage that in performance would last barely a minute. Composing would be easy, were it not for music's propensity to outpace its material inscription. Nor is this a problem confined to musical composition. The performer, writes Merleau-Ponty, who feels that the music 'sings through him', finds that he 'must "dash his bow" to follow it' (Merleau-Ponty 1968: 151). The celebrated Portuguese architect, Alvaro Siza, compares the task of designing a building to tracking a character, or rather a host of characters, who are always slipping away from him. His predicament, he says, is not unlike that of the novelist, whose characters have a way of outrunning his capacity to write them down. It is vital not to lose them (Siza 1997: 51). Even painters are challenged to rein in their fleeting visions of an evanescent world before they escape. These visions – these imaginings – may excite and terrify in equal measure, or inspire joy or anguish. Yet even as they are felt as an urge or impetus that carries practitioners forwards as though on the crest of a wave, the heaviness of materials perpetually holds them back. It seems that composer, performer, architect, novelist and painter alike are ever caught between the anticipatory reach of the imagination and the tensile or frictional drag of material abrasion – whether of pen on paper, bow on strings, or brush on canvas.

The trick, then, is to be able to hold the imaginative foresight that pierces the distance like an arrow in check with the close-up, even myopic engagement that is necessary for working with materials. In a recent article, anthropologist Rane Willerslev has argued that one of the singular properties of vision, by which it is distinguished from other sensory modalities (including hearing and touch), is that it brings foresight and the close-up together, to the extent of making the former a *condition* for the latter. The inspiration for this move comes from Merleau-Ponty's claim that 'to see is *to have at a distance*' (Merleau-Ponty 1964: 166). With hearing and touch, if you come close to something, then the boundary between yourself and the thing begins to blur and eventually dissolves altogether. You merge with it. In vision, by contrast, if you are too close to something, you cannot see it. To see, at least with binocular vision, you must take a certain distance. And in this distanciation lies the possibility for a kind of reflexive self-awareness. You do not just see, but see yourself seeing. It is this self-awareness, then, that makes it possible to come close to another thing or being, and hence to engage with it materially, without actually merging with it. This is a prerequisite for hunting, for example. To succeed, the hunter must identify with his prey, but were he to merge with it the consequences would be fatal. Likewise the artist painting a landscape must immerse himself in the sensory environment, whilst remaining afar from it. And even in the practice of ethnography, the fieldworker who participates with all his being in an alien reality must all the while maintain his separate identity as a scholar. It is difficult to conceive, Willerslev concludes, how this could be pulled off without vision (Willerslev 2006: 41).

I have some reservations about this argument. For one thing, if vision is a condition for self-awareness, then this leaves us wondering how human beings with visual impairments can be aware of themselves – as they manifestly are – or why non-human animals (even those endowed with binocular vision) apparently are not. For another thing, anyone who has had to make their way in pitch darkness, relying on haptic and aural perception alone, knows that touch and hearing, too, can induce a sense of distance, just like vision. You may be startled by sounds, and recoil from what is touched. Be that as it may, the general point that a perception that is imaginative is one whose close-up engagements are guided by foresight is a powerful one. It has been said, as Deleuze and Guattari note (with reference to Cézanne), that painters cannot see what they are painting, since they are too close to it, and likewise that composers cannot hear – even that writers cannot remember what they are writing about (Deleuze and Guattari 2004: 544). But it would probably be closer to the mark to say that the particular skill of painters, composers and writers – and indeed of ethnographers – lies in their practised ability to keep their distance whilst in the thick of the labours of proximity. The parallel with hunting, as Willerslev (2006) intimates, is precise. Hunters often dream of animals before they encounter them. Artists, composers and writers, likewise, are bent upon capturing and reining in the insights of a fugitive imagination, always inclined to shoot off into the distance, before they can get away, and on bringing them back into the immediacy of material engagement. Like hunters, they too are dream-catchers.

Imagining in the Flesh

Perhaps we might also draw a parallel with the world of nomadic pastoralists, as Stefano Biagetti and Jasper Morgan Chalcraft suggest in Chapter 5. For generations, the Tel Adrart Tuareg have been husbanding their herds of mainly sheep and goats in a region of south-western Libya bordering on Algeria. It is an environment that, in the 'official' discourse of climate science, is deemed to be *arid*. This discourse is one of projection, in which model scenarios are built to be tested against data obtained by precise scientific measurement. For the Tuareg, however, climate is not a state of affairs but a many-stranded process. Like the inhabited landscape, it goes on. Remembered rather than measured, this process leaves its dispersed but emplaced marks in the remains of shelters, traces of rock art, deposits of dung and the filling and drying of rock pools, and is performed in on-going grazing strategies. This is not to say, however, that the Tuareg, living 'up close' to the land and responding continually to immediate variations in pasture quality and water supply, lack a more distanced view. On the contrary, theirs is as much an imagined landscape as the arid desert imagined by science. But their imagining is part and parcel of their on-going perceptual engagement with a highly dynamic environment. The art of pastoral herding lies precisely in being able to attend to these dynamics, to join with them, and to follow where they lead. Whereas in the concept of aridity, science postulates an absolute, external constraint on the possibilities of human social life and habitation, it is through the imaginative exercise of foresight that Tuareg herdsmen open up the paths that enable them to carry on. For them, and indeed for their animals, the landscape is imagined kinaesthetically in modalities of movement.

In Chapter 6, Sophie Haines describes the contestations over land use and indigenous entitlement which accompany processes of 'development' in rural Belize. One example of development was the construction of a road, through dense tropical forest, to the village of Mahogany Bank in the district of Toledo. In the language of development, which mirrors that of climate change in its commitment to predictive modelling and projected futures, road-building connects previously isolated villagers to the modern world, giving them access to objects and commodities not seen before. For the villagers themselves, however, the road literally opened up a visionary pathway – a way of bringing the world to light. It was seen as a potential source not just of material innovation but of revelatory insight. People wanted to move their homes near to the new route, according to one resident, 'because they say the light is coming'. Cutting through the forest canopy, the road let in the rays of the sun, bringing illumination. With roads, too, comes electricity, lighting the world even in hours of darkness. But development brought sound as well as light, as traditional timber-and-thatch houses began to be replaced by houses of cement blocks roofed with sheets of zinc. The drumming of heavy rain on the roofs can be so loud as to drown out any conversation. Thus for the villagers of Mahogany Bank, modernity was experienced up close not in the objective forms of roads and buildings but as an overwhelming experience of light and sound – that is, as an *atmosphere* (Böhme 1993, Ingold 2010: 247) – pervading the awareness of perceivers and underwriting (or undermining) their very capacities to see and to hear and, by the same token, to imagine.

I have already suggested that 'having at a distance' is not necessarily limited to vision, and that it could extend to tactile and auditory perception as well. But could it even extend to gustation? The monastic practices of medieval Europe show us that imagination need not be the activity of a mind cocooned in silence, locked in an inward-turning self-contemplation. Monastery libraries were abuzz with the sounds of reading as, murmuring the words of liturgical texts, resident monks would bring to life the 'voices of the pages' (*vocespaginarum*) and engage with them as though they were present and audible. Bodily performance and imaginative contemplation were, for them, as viscerally related as eating and digestion (Ingold 2007: 14–15). The digest of beautiful words would be released in song, just as –

according to explicit analogy – a stomach filled with rich food would find relief in a pungent belch or fart (Carruthers 1990: 166). The monks appreciated their food! So too, as Kaori O'Connor explains in Chapter 7, in the contemporary discourse of *terroir*, 'certain foods are believed to take on the unique physical qualities of the locality where they were grown, gathered or made, as well as the metaphysical essence of events, values, practices and forbears grounded in the ancestral "soil"'.

For medieval monks as for inhabitants of the 'heritage coast' of Gower in South Wales, who are the focus of O'Connor's account, we can see how the very process of digestion, in which consumed food merges with the living body, is also an imagining that both takes in and releases the body into the fullness of the world. As the monks imbibed their liturgical texts, so the people of the Gower Coast, in the consumption of cockles and edible laver seaweed, imbibe a reverence for the littoral environment which nourishes them both bodily and spiritually. 'The most important relationship between persons and landscape', as O'Connor writes, 'is not being in it, but having it be in you'. In a perception that is at once material and imaginative, at once up close and distant, the landscape (as we have already seen in the case of Orkney) imagines and re-imagines itself through the awareness of its perceivers. Thus 'coiling over' on itself, as Merleau-Ponty put it (1968: 140), landscape becomes flesh.

Imagining is Being Alive

I have shown in the foregoing sections that perception and imagination are one: not however because percepts are images, or hypothetical representations of a reality 'out there', but because to perceive, as to imagine, is to participate from within in the perpetual self-making of the world. It is to join with a world in which things do not so much *exist* as *occur*, each along its own trajectory of becoming. In the life of the imagination, the landscape is a bundle of such trajectories, forever ravelling here and unravelling there. One could, with geographer Doreen Massey, think of every trajectory as a story and of the totality of the landscape at any particular moment as the 'simultaneity of stories-so-far' (Massey 2005: 12). Human beings have their stories, of course, but so do animals, trees, mountains, mud and water, in so far as in their growth, movements and displacements they continually and mutually respond to each other's presence – or in a word, they *correspond*. Life, as I have argued elsewhere, is lived in correspondence (Ingold 2010: 243–4). To imagine the landscape, then, is to enter into correspondence with it, or as anthropologist Stuart McLean puts it, 'to respond creatively to the creativity of the world's ceaseless self-transformation' (McLean 2009: 231). This is to intuit an essential continuity, McLean argues, between 'human acts of imagining and fabulation' and 'the processes shaping and transforming the material universe' (ibid.: 232). Such intuition, which flows like an undercurrent though myth and folklore, art and literature, philosophy and science, presents a fundamental ontological challenge to any division we might attempt to force between the reality of the world and its representation.

This is a challenge, however, with which the people of the Kelabit Highlands of Sarawak, whose understandings of their rainforest landscape are described by Monica Janowski in Chapter 8, would be entirely comfortable. Central to these understandings is the idea of *lalud*, which Janowski renders as 'life'. For the Kelabit, as Janowski explains, the landscape is animated by the flow of *lalud*. It runs through everything. All things considered alive, from humans and other animals to stones and mountains, while immersed in the flow, nevertheless have their own distinct trajectories. Things are composed of materials, but these materials do not just contain *lalud*, they are *lalud*. This is as true for human beings as it is for everything else. Yet humans are not just carried along in the current. They rather participate creatively in taking it forward, not just by actively tracking the flow but by bending or diverting it to their own evolving purposes. As powerful makers, their role is not to impose form on matter but to impart direction: for example through the construction of earthworks or the straightening of meandering rivers. It is as though, by entering into the stream of life, of flowing material, one could deflect it to a certain degree, enough to set up eddies that eventually form and coalesce into things, such as stones and mountains, that have all the appearance of solidity. The older things are the more solid or stone-like they become, and the more *lalud* is condensed in them. Yet nothing lasts forever. Entities in the Kelabit landscape continually form and dissipate. They only 'feign immobility', as the philosopher Henri Bergson would have said, for in truth the permanence of their form is but the envelope of a movement (Bergson 1911: 135).

The example of the Kelabit focuses our attention on the relationship between the individual as a locus of imagining and the landscape – or rather, the cosmos – of which he or she is part. This is an issue that has already arisen in our discussion of how, for the people of the Orkney Islands, the land shapes itself by way of the entrepreneurial visions of its inhabitants. For the highlanders of Kelabit as for the islanders of Orkney, imagining is a way of creatively participating in the ongoing self-creation of the world. This is something to which, to some degree, every living being contributes. Each being's imaginative acts lend a certain direction to the whole living landscape to which it belongs. As a 'line of life' travelling through the world, every organism shapes the future both for itself and for the whole landscape, through imaginative processes that are carried on in correspondence with those of other organisms of the same or different species. But how much imagining should an individual engage in? For the Kelabit, sensitive as they are to the presence of other 'lines of life' in the landscape, the emphasis is on the expectation that an individual should not merely follow but strive to shape the flow of life around the landscape, moulding and moving other 'lines of life' while remaining respectful of their presence. This relatively active way of imagining the landscape is the basis, in Kelabit society, for respect and esteem. And so it is, too, in Orkney.

To appreciate the distance we have come, let me finally return to Magritte's characterisation of the human condition, as that of a being who can only know what is 'out there', on the far side of our eyes or beyond the skin, through an imaginative process of internal mental representation. Our review of the contributions to this volume leads us to conclude, to the contrary, that if imagination is the work of the mind, then it is a mind that far from remaining disengaged, wrapped up in its own auto-generative deliberations, mingles freely with the world along multiple lines of sensory participation. It is, as philosopher Andy Clark contends, a 'leaky organ' (Clark 1997: 53). Perhaps we could highlight the contrast between this latter understanding and the one from which we began by introducing the work of another artist, Richard Long. Long walks lines into the landscape, whether it be a grassy meadow, a wood, desert sands, a snowfield or a mountain plateau. He is, much like the Kelabit, a direction-maker. His lines tend to be straight, and they make their mark precisely because of the direction they impart. For Long, it is in this very casting forward – of his whole being in the world, on the ground, along a line of movement – that the work of art consists. It is not in this form, however, that his works are generally rendered accessible to others. Instead, what we (as his public) get to see are mainly photographs, conforming in every respect to the romantic ideal of the scenic panorama, each showing an already completed line stretching from the foreground into the middle distance. These photographs are assembled into sumptuously illustrated books (Fuchs 1986, Long 2002) which adorn the occasional tables of many a discerning, art-loving household, as an index of good taste. Such books, and countless others like them, are designed to appeal to an aesthetic sensibility that perceives beauty in finished forms, and not in the processes that give rise to them. They are, indeed, very attractive.

Yet paradoxically, the very medium of photographic representation, while it affirms the work of art in the sight of others, wipes out the artistic intention that motivated its original production. Is the point of the photographs, then, to release or slough off the burden of representational aesthetics so as to leave intact the artistic integrity of the real work, the walk itself? Can they be seen, as philosopher and critic Herman Rapaport suggests, as epitomising 'the very aesthetics that the walks have dropped by the side of the road'? (Rapaport 1997: 91). Are they the cast-offs of artistic production? It seems that the art's real purpose is both concealed and confirmed by way of its deliberate and exaggerated negation in the scenic picture-book. What it negates is the very premise upon which Schama builds his account of landscape and memory, according to which it is the mind, in its recollections of things past, that contributes design to the raw material of sensory experience, allowing us to discern forms and derive pleasure from their perception (Schama 1995: 10, 12). Perhaps, with Long, we can leave this view, along with the picture-book images it yields, at the roadside, as bait to feed the market in fine art. For in walking the line, Long shows us how the apprehension of landscape lies not in the unification of memory and rock, image and object, appearance and substance, or mind and matter, but in the never-ending, contrapuntal interweaving of material flows and sensory awareness. The walk of life advances in an alternating movement of casting forward and drawing up, of imagination and material practice. But these are movements of the entire being in its world, not alternately of cognition and locomotion. Perceiving the landscape is, in short, tantamount to imagining the landscape, in so far as we do not just to live *in* the world but are simultaneously alive *to* it.

References

Bergson, H. 1911. *Creative Evolution*, trans. A. Mitchell. London: Macmillan.

Böhme, G. 1993. Atmosphere as the Fundamental Concept of a New Aesthetics. *Thesis Eleven* 36, 113–26.

Carruthers, M. 1990. *The Book of Memory: A Study of Memory in Medieval Culture*. Cambridge: Cambridge University Press.

Clark, A. 1997. *Being There: Putting Brain, Body and the World Together Again*. Cambridge, MA: MIT Press.

Deleuze, G. and Guattari, F. 2004. *A Thousand Plateaus: Capitalism and Schizophrenia*, trans. B. Massumi. London: Continuum [originally published as *Mille Plateaux*, vol. 2 of *Capitalismeet Schizophrénie*, Paris: Minuit, 1980].

Fuchs, R.H. 1986. *Richard Long*. London: Methuen.

Gibson, J.J. 1979. *The Ecological Approach to Visual Perception*. Boston: Houghton Mifflin.

Gombrich, E.H. 1960. *Art and Illusion: A Study in the Psychology of Pictorial Representation*. London: Phaidon.

Gregory, R.L. 1973. The Confounded Eye, in *Illusion in Nature and Art*, edited by R.L. Gregory and E.H. Gombrich. New York: Scribners, 49–95.

Hartley, L.P. 1953. *The Go-Between*. London: Hamish Hamilton.

Ingold, T. 2000. *The Perception of the Environment: Essays on Livelihood, Dwelling and Skill*. London: Routledge.

Ingold, T. 2007. *Lines: A Brief History*. London: Routledge.

Ingold, T. 2010. Epilogue, in *Conversations with Landscape*, edited by K. Benediktsson and K.A. Lund. Farnham: Ashgate, 241–51.

Ingold, T. 2011. *Being Alive: Essays on Movement, Knowledge and Description*. London: Routledge.

Ingold, T. and Hallam, E. 2007. Creativity and Cultural Improvisation: An Introduction, in *Creativity and Cultural Improvisation*, edited by E. Hallam and T. Ingold. Oxford: Berg, 1–24.

Klee, P. 1961. *Notebooks, Volume 1: The Thinking Eye*, edited by J. Spiller, trans. R. Manheim. London: Lund Humphries.

Long, R. 2000. *Walking the Line*. London: Thames & Hudson.

Lowenthal, D. 1985. *The Past is a Foreign Country*. Cambridge: Cambridge University Press.

Manning, E. 2009. *Relationscapes: Movement, Art, Philosophy*. Cambridge, MA: MIT Press.

Massey, D. 2005. *For Space*. London: SAGE.

McLean, S. 2009. Stories and Cosmogonies: Imagining Creativity Beyond 'Nature' and 'Culture'. *Cultural Anthropology*, 24(2), 213–45.

Merleau-Ponty, M. 1964. Eye and Mind, in *The Primacy of Perception, and Other Essays on Phenomenological Psychology, the Philosophy of Art, History and Politics*, edited by J.M. Edie, trans. C. Dallery. Evanston, IL: Northwestern University Press, 159–90.

Merleau-Ponty, M. 1968.*The Visible and the Invisible*, edited by C. Lefort, trans. A. Lingis. Evanston, IL: Northwestern University Press.

Popper, K. 1950. *The Open Society and its Enemies*. Princeton, NJ: Princeton University Press.

Rapaport, H. 1997. *Is There Truth in Art?* Ithaca, NY: Cornell University Press.

Schama, S. 1995. *Landscape and Memory*. London: HarperCollins.

Siza, A. 1997. *Architecture Writings*, edited by A. Angelillo. Milan: SkiraEditore.

Uexküll, J. von 1982. *The Theory of Meaning*, trans. B. Stone and H. Weiner from *Bedeutungslehre* (edited by T. von Uexküll). *Semiotica*, 42(1), 25–82 [originally published in 1940].

Willerslev, R. 2006. 'To have the world at a distance': Reconsidering the Significance of Vision for Social Anthropology, in *Skilled Visions: Between Apprenticeship and Standards*, edited by C. Grassemi. Oxford: Berghahn, 23–46.

Chapter 2

Seeing Ruins: Imagined and Visible Landscapes in North-East Scotland

Jo Vergunst

In this chapter I explore the landscapes of a particular hill in north-east Scotland. There, community-based archaeological research does not just inform a reconstruction of the past but is a site of active social relations between generations of inhabitants and various landowners. For current inhabitants a primary concern is to make visible and keep visible the archaeological remains against both the encroaching undergrowth of a forest environment and the threat of further industrial afforestation. I explore how members of the community learn to make their own landscape physically and bureaucratically visible through the techniques of archaeological drawing. These archaeological imaginations start from an involvement in the world as landscape rather than from a discrete cognitive process.

Imagining is not a purely cognitive activity that is separate from a person's involvement in the world around them. The imagination cannot be understood as a faculty locked away 'in the mind', on the one hand disembodied from the person and on the other displaced from the landscape. Better instead to consider the verb rather than the noun form and explore the process through which cognition, body and landscape come together in imagining. As Ingold and other phenomenologically-inspired anthropologists have argued, cognition occurs through engagement with the world, rather than prior to it (Ingold 2000). It might be thought that imagination would provide a counter-case to a theory of embodied cognition, because imagination above all is thought to be located 'in the head'. But I want to explore its links to memory, the body and place. To start with a hypothetical example: if we sit down to draw a picture of a house 'from our imagination', as we might say, at the same time we are remembering when we were present inside or in front of a house, or we think of another picture of a house as the drawing is made. Drawing or even building a new house involves setting up real relationships with materials and people that quickly preclude any sense of the imagination locked away in the head. In drawing, thoughts and perceptions are both made visible and extended into the environment through bodily gestures of the hand moving over the page.

Understanding drawing techniques as gestural activity may not be an immediately obvious step if gesture is thought to be just a supplement to conversation or a kind of utterance (Kendon 2004). A broader reckoning of gesture would involve a repertoire of bodily actions with a creative basis rather than being specifically linguistic or part of language as such. Henri Lefebvre argued that 'the everyday micro-gestural realm generates its own spaces' in ordinary areas such as corridors or eating places, in the same way that movement can organise formalised large-scale settings such as pilgrimage sites (Lefebvre 1991: 216). These spaces are created by the type of bodily movement that happens in them: a corridor is a corridor because it allows movement between rooms. We might think of gesture as creative expression that can be learned and shared through bodies. How then does it work as an imaginative interaction with landscape? The gestures of drawing form the case material in this chapter.

Holding the pencil and other tools in a particular purposeful manner and orienting oneself towards the paper, a drawing is made as the expression and performance of movements and interactions the artist is engaged with. Following Lefebvre, these gestures must entail a particular relationship with the surrounding space. Sitting down at a table in a studio might suggest that the artist is controlling the conditions of the production of the drawing quite carefully. In this chapter I will explore drawing outside, on the move, sometimes in low light and rain, with an indeterminate subject matter, and while the drawer is trying to take account of the positions and perspectives of other various people involved in the activity of drawing. If, as Ingold (2007) puts it, a drawing can be understood as a trace of the gesturing hand, following the gestures of drawing could be one way into the relationship between cognition, the body and landscape. The resulting marks made on the paper bear their own relationship to these gestures that explore the landscape.

This chapter has a particular focus on houses so I will pursue the example a little further. While anthropologists have demonstrated a wide variety of social meanings and purposes of houses around the world, Bachelard's *Poetics of Space* is as good an account as any of what he calls a 'phenomenology of imagination' of the Western house. Bachelard writes that: 'A house consists of a body of images that give mankind proofs or illusions of stability' (Bachelard 1969: 17). But these are images not in the sense of representational pictures; rather, he explores moments of imagination in the house through its cellars and attics, walls and wardrobes. Perhaps an image is then best understood as that which is produced by the activity of the mind and body known as imagining. The house is present in Bachelard's phenomenology as a series of shelters, nests and corners that are tied up with the biographies of its inhabitants moving from childhood to adulthood. Walls are at the same time load-bearing and lifeworld-defining. If this imagination is to do with cognition, it is in the distinctly ecological framing of Gregory Bateson, apparent through bodily and perceptual relationships with the environment rather than just mental process. Early in the *Poetics of Space*, Bachelard briefly celebrates the 'muscular consciousness' of the body moving along a path before returning again to what he describes as the more 'introverted' imaginative capacities centred on the house (Bachelard 1969: 11). Yet imagining in Bachelard's sense must involve dwelling in places rather than in heads (and outdoors as well as in), and be productive of images that can be explored by foot and hand as well as sight.

A house is above all a place that the inhabitant has learnt to move through in an intimate way. We know the shape of a familiar room even in the dark and can move through it by way of a sequence of gestures learnt through the body – stepping, reaching out, sitting, lying and so on. Bachelard imagines returning to a familial house:

> After twenty years, in spite of all the other anonymous stairways; we would recapture the reflexes of the "first stairway", we would not stumble on that rather high step. The house's entire being would open up, faithful to our own being. We would push the door that creaks with the same gesture, we would feel our way in the dark to the distant attic. The feel of the tiniest latch has remained in our hands. (Bachelard 1969: 15)

Gestures informed by memory and learning express the relationship with space that is at the heart of this imaginative work. So rather than confining imagination to the cognitive realm we need to make connections with what we might describe as landscape – by which I mean a place 'gathered together' through the activities of dwelling (Heidegger 1978: 354). Here I want to explore how relationships with landscape can be explored through an ethnography of a particular kind of drawing, that used in archaeological investigations.

Farming, Crofting and Forestry at Bennachie

Since 2007 I have been carrying out fieldwork around the hill of Bennachie in Aberdeenshire, north-east Scotland. I was initially approached by a community group there, the Bailies of Bennachie, to begin an oral history project centred on people who have lived, worked and enjoyed recreation on and around the hill. The oral and archival history has been pursued in doctoral research by Jennifer Fagen. The hill itself rises sharply above a large region of flat farmland to the east, and its distinctive outline is visible from many places in north-east Scotland. In the past and sometimes the present the hill is used by sailors as a navigational aid despite being some 20 miles from the sea. Helicopter pilots journeying between the mainland and the North Sea oil rigs use the hill in the same way. To the west lie higher ground and the foothills of the Cairngorm Mountains.

Bennachie is often the subject of postcard photographs. One informant in the oral history project showed me his collection of dozens from over the decades. Typically they have a foreground of a village, cattle or a harvest scene and the hill rising up in the middle and background. I took the photo in Figure 2.1 as a re-creation of the kind of view in which Bennachie takes on an iconic quality. Fagen has described how emigrants from the north-east often retain the hill in memory as a symbol of belonging and connection to the region. Return visits will often

Figure 2.1   Bennachie in Aberdeenshire, north-east Scotland
Source: Image courtesy of the author.

include a trip to the hill. In these renditions the hill is a generic marker of home in its totality and its overall shape: a person sees Bennachie and feels they are here in north-east Scotland, or sees a picture and remembers their connection with it.

While Bennachie is a symbol of north-east Scotland, it also exists as a place apart from the strict landscape schemes of farms and towns to be found there. In the mid-nineteenth century, similarly to much of the rest of the United Kingdom, agricultural land was rationalised into larger farmsteads (known as 'fermtouns') with various farm hands and labourers working on them (Carter 1997). Much land was broken out and formed into characteristic large, straight field systems. Discourses of 'improvement' meant that there was a kind of moral prerogative to use every inch of the land for production. In Orkney, where I have also carried out fieldwork, contemporary farmers spoke of carrying on up the hillsides until the tractors tipped over, at least until recent nature conservation schemes were introduced (Lee 2007). This leaves the coastline and hilltops to offer the chance for alternative kinds of landscape practices to take place, based on movement much less constrained by the barbed wire fences and roads – now nearly the sole preserve of fast traffic – of the farming areas.

Bennachie is recognised as the place to go for a walk through woods and over the open heathery tops. Visitor surveys by Aberdeenshire Council show that people mostly walk there 'to get the top' or to walk dogs through the forest in the lower areas (Fiona Banks, Aberdeenshire Council Ranger, personal communication). Many informants in my oral history fieldwork spoke of going to have picnics on the hill, which is a tradition mostly lost today, when the walk in itself has taken precedence. There remains however a notion of common use rights on the hill. The use rights, while contested in practice, endured on the hill through the period of around a hundred years from the mid-nineteenth to the mid-twentieth century. At the start of that period, the surrounding estates first divided up between them the commonty (as land held between more than one owner in Scotland's feudal land tenure system was known) and at the end of it sold most of their land to the Forestry Commission. Since the 1970s the Forestry Commission have had an agenda to balance their economic forestry activities with providing public access to their land (Mackay 1995, Tsouvalis 2000), although there are still swathes of dense conifers on most Forestry Commission land. A triangle of the hill remains in private ownership together with some of the lower reaches. At the moment, visitors may walk along various footpaths and forest tracks both on the hillsides and on the open hilltops. From this perspective the picture-postcard images of Bennachie replay the distinction in Scottish landscape between a productive but privatised lowland landscape and a recreational highland that symbolises a common legacy (Nadel-Klein 1997).

The period of estate ownership up to the mid-twentieth century is still significant to many people living around the hill. When the estates divided the commonty between them in 1859 the status of a small group of crofters who had settled on the sides of the hill became even more insecure. Their collection of crofts and dwellings on the hillside were known as the Bennachie colony. Marginalised from the fermtouns and making their living from the granite quarries on the hill, small-scale farming or a variety of other low-income occupations, the colonists were now brought into a landlord-tenant relationship. Fagen's research describes how rents were introduced and increased if the colonists improved their houses or holdings. There are stories of 'clearances' happening on Bennachie in the latter part of the nineteenth century as tenants were removed from their homes to make way for the estates' sporting interests in grouse and deer, and for sheep. The last of the Bennachie colonists still dwelling on the hill died in 1939.

Interest in the colony has increased again since the 1970s in the context of research into crofting and folk life in Scotland (Hunter 1976) and the development of various heritage and conservation interests. Around Bennachie, the Bailies of Bennachie community group was formed, initially with a nature conservation and access ethos, but now also to promote the history of life around the hill and to encourage community involvement in its current management. They are interested in the history of the Bennachie colony and are keen to make connections between the colony and current life and activity around the hill. A key theme in their work has been relations between landowners and people living and using the hill in the present and the past. Connections between past and present life at Bennachie are partly imaginative, based on the symbolism of the hard work and down-to-earth existence of people in the colony as authentic dwellers in the landscape, close to the land in their croft and quarrying work. But it is an imagination firmly based in practical activities of both looking after the hill and finding out about it. Coming to know about life in the colony in the nineteenth century plays into social relations in the present as well, and this is where field archaeology comes to be part of the story.

Coming to Know Through Drawing

The ethnographic fieldwork presented here centres on the 'work parties' which the Bailies organise each month to carry out practical work on the hill. The work varies from archaeology to path building and maintaining areas of woodland, but here I will mainly concentrate on a programme of archaeological surveying that has taken place over recent years. Although there have been a number of professional archaeological digs on various sites around the hill, the initiative of an archaeologist by the name of Colin Shepherd has meant that this particular project has anthropological significance too. Colin tells me that his relatively late entry into archaeology came through a local history society, an amateur involvement rather than direct professional training. Since moving to north-east Scotland 25 years ago he has retained an interest in community participation in archaeology and has started another local archaeology group where he lives in Huntly, north of Bennachie. He is now also contracted by the Forestry Commission to advise them on archaeological sites on their land, and it was the combination of Colin's personal and professional interest that led to the Bennachie colony survey being started by the Bailies. Through this archaeological practice the landscape is explored, relationships between past and present are forged, and a community of interest and practice is formed around the colony. What I want to investigate here are the specific modalities of gesture practiced in the archaeology, and especially the drawing, and what kinds of knowledge they allow.

The volunteers who turn up for the work parties are a mixed group of 'locals' ranging from teenagers doing Duke of Edinburgh awards to older folk, some of whom have lived near the hill all their lives. Others are from the city or are more recent incomers to the area. Yet others have a semi-professional interest through working for the Forestry Commission itself or for Aberdeenshire Council. Colin is keen for everyone working on the colony to develop their own skills as archaeologists in surveying and drawing. As a result everyone is learning about drawing on the job itself, partly through following Colin's instructions and partly working it out as they go along.

As an undergraduate taking classes in archaeology I was not taught to draw and as 'trowel fodder', an ordinary digger-archaeologist, it takes a long time before one is trusted to try drawing. But when one does get the chance, the comportments of body, tool and observation needed for this kind of drawing become clearer – drawing is a practical activity that does not transfer particularly well to the classroom. The procedure for on-site drawing in archaeology is, in my still very amateur reading, as follows: Tape up some translucent paper over graph paper on a rigid wooden board. Set up the baseline and measuring tapes from the appropriate points on the site and work out scale and guidelines on the paper. Sharpen your pencil. Have a rubber and measuring tape handy. Manipulate the drawing board, hold it or lean it against something, stretch the measuring tape and find the distance between the baseline and whatever is being drawn. Use the pencil to make dots on the paper, to be joined up later with lines. Points of contact of the tape between the baseline and the thing are related to counts along the graph paper. The work is sometimes done in pairs with one person calling out the measurements and the other marking the paper. Drawing can thus take place together, in a social form very unlike that of a solitary artist sitting in a studio. The appropriate textual information is added – site name, date, north arrow, legend. The symbols for topsoil, for stones or for almost any other material are added too, if you're doing a section. The key relations are yourself, the tools, and the site. Then the dig supervisor passes judgement at the end: 'yes, very neat', you hope.

At Bennachie everyone goes through a version of this story. A textbook on archaeological illustration in my university library says that this type of learning is characteristic: 'Formal teaching and courses in archaeological illustration are

Figure 2.2 An area in the forest to be surveyed
Source: Image courtesy of the author.

Figure 2.3 Drawing together
Source: Image courtesy of the author.

extremely limited; most illustrators learn their techniques through experimenting, watching other people and by talking to other illustrators' (Adkins and Adkins 1989: 40). Archaeology as field practice is emphasised here: a set of bodily and social activities learned in practice rather than in theory. This practical aspect resonates with the very nature of what is going on, which is an exploration of the specific and immediate place one is in. There would therefore be no generic 'house' of the imagination, which might be learned or rehearsed in an abstract context. Instead there is only the particular gathering of stones, bricks or other materials that the archaeologist is in the midst of. While the textbook helps the trainee drawer prepare for this encounter, it cannot shape the content or result of it.

On the occasional Saturdays when the Bailies do the surveying at the colony, everyone gathers at the Bennachie visitor centre and walks the few minutes up the hill to the main part of the colony. Colin sets the agenda for the day, then those who know what they are doing get things set up, split into groups of two or three on different parts of the site, and get to work. We try and keep the measuring lines tight. The straight lines are made by eye, once the baseline for each area to be surveyed has been triangulated from the main site baseline, although lines of sight need to be negotiated as we work through trees and bushes. In some groups people have learnt what to do and, perhaps having spent some years working together on the hill, they communicate well together. In other groups the people might not know each other so well: they are not quite sure what to do, and the process is slower. The gestures are made collectively as one person holds the line and calls out the measurements and another marks the paper. We all question what we're doing as we go along – no-one amongst this group of volunteers would want to claim an expert knowledge. Should we cross-check the other way or not? Where to stop drawing on the piece of paper, and where to stop measuring on the site itself? Should we do this extra bit of wall or stop at the baseline? Ultimately, what is actually there, on the ground? Is this a piece of wall, amongst the bracken and tree roots? Is it linked to that piece? Could it be a doorway? These are questions that everyone talks about in their groups. There is an egalitarian and open feel to it that is rather different from what I remember from student and professional digs.

Everyone is physically involved in the site. We climb around the trees, over the low walls and balance on heaps of stones. We pull some material away (broken branches or a small fallen trunk, heaps of larch needles, a patch of moss) and hold the tape tight. Using lines of sight and calling out to each other we orient the measuring tapes and drawing tools to the site itself, peering through the trees in the gloom of the dense plantation, or amongst the gorse and bracken of the open areas. When it starts raining those holding the drawing boards crouch over them to stop the paper getting wet.

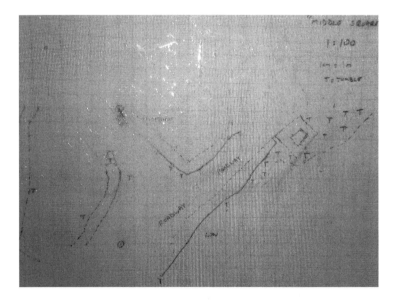

Figure 2.4 'Middle Square' – one of the drawings photographed at the end of a day's work

Source: Image courtesy of the author.

Brian marks Ts in the drawing for 'tumble', the loose and fallen stones, and is asked to turn them into a clear boundary line. Colin wants us to be clear where the fallen stones from the walls of the colony buildings are. The ideal is to have well defined lines that translate easily into tracings and final versions. What is a stone *in situ* and what is fallen is hard to tell and can only really be determined by following a regular line of a wall. These decisions are made as the drawing progresses, and the resulting drawing sums up all these decisions and the conditions in which they were made.

When I brought up the subject explicitly, others in the group agreed that drawing and doing the surveying meant having 'a really good look' at the stones. The drawers have to decide where walls start and end, what is actually 'there' and what not. After one session I asked Colin to reflect on this kind of drawing in archaeology. 'It forces you to ask questions of the site … How does each wall join up, how on earth does that work? You disentangle it through drawing', he said.

On one occasion Colin dug in to the turf with his trowel in order to trace where one of the walls was going. It is not just he who digs, however, as occasionally someone asks to have a dig at something. Is this section of road paved, we ask? Someone else grabs a piece of cut branch from the forest floor and uses it to dig away at the end of a wall to find where it finishes. On other Saturdays, the whole group is involved with digging at a different part of the hill, uncovering the shape and extent of another colony house with shovels, spades and trowels. These gestures are not so different from those involved in drawing, pulling away vegetation and following the lines of stones. On one corner Mick and I head towards each other from different sides, aware of where the walls should be if they follow the pattern of the opposite corner. The tumble of stones stops us ever getting a clear view. We draw out the lines of the walls by levering away the grass and rushes that have grown over the old house.

Drawing Landscape into Anthropology

Archaeologists, unlike anthropologists, have long maintained drawing at the heart of their discipline. Where anthropology has relied much more in recent years on ideas of text and symbol and metaphors of meaning and interpretation, archaeological drawing, like other kinds of technical drawing, seems to be an archetypal example of objective and reliable data recording. It is based on point-to-point measurements in which the notion of scale is key. The proportions of a feature are transferred from the landscape to a piece of paper, and nowadays to a computer. What is objectively there on and in the ground needs to be recorded on the paper. This is achieved in part through a denial of perspective and the judgement of the drawer in favour of a cartographic rendering. The techniques of surveying in archaeology are of course related to drawing practices in allied professions such as architecture and cartography, and such powerful visions have their own history. Dixon, for example, describes the imaginative mapping out, in the eighteenth century, of an atemporal ancient Rome in which all the most magnificent buildings are presented as existing simultaneously (Dixon 2005). The emergence of 'naturalised' state power occurred in part through landscape imagery that has developed from perspectival art to include cartographic rationalities (Olwig 2002).

Archaeologists do not deny that there is an interpretive or subjective aspect to archaeological drawing. My textbook makes this clear, both reacting against the picturesque tradition in archaeological or antiquarian research and warning of the dangers of an overly 'scientific' or positivistic approach to drawing. 'The modern approach to illustration', the authors say, involves 'the conscious realisation that the purpose of the illustration is to convey not only information but also an interpretation of that information' (Adkins and Adkins 1989: 5). In a more reflexive vein, Colin Renfrew writes that 'drawings of the stonework have their own style and bring their own satisfaction, as well as enhancing one's appreciation of the skill of the ancient masons. Archaeological draughtsmanship is an art in itself, and can illuminate the methods of manufacture and the style of the original object or structure' (Renfrew 2003: 43).

The first time I tried to excavate and draw a posthole comes to mind as a good example of the difficulties of being a novice drawer, caught between 'object' and 'representation', and it has stayed with me off and on during this research. Postholes are dug to accommodate a wooden post during a building's construction, and remain visible long after the post has decayed or been removed. Shortly after finishing my undergraduate degree, I was taking part in a dig that was working through very sandy soil in which only faint changes in colour marked the different layers. I tried to dig out the slightly darker fill of the posthole, and then set up my base line, measuring tape and so on to draw the section, despite the tendency of the sides to collapse on contact with the trowel or even the tape measure. The resulting drawing was, like the posthole, rather indistinct. The leader of the dig straightaway told me to 'make it look like a posthole' – to dig it deeper, wider, more regularly, and then to communicate the interpretation of the feature in my drawing.

It would be possible to have a discussion around the objective existence of landscape and its subjective, or cultural, interpretation but I am not sure that this dichotomy offers a fruitful direction for an anthropologically useful understanding of landscape. However there are things going on in archaeological drawing that relate to the sense of imagination as an engagement with landscape rather than a cognitive process. What seems important to me in the archaeological drawing I have been involved with is not just the final result, or the extent to which our drawings are – depending on one's archaeological paradigm – either objectively accurate or adequate to an interpretation. Significance lies rather in the process through which the drawers come to know and enter into a relationship with what they are working on. This is achieved through particular gestures that engage the body with the site, moving, uncovering and measuring.

What then does an archaeologist actually achieve in making a drawing? At Bennachie, from the mixture of stones, undergrowth and trees comes the house,

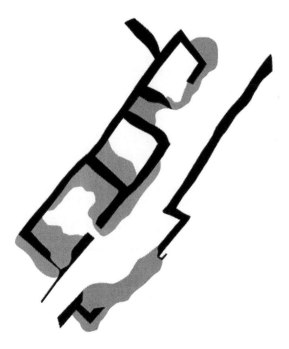

Figure 2.5 A detail from the finished result
Source: Image courtesy of Colin Shepherd and the Bailies of Bennachie.

the enclosures, and the colony with an almost piercing clarity. It is, as Colin says, an untangling. Colin emails me his completed PDFs of the colony drawings. He has re-traced our smudgy efforts onto new paper and used a computer to scan and produce the final images. The binary black and white of the walls and surroundings is leavened slightly by grey areas of now clearly defined tumble, but there can no longer be any doubt about the presence of the walls and the houses on Bennachie. The space of the colony has been generated through the sequences of gestures I have described.

Drawing Out Relationships at Bennachie

To the members of the Bailies' work parties, the drawings are not simply a summary of what is present. They are also a record of the efforts made during the drawing, efforts which involve both their own gestures and the landscape itself, which is part of the whole enterprise. Although the marks are made through measuring, and making and joining up dots, just as important are the movements of clearing the ground, of feeling where the stones do and do not touch each other, of clambering over tree roots and branches to hold the tape measure tight and straight. At this stage of the archaeological work at least, the members of the work parties are not too worried about how Colin produces the final images. They are learning about the site by the practice of drawing, rather than by looking at the images. Drawing is an activity of the archaeologists' bodies, the sum of their gestures and the processes of engagement and interaction with their surroundings. It is a way of coming to know something, and as one comes to know it, one enters into a relationship with it. This relationship happens imaginatively, but not being confined to the internal mind, it acts through the material landscape to make visible what, and who, was hidden before. Above all, then, drawing is a *drawing-out*, an encouragement of openness, as if there was a quiet guest needing to be encouraged to join the conversation at a party. But what sorts of conversation are happening? What kinds of relationships are being formed here?

At Bennachie, it is the absence of people from the croft houses that we are working to overcome. It turns out that the work is happening in the actual houses of people. From her archival work, Jennifer Fagen tells the group that the Littlejohn family lived in this particular house in the latter part of the nineteenth century, and the Garden family lived in that one. We draw out their presence not as guests in our work, but as hosts in their own houses. Thus far, the relationships are still not as full or complete as the Bailies would wish. Now that some information and stories are becoming known, even more questions crowd around the houses. What was their environment like then? What were the gender relations? What kinds of things did they make? How, in the end, did they manage to live on the side of this hill?

Many of the answers are not yet available to those working in the colony, and so the relationships they have with the houses and those who lived in them is still one that is full of questions – either to be mulled over during lunch breaks or set out in meetings as the basis for future work. Some answers might come through further archaeological and archival work, but others become apparent more gradually through the material of the hill itself. The group is dealing first and foremost with the stones. Much of the colonists' work involved the stones too, as they were often quarrymen, dykers and builders. Sometimes there are historical resonances between the Bailies and the colonists in working on the hill. In one quarry at the top of the hill, lintel stones lie on the ground still waiting to be taken down the hill. Algy Watson, a retired schoolteacher who lives just near the hill, tells a half-read, half-heard story about the end of that quarry in 1891.

Aye, there was a cloudburst, that's not what they called it, but I think the water, my own theory is that the water collected on the plateau and then burst through at the lowest point, and came right down the hill and the rumble of stones coming down with that water could be heard in Oyne, about a mile and a half away. So I'm told, so the book says. But that was the end of quarrying, although some of the lintels, the cut lintels are still lying in Little Oxen Craig. And some people say 'Oh, I'm building a house, I could be doing with a lintel, have we permission?' I said no, it's part of the social history of Aberdeen or of Bennachie, please leave the lintels alone, you know?

The lintels are present on the hill. They have been drawn out of the rock by the quarrymen and they now embody those absent workers. The granite at Little Oxen Craig is fissured and one can imagine the gestures of the quarrymen's work. Harry Leil, one of the work party archaeologists, remembers the techniques his grandfather used. Finesse as well as strength would have been required to form the lintels from the wide slabs – not hacking, but a careful drilling of a borehole and levering to release the rock a little at a time, and then chiselling by hand into the required shape. Horses were used to move the stone down the hill until, as Algy explains, a flood washed the road away and it was never remade. The lintels have become *social* history, formed through the productive relations of labour and landscape, and a contrast is implied with the histories of the various landowners living in the castles around Bennachie.

Social history has a very material form here. The colony houses are connected up to the quarries on the hill through the stone and the inhabitants who lived and worked there. The paths between the houses and quarries must have been well-trodden, and perhaps in the imagination of the crofter-quarriers the quarry and the houses even had similar qualities. Each envelops its inhabitants in shaped stone which in itself is cold, but is capable of providing shelter. Where the stone is drawn out of the one, creating an indent into the landscape, the other is built up into a protrusion that is no less part of that landscape. The nest-like qualities of houses that Bachelard touched on were also noted by a visitor to the last active croft in the colony, retired farmer Alan Mackie, who told me he called it 'the eagle's nest', perched on the side of the hill and visible from afar.

Between 'then' and 'now', of course, the stones of the houses have moved again. There were violent evictions on the hill when the land was enclosed and rents were imposed at a high level for these dwellers on the margins of the habitable landscape. At least one house was set alight and the walls pulled down at this time. Other crofters left as the economic viability of life on the hill changed and other opportunities in towns presented themselves, as Jennifer Fagen is exploring (Fagen, forthcoming). Many stones will have been removed purposefully from the houses and incorporated into neighbouring dry-stone dykes. The stones seem to mark a certain stability in each of these contexts – the hill itself, in a house wall, or a field dyke – despite the movement between the settings. Other stones now form the 'tumble' that we struggle to delineate in our archaeological drawings, and these stones seem to be in the midst of movement despite the moss that grows over them. But recognising the routes between the quarries, the houses and the dykes means that all of the stones have a potential for imagining movement in just the same way that Massey (2006) recognises in glacial erratics: landscape is not after all a stability but a flux of coming and going, intrusion and protrusion. The relationships that are developed with the colonists are similarly transient, coming into existence and needing work to maintain them as all relationships do. Perhaps Algy's protection of the lintels in the quarry removes the stone from its normal circuits of use, but in so doing he has helped to preserve evidence of the gestures of the quarrymen and allowed future relationships based on them to be formed.

The archaeological drawings are, in a similar way, an attempt to provide the stones with a recognisable presence as walls. In some ways, of course, archaeological drawing is not faithful to the movements of the stone and the actual entangled nature of the forest landscape. In the drawings we do not worry about the tree roots, the bracken and moss, the odd piece of bedrock. But I think it would be truer to say only that such drawing does not *represent* such landscapes well. For the volunteers, it does allow them to come to know their landscape in the way they wish. As Colin put it, this drawing is a disentanglement of the stones and walls. The marks on the paper are the working-out of the lines of walls in the face of the upheavals of the end of crofting and the encroachment of recent forestry activities.

More broadly, drawing – whether it is archaeological or not – does not have to be thought of as a copying, a representation or an interpretation of a separate physical reality. It is precisely the kind of drawing that is non-representational to which Chris Tilley directs our attention in his analyses of rock art and stone monuments. There is considerably more going on in these monuments than just inscriptions of a tool in a surface that might 'look like something'. Rather, the shaped or marked stone itself invokes and brings into being relations amongst people and with the landscape. In southern Sweden cold, undulating marble brings the sea inland. Narrow entrances to Maltese temples require a prostrated approach, rather than representing anything (Tilley 2004).

What is equally important at Bennachie is that the drawing does not just make the ruined croft houses visible for those doing the survey on the day. For current inhabitants a primary concern is to make visible and keep visible the archaeological remains against the possibility of afforestation and clear-felling deforestation, as well as the gradual encroaching undergrowth of a forest environment. Colin is able to write reports and talk with the forest managers about the colony. The Bailies keep up their round of public talks, visits to the hill, and occasional funding of research projects.

This ties in with the narrative about the Forestry Commission shifting from producing timber as a commodity to the provision of biodiversity and services such as recreation, as I described earlier (see also Robbins and Fraser 2003). To my mind, however, the FC is somewhat ambiguous in its practical commitment to these agendas. In Scotland outdoor access reforms are resulting in a higher profile for the kind of access and user rights that I have described at Bennachie. In terms of management, Bennachie is an example of where there is a relatively strong consultative approach, although it is not constituted as one of the formal 'Forest Partnership' co-management groups that exist elsewhere in the country. However, especially in Scotland and the north of England, there are large areas of dense industrial forestry. Clear felling, leaving stands of 'snags' reminiscent of gravestones, is common. Often only small areas are set aside from intensive forestry, mostly where visitor facilities are added. Fringing stands of Sitka spruce with larch, or a thin line of broadleaf trees in the name of 'landscape design', hints at an alternative approach, but volunteers at Bennachie need to work to keep their site visible in such a context. This is by no means to downplay the importance of

Figure 2.6 A new path being made up the hill
Source: Image courtesy of the author.

forestry and forest products in themselves. My concern, however, is to explore kinds of landscape-based activities and land management that are different from those possible in strictly regulated urban and agricultural contexts.

For the members of the work parties, the significance of the gestures I have described goes beyond archaeological drawing. Drawing takes place alongside other activities they carry out on the hill. Each month the work parties carry out one task or another – cutting back vegetation, maintaining the paths, planting trees, as well as the surveying – and get involved with materials other than stone on the hill. I think there is a synergy between many of these activities. Similar gestures are involved in clearing and making paths as are involved in surveying and drawing the colony. In clearing the paths, we draw the lines back into the landscape with our shovels and loppers, making the paths present again. We cut gorse and bramble branches out of the line of the path, gather them up and throw them over the side of the path. As the rain falls Mick leans over a drain beside a path and digs out the vegetation that blocks it. Water follows the trace of his shovel, eight inches at a time, as a puddle in the path empties into the newly-cleared drain. Mick makes a small pile of mud and weeds dug from the drain slightly away from the path, much like the spoil heap in an archaeological dig. In 2008, a small but dedicated group of us spent a weekend each month learning how to build hill paths. We drew out a line on the hill as we progressed up it, painfully slowly, digging turf, hauling and levering rocks as we went. These are mark-making gestural activities just as survey drawings are.

Presence, Absence and Imagining

John Wylie (2009) recognises a strand in recent research in geography and anthropology concerned with the interplay of absence and presence in landscape. Where 'classic' landscape phenomenology has described bodily presence '– of sensuous, tactile and experiential being – in the co-constitution of self and landscape', others have worked at the 'threshold of presence/absence' (Wylie: 279). He cites, among others, Edensor's enormously engaging work on urban industrial ruins (Edensor 2005, 2008) in which the tactile affordances of abandoned factories offer their own comments and silences on the post-industrial economy and the regulated spaces of modern cities. The labourers are missing from the factories, but they have a kind of presence, if only as ghosts, through the things and the spaces they have left behind. Wylie finds amongst memorial benches next to a path on the Cornish coast that there is as much possibility for affective relations through absence as there is through presence. In the industrial ruins, however, the gestural performances of the space have a directness and a mobility to them that evoke the very people who were there themselves, and not merely the memory of them. Edensor can sit at the same boardroom tables and lean against the same walls. Moving around the dwelling place of an absent being, we can take on something, at least, of their gestures, and form some kind of relationship with them. Elsewhere I have argued that walking together is often such a sociable and even intimate experience because of the shared gestural rhythms that the walkers enter into (Lee and Ingold 2006). There is something similar with the ability to move around a familiar room in the dark: the room is absent, but the gestures guide, and the relationship with space is – if anything – more profound.

Archaeologists, of course, work perennially at the threshold of presence and absence, and indeed of present and past, through the scraping of their trowels and the way they move around sites and landscapes. Christopher Tilley has based his archaeological fieldwork practice in 'the phenomenological walk' – the 'walk of the walk' as he puts it – in which he is attentive to all relationships and all possibilities of being in the landscape as he wends his way on foot around sites

(Tilley forthcoming). He makes present the experience of the weather and the shape and feel of the land in a way which is much more difficult to achieve when one is merely 'on site' in a dig. At Bennachie, realising that there is a doorway, and walking through it rather than climbing over the ruckle of stones next to it, similarly brings the house into the present again. While in the absence of their dwellers houses may change and decay, the very act of moving *as if one were dwelling there* makes it over as a house once again.

In this chapter I have considered the extent to which images in landscape are produced through gestures of the body. In an attempt to pull together the ways that cognition, body and landscape interact, I have argued that understanding gestures as broadly expressive and creative may allow us to begin to grasp some of these connections. If landscape at this hill is imagined, it is an imagination that leads to the cultivation of gestural skills on the hill that in turn, lead on to skills in dealing with landowners. As the community becomes confident in moving around and recording the colony, so they build up a status and a voice amongst other organisations. The gestures of archaeology are transferred, gradually, to the language of bureaucracy and management. Habitation of the hill takes place not through permanent residence any more but through these activities that allow for the landscape to be explored. The colonists who did live there are remembered, imaginatively, and in a way made present again. Drawing on an amateur tradition of archaeology, the work has forged an enduring connection with the activity of their local landscape. Finally, it is also a counterpoint to the postcard appeal of Bennachie as a symbol of dwelling in outline. The close-up and hands-on exploration of the hill in its immediacy comes before its place in any overarching landscape scheme.

Acknowledgements

This chapter has benefited from the insights of Tim Ingold, Jennifer Fagen and the participants at the ASA 2009. I also acknowledge the help of the Bailies of Bennachie community group in Aberdeenshire, Scotland.

References

Adkins, L. and Adkins, R. 1989. *Archaeological Illustration*. Cambridge: Cambridge University Press.
Bachelard, G. 1969. *Poetics of Space*. Boston: Beacon Press.
Carter, I. 1997. *Farm Life in Northeast Scotland, 1840–1914*. Edinburgh: John Donald.
Dixon, S. 2005. Illustrating Ancient Rome, or the Ichnographia as Uchronia and Other Time Warps in Piranesi's Il Campo Marzio, in *Envisioning the Past.*

Archaeology and the Image, edited by S. Smiles and S. Moser. Oxford: Blackwell, 115–32.

Edensor. T. 2005. *Industrial Ruins*. Oxford: Berg.

Edensor, T. 2008. Walking Through Ruins, in *Ways of Walking. Ethnography and Practice on Foot*, edited by T. Ingold and J. Vergunst. Aldershot: Ashgate, 123–41.

Fagen, J. forthcoming. PhD thesis, University of Aberdeen.

Heidegger, M. 1978. Building Dwelling Thinking, in *M. Heidegger, Basic Writings*, edited by D. Krell. London: Routledge, 347–63.

Hunter, J. 1976. *The Making of the Crofting Community*. Edinburgh: John Donald.

Ingold, T. 2000. *The Perception of the Environment*. London: Routledge.

Ingold, T. 2007. *Lines*. London: Routledge.

Kendon, A. 2004. *Gesture: Visible Action as Utterance*. Cambridge: Cambridge University Press.

Lee, J. 2007. Experiencing Landscape: Orkney Hill Land and Farming. *Journal of Rural Studies*, 23(1), 88–100.

Lee, J. and Ingold, T. 2006. Fieldwork on Foot: Perceiving, Routing, Socializing, in *Locating the Field. Space, Place and Context in Anthropology*, edited by S. Coleman and P. Collins. Oxford: Berg, 67–86.

Lefebvre, H. 1991. *The Production of Space*, trans. D. Nicholson-Smith. Oxford: Blackwell.

Mackay, D. 1995. *Scotland's Rural Land Use Agencies. The History and Effectiveness in Scotland of the Forestry Commission, Nature Conservancy Council, and Countryside Commission*. Aberdeen: Scottish Cultural Press.

Massey, D. 2006. Landscape as a Provocation. Reflections on Moving Mountains. *Journal of Material Culture*, 11(1/2), 33–48.

Nadel-Klein, J. 1997. Crossing a Representational Divide. From West to East in Scottish Ethnography, in *After Writing Culture: Epistemology and Praxis in Contemporary Anthropology*, edited by A. James, J. Hockey and A. Dawson. London: Routledge, 86–102.

Olwig, K. 2002. *Landscape, Nature, and the Body Politic. From Britain's Renaissance to America's New World*. Madison, Wisconsin: University of Wisconsin Press.

Renfrew, C. 2003. *Figuring it Out*. London: Thames and Hudson.

Robbins, P. and Fraser, A. 2003. A Forest of Contradictions: Producing the Landscapes of the Scottish Highlands. *Antipode*, 35(1), 95–118.

Tilley, C. 2004. *The Materiality of Stone*. Oxford: Berg.

Tilley, C. forthcoming. Walking the Past in the Present, in *Landscapes Beyond Land*, edited by A. Árnason, N. Ellison, J. Vergunst and A. Whitehouse. Oxford: Berghahn.

Tsouvalis, J. 2000. *A Critical Geography of Britain's State Forests*. Oxford: Oxford University Press.

Wylie, J. 2009. Landscape, Absence and the Geographies of Love. *Transactions of the Institute of British Geographers*, 34(3), 275–89.

Chapter 3

Scottish Blackhouses: Archaeological Imaginings

Tessa Poller

Introduction

Blackhouses are dwellings most associated with the agricultural system of crofting that was practised from the nineteenth century throughout the Scottish Highlands and Islands (Fenton 1978, Stoklund 1984, Holden 2004). These had largely been abandoned as homes by the mid-twentieth century. Compared to any other form of later historic building, it is the blackhouse that has captured the imagination of generations of academic researchers. For archaeologists this fascination may be mainly due to the materiality and physical form of these houses: thatched roofs sitting on low thick walls of earth and turf held together with skins of rough unhewn stone. Archaeological interest also stems from the imagined rural and traditional life within and around these houses. Ultimately the archaeological aim of exploring blackhouses, as Shannon Fraser suggests, has been 'to embody the human project of making sense of who we are, and of what we might be' (Fraser 2000: 397).

Romantic notions certainly influenced the study of blackhouses in the early part of the twentieth century, when many archaeologists saw blackhouses as 'living' examples of 'primitive' architecture still in use in their contemporary world. The construction of blackhouses, employing, as they did, readily available materials, was thought to be strikingly reminiscent of prehistoric buildings (Childe 1931, Curwen 1938, Piggott 1966). More recent archaeological studies have emphasised the importance of considering the construction of blackhouses within their specific economic and social contexts of the late eighteenth, nineteenth and early twentieth centuries (Fenton 1978, Stoklund 1984, Holden 2004). Yet there is still a view that blackhouses are the last in a genealogical line of vernacular architecture that stretches back into prehistory (Walker and MacGregor 1996, Holden et al. 2001). It is clear that blackhouses have a complex history and as a type site have come to embody both change and continuity (Fenton 2003). Blackhouses as they are imagined now are dynamic reflections of those who dwell in their landscapes, both in the present and in the past.

In this chapter I will explore the imagined Scottish blackhouse from an archaeological perspective – drawing and reflecting on past research as well as on my own practical archaeological experience of recording blackhouses within the contemporary landscape of Ness, located at the northern tip of the Hebridean island of Lewis. Influenced by reflexive approaches to archaeology and through my interactions with the local community I came to consider in more detail my relationship with the blackhouses I was recording. It was particularly through these interactions that I became more aware that my relationships were rooted in a very specific perspective, that of the archaeologist, who interprets a past through the observations and experiences of materials in the present. These relationships both contrasted and complemented those of the local community I was confronted with.

Ingold's 'dwelling perspective' offers a way of viewing these differing relationships as part of a singular endeavour. From this perspective the blackhouse in the Ness landscape can be seen as 'an enduring record of – and testimony to – the lives and works of past generations who have dwelt within it, and in so doing, have left there something of themselves' (Ingold 2000: 189). Although this statement can easily be said to apply to those who actually lived in the blackhouses during the nineteenth and twentieth centuries, and perhaps even to those who dwell in the landscape today, Ingold further proposes that '*the practice of archaeology is itself a form of dwelling*' (Ingold 2000: 189, original emphasis). Therefore the practice of archaeology, as it has focused on blackhouses and their associated settings, can also be seen as part of the wider enduring record of understanding, interpreting and dwelling in the Hebridean landscape. The imagined blackhouse has thus been created from many interconnected life stories.

Historically the archaeological perspective on blackhouses has been that of an outsider wanting to observe and record something of the past preserved in the present, much as the returning diaspora wish to see what they left, preserved in a timeless, traditional landscape. From the time of the first archaeologists who recorded blackhouses in the Hebridean landscape both theory and practice have changed, but how has this affected the way we view these dwellings within their landscapes?

Archaeology and the History of Research into the Hebridean Blackhouses

Since the seventeenth century, the vernacular Scottish rural house has interested visitors to the Western Islands, such as Martin Martin c. 1695 (see MacLeod 1999) and Pennant (1790), who saw it as worthy of particular mention and description, as its physical character was strikingly different from what they were accustomed to on the mainland and in the cities. At the end of the nineteenth century, incorporating the accounts of these travellers and other antiquarians (e.g., Thomas 1867) together with observations from his own travels, Sir Arthur Mitchell featured the blackhouses of Lewis in his 1878 Rhind Lectures, entitled *The Past in the Present: What is Civilisation?* In these lectures Mitchell combined what he saw as a science-based archaeological method of inquiry with an anthropological approach in order to identify 'primitive' forms of technology and culture (Mitchell 1880: iv). In his paper blackhouses were presented as an example of 'primitive' culture, but Mitchell was careful to emphasise that the 'primitiveness' associated with the 'wretched condition' of the houses did not directly reflect on to the people who inhabited them, who, for Mitchell, were worthy people with a strong sense of community (ibid.: 55).

It was the organic and rough physical character of these buildings that still captured the imagination of archaeologists nearly 50 years later, during the interwar years. Archaeologists such as Gordon Childe drew parallels between the blackhouse and prehistoric architecture, such as the Neolithic houses of Skara Brae (Childe 1931). Cecil Curwen, a contemporary of Childe's, explored the character and setting of the Hebridean blackhouse in more detail and suggested that at the end of the nineteenth century the Hebridean culture 'was more like that of the pre-Roman Iron Age in southern England than any succeeding phase' (Curwen 1938: 261). Other studies of the time, such as that conducted by Danish architect Aage Roussell (1934), proposed cultural links between the Hebrides and the Norse world based on the morphology and construction techniques of the blackhouses. In each case, the image of the blackhouse as a living ancestor to a prehistoric tradition was reinforced. For archaeologists these buildings predominantly figured within a culture-historical approach to archaeology aimed at understanding the distant past. To study blackhouses within their contemporary setting was not seen as a valid archaeological exercise.

During these interwar years blackhouses were increasingly abandoned by their occupants. New housing, resembling mainland forms, was adopted. Communities on the Isle of Lewis were actively encouraged to build 'white-houses', so named due to their white lime-washed walls, through grants provided by the Department of Agriculture and Fisheries (Hance 1951, Holden 2004). Blackhouses themselves were also changing as many were being modified and adapted. Curwen (1938) was acutely aware of these changes. He wanted to preserve what he saw as 'pristine' blackhouses, which he saw as an important resource for archaeologists. Influenced by such academic arguments, the National Trust of Scotland purchased a blackhouse at Callanish on the island of Lewis in order to renovate it and open it to the public. However, as Shannon Fraser (2000) discusses in detail, this process was not as straightforward as the academics had envisioned. The image of a 'pristine' blackhouse as presented by Curwen did not reflect reality: blackhouses were variable, complex and dynamic structures. Since the nineteenth century many houses had been rebuilt, modified and improved in response to 'Articles of Set' issued by the landlord Sir James Matheson in 1879, which specified improvements to be made to blackhouses (MacDonald 2003, Holden 2004: 22, Lawson 2008). Moreover, in the case of Callanish the process of constructing a typical blackhouse was further complicated by the conflicting agendas held by the different groups involved in the reconstruction. Some local community members rejected the idea of presenting the old, supposedly 'pristine' blackhouse because they saw it as backward and believed that it would present the wrong impression to visitors. Instead they championed the construction of a modified blackhouse, which would encapsulate both traditional and modern aspects of their identity

(Fraser 2000: 393). In the end the blackhouse at Callanish became an amalgam of the differing views and perspectives of the time (loc. cit.). The complex and variable character of blackhouses enabled them to be used as a symbol of identity for various communities.

During this time the rural life of the Highlands and Islands was deliberately idealised as part of a process of a renegotiating a shared Scottish identity (MacDonald 1998, Lorimer 1999). The blackhouse became a symbol of a romanticised Scottish rural heritage and was promoted as such through 'official' expressions of national identity, exemplified by the construction of a blackhouse village by the National Trust of Scotland at the Glasgow Empire Exhibition in 1938 (see Lorimer 1999). In this context the blackhouse was seen as a timeless symbol, representing both the wild and rugged environment and the heroic character of the people, who had lived through harsh conditions. This was despite the fact that, as mentioned above, blackhouses were not timeless. The inhabitants of the Hebridean landscape were constantly renegotiating their own identities and their relationship with the wider 'modern' world (Webster 1999). The system of crofting was changing; new technologies were adopted and many crofters had gained more control over their land. For others employment opportunities had shifted; some had to leave the Hebrides and emigrated to distant lands. As generations had done before, the Hebridean people were adapting to their ever-changing situation, finding their own identity between the traditional and the modern.

In the years following the Second World War archaeological interest in the blackhouse virtually ceased. The value of studying the recent or the 'contemporary past' was still not fully appreciated. However, some interested individuals and scholars from disciplines such as human geography continued the study of Hebridean blackhouses (e.g., Kissling 1943, Hance 1951, Jaatinen 1957). With these studies the emphasis changed to a focus on the physical and economic environment in which the blackhouses were situated. This marked a shift in how these places were viewed – as part of a dynamic social, economic, environmental and historical process.

In the 1960s Alexander Fenton became a dominant figure in the study of Scottish rural material culture. His aim was to investigate Scottish rural life and traditional crofting techniques, which he saw were at risk of being completely lost if they were not studied and preserved (Fenton 1985: chapters 1 and 2, Fenton 1987). Fenton also wanted to position Scotland's heritage onto a wider global stage of ethnological research. His position within the National Museum of Scotland facilitated a dialogue with archaeologists and the developing cultural resource management sector. In 1964 Fenton first visited the village of Arnol, situated in the parish of Barvas on the island of Lewis. During the eighteenth century the original site of Arnol on the coast became less tenable for the ever expanding population and therefore the village was relocated inland. At this time the whole population of Arnol lived in the blackhouses, which were erected along the length

Figure 3.1 Reconstruction of No. 42 Arnol blackhouse in 2004
Source: Image courtesy of the author.

of the main road with the croft lands extending in thin strips behind them. Over time these blackhouses were adapted, modified and abandoned in favour of newer house forms. Notably in Arnol many of these new houses were built beside the ruins of the older blackhouses. By the time of Fenton's visit in the 1960s the house at No. 42 along the main road of Arnol was one of only nine blackhouses that were still occupied in the village. Fenton's aim was to oversee the hand-over of the blackhouse directly into state care. As the former occupants took up residence in a new whitehouse next door, Historic Scotland opened the blackhouse at No. 42 Arnol as a museum for the public (Fenton 1978).

Through an integrated knowledge of historical records and environmental studies, as well as a detailed analysis of material culture, Fenton appreciated that 'however crude a blackhouse may appear to an uninformed observer, it nevertheless represents a highly sophisticated reaction to the environment and its resources' (Fenton 1985: 39). He emphasised that the blackhouse was a product of the particular social and economic circumstances of the Scottish highlands and islands in the nineteenth century, embodying both change and conservatism (Fenton 1978, 2003). This view was a marked change from Curwen's idea of a 'pristine' blackhouse.

Figure 3.2 The dark interior of No. 42 Arnol blackhouse
Source: Image courtesy of the author.

Recent Archaeological Approaches to Blackhouses

Since the 1960s archaeological perspectives have changed. Two main trends in British archaeology have influenced the few recent studies of blackhouses. Firstly, the importance of viewing archaeological sites within their landscape setting is now emphasised; and secondly, there has been a greater appreciation of the employability of archaeological methods in the study of historic and contemporary periods (e.g., Buchli and Lucas 2001). An opportunity to use these new archaeological perspectives in the context of a crofting township came when the museum at No. 42 of Arnol was renovated and expanded in the 1990s

(MacGregor and Walker 1996, Holden et al. 2001, Holden 2004). Influenced by recent landscape approaches to archaeology, this study aimed to explore the wider social, political, physical and material context of the blackhouse. Fieldwork included landscape survey, historical and aerial photographic survey, as well as excavation of the newly acquired blackhouse next to the existing museum (No. 39) (Holden 2004). This archaeological project signalled the shift from simply examining the form and material of blackhouses as a site type to situating them within the practices of everyday life.

The results of this archaeological investigation illustrated clearly the complexity of blackhouses in relation to the landscape. The settlement of Hebridean population from the eighteenth to the twentieth centuries was in a constant state of flux. Not only did settlement move across the landscape as the land was allotted and re-allotted, but the buildings themselves went through substantial change. Blackhouses were an integral part of the crofting cycle (Holden 2004, Fenton 2005). For instance, not only were animals housed within their walls; their thatch roofs – full of soot from the peat fire – were also renewed annually and spread onto the fields as manure (Fenton 1978, Fenton 2005). These buildings were adaptable, constructed in relation to both the physical and social landscape. The excavation at No. 39 Arnol uncovered at least five phases of building within the forty years of its use as a dwelling (Holden et al. 2001: 26). It has also been suggested that as certain modifications were imposed on and incorporated into the vernacular architecture, the building became less flexible and therefore its form more fixed (ibid.: 30).

Within the current archaeological perspective the image of Hebridean blackhouses is still being actively remodelled and repositioned. The detailed study of the Arnol blackhouses remains an exception rather than the rule. At the heart of this study was the museum, the aim of which was to present a more integrated story of the recent past to the public. Reflecting on the process of presenting the Arnol blackhouse within a modern cultural management service, Chris Tabraham (2006) highlighted the very deliberate way in which the blackhouse was cleared of the 'modern clutter' such as a fax machine and displays. These items were put into a separate visitor centre, a whitehouse, which was seen as 'a 'run-of the mill' building by comparison to the blackhouse (Tabraham 2006: 67). The outcome was a blackhouse described 'more or less as an "interpretation-free" zone, which would be better able to arouse emotions in visitors and provoke reactions' (ibid: 68).

Around the same time as the Arnol museum was being redesigned, Shannon Fraser (2000) from the National Trust of Scotland was tasked to devise a new cultural heritage management plan for the aforementioned Callanish blackhouse, which had been acquired in the 1930s. Aware of the complex political and social history of the original reconstruction and influenced by reflexive approaches to archaeological practice and theory (e.g. Shanks and Tilley 1993), Fraser advocated a more self-aware presentation of the blackhouse at Callanish. Instead of completely renovating the blackhouse (as at Arnol) or leaving it as a ruin, her proposal was to consolidate what was there and to provide sufficient interpretive resources to enable people to work out the complex history of the building for themselves, thus 'allowing insights into the way in which archaeologists and architectural historians tease out histories of inhabitance from the fabric of lived space, and ... enabl[ing] understanding of the various aspirations and tensions surrounding the perceptions of the blackhouse and the crofting system at different points in time' (Fraser 2000: 396). Fraser wanted to enhance the transparency of the process of archaeological interpretation as well as to promote self-critique through the eyes of the visitor. This project has yet to be realised, but it demonstrates the shift in how the role of the archaeologist is seen in the contemporary world. Fraser's ideas exemplify how the practice of archaeology is both a form of dwelling and plays an important role in how blackhouses are experienced, remembered and lived in the everyday.

The Ness Archaeological Landscape Survey

In 2005 the Ness Archaeological Landscape Survey (NALS) continued the practice of archaeological 'dwelling' in the Hebridean landscape. As part of this survey I recorded and surveyed some of the blackhouses in Ness. Applying

**Figure 3.3 Collage of images of people and places from
the NALS survey report**
Source: Image courtesy of Chris Barrowman.

Ingold's 'dwelling perspective' to the practice of archaeology, it can be suggested that my archaeological practice added to the enduring record and image of blackhouses created and recreated by the generations of scholars before me (Ingold 2000: 189). Like these previous archaeological studies of blackhouses, the Ness Archaeological Landscape Survey was framed by its specific social and political setting and not only in terms of the current archaeological practices and theories adopted during fieldwork.

The basic aim of the *Ness Archaeological Landscape Survey* (NALS), directed by Chris Barrowman, was to identify and record all the archaeological sites within the survey area located on the northern tip of Lewis (Barrowman 2006: 7, 2007a :8, 10, 2007b: 10). This aim guided the field methodology; but the ultimate goal of the survey will be to show how the sites are inter-related and index change in the Ness landscape through time (Barrowman 2006: 31, 2007b: 10). The archaeological sites recorded were of various forms and included structures and features of all periods up to the Second World War.

In practice the survey area was divided into 1km grid squares and shared between three teams. Each team was given recent and historical maps of the area, which included data from the 1st and 2nd Ordnance Surveys dating to the nineteenth century, as well as the locations of sites already recorded in the Sites and Monuments Record (Barrowman 2007a: 10). Further detailed information regarding previous investigations and surveys was also available. The process of fieldwork involved systematically walking the given area, recording each archaeological site encountered. All the information was drawn together into a searchable and integrated database and Geographical Information System (Barrowman 2007a, 2007b). The intention was not only that this data be analysed by professionals, but also that it be 'a valuable asset to the Ness community' as it would be made available in the local heritage centre *Comunn Eachdraidh Nis*, interlinking all the field notes and descriptions of archaeological sites together with maps and aerial photographs (Barrowman 2007a: 42). Integrating all aspects of the survey, such as the field notes, directly into the database was a way of enabling the public to see not only what was surveyed but also the *process* of the survey.

The survey was rapid, and therefore in most instances only the general character of the archaeological features could be recorded. Although there had been previous archaeological investigations within Ness, such an inclusive and large-scale survey had not been conducted before. The results would give a sense of what kind of archaeological sites were preserved in this landscape, and their condition. The focus was not on one site type, and thus blackhouses were treated like other archaeological sites, identified and recorded as part of a wider landscape study.

Much of the area I surveyed fell within the inland townships, where most of the people of Ness live today. Since the late nineteenth century, the houses have been predominantly built along the main roads, with long fenced strips of arable fields stretching out behind the houses. To the uninitiated the towns appeared to

**Figure 3.4 NALS surveyor with dGPS enroute between sites in
the townships of Ness**
Source: Image courtesy of Chris Barrowman.

merge into one another, sandwiched between the coast and the moors. From the
initial historical research and fieldwork it was anticipated that most of the remains,
particularly within the crofts, would date to the nineteenth and twentieth centuries
(Barrowman 2007a: 29). As expected, in the fields of the crofts few archaeological
features were discovered, supporting the suggestion that here any earlier sites
would have been ploughed over and destroyed (Barrowman 2006, Holden 2004).

Recording Blackhouses in Ness

Some of the roofless stone ruins with characteristic thick stone and earth walls
stood out from the modern cottages and bungalows which lay on either side of
them. These were easily classifiable as blackhouses. However, the blackhouses in
Ness survived in different states of ruination: some were difficult to distinguish
amongst the modern houses and constructions, only visible as low grass-covered
undulations, having been largely demolished (Barrowman 2007a: 8).

Whether the walls were still upstanding or only survived as low mounds,
the remains of these buildings were measured and any basic architectural
features recorded. We traced the outline of the walls with a differential GPS
so they could be mapped; key features and elevations were photographed, *pro*

forma sheets were filled out and sketches drawn. Despite clear and important differences in the technologies used and theoretical approaches adopted, the basic practice of observing and describing the material nature of blackhouses was comparable to archaeological studies of more than 60 years ago. This underlying methodology forms a very particular relationship with and understanding of the past in the present.

Over the short course of the survey, the complexity of the blackhouses became more apparent. As noted in other recent surveys of blackhouses, it was clear that many of the houses in Ness had also undergone various architectural modifications: concrete walls had been inserted, chimneys added and porches remodelled. Some had been converted into barns, storage areas or places for livestock to shelter and feed. In Ness there were few, if any, examples of what Curwen would have described as 'pristine' blackhouses. Indeed, to have classified all the houses I encountered under the single label of 'blackhouse' would have been to fail to take into account the many perceptible alterations and uses of these structures.

It also became clear how much the blackhouses were only one part of a dynamic tradition of settlement of the Ness landscape. The blackhouses of Ness that were still visible as ruins were not equally distributed across the townships. For instance,

**Figure 3.5 An example of a modified and reused house
and outbuilding in Ness**

Source: Image courtesy of Chris Barrowman.

**Figure 3.6 The remains of another blackhouse in Ness that has a complex
history of adaptation and change**

Source: Image courtesy of Chris Barrowman.

very few remains of blackhouses were recorded in Port. This township developed as a result of the fishing industry in the mid-nineteenth century, and although at that time fishing was a good source of income and a new pier was constructed, the people were still living in the traditional blackhouses (Lawson 2008: 26). The fishing industry declined after the Second World War, but here – more, it would seem, than in the neighbouring towns – many new cottages and whitehouses were built and the old blackhouses were removed as the town was transformed from the late nineteenth and into the twentieth century (ibid: 29). Some of these late nineteenth and twentieth century houses have been replaced and modified in the contemporary landscape.

The NALS project explored the whole landscape, observing and recording what was visible in the landscape in 2005. This raised issues and discussions about archaeologically recording more recent abandoned buildings. Although time limited what could be surveyed, it became clear that settlement in Ness was constantly changing and that the blackhouses as they are did not mark a definitive end of traditional vernacular architecture. Not only were most of the remaining Ness examples of blackhouses adapted and modified using some imported materials and techniques; some of the whitehouses and even modern cottages were also built from locally available materials in the same tradition as blackhouses, using the same stone quarries and locally dug clay. In many ways, such as in relation to plan and form and also some building techniques, the whitehouse and the more modern houses can be distinguished from blackhouses; however, there are other elements and characteristics that link these structures with the blackhouses. It is clear, in other words, that the whitehouses and more modern houses remain part of a particular settlement tradition in Ness.

Recording and interpreting this settlement tradition by directly engaging with the material remains underlies the archaeological practice undertaken as part of the NALS project. As already touched on above, in recent decades more reflexive methodologies involving the deliberate recording and observation of archaeological practice in the field, and used alongside more traditional methodologies, have highlighted the subjective nature of the interpretation of past material culture (Shanks and Tilley 1993, Lucas 2001, Hodder 2003, Chadwick 2003). Although a reflexive methodology was not integrated into the NALS fieldwork, there was an underlying reflexive appreciation of the practice. I was certainly very aware of my own practice of archaeology and its role in the interpretation of the past for the present, through my conversations with people from the local community. Through these interactions I came to realise that the archaeological perspective on blackhouses, in surveying their material character, both complemented and differed from the perspectives of local communities which relate to them through everyday practices.

When confronted with the different perspectives of the local community it became clear that archaeologists form a very specific relationship with past *and* the present through the very process of doing archaeology – a *materialising* relationship (Lucas 2001). Walking amongst the modern houses during the survey of the townships we would meet local people and have the opportunity to discuss what we were doing and more generally to discuss the past. Everyone we met was very open and helpful, even if some were not exactly certain what the purpose of our survey really was. Blackhouses would often come up in conversation and it became clear that my *materialising* archaeological relationship with these features was different from the way those living in the contemporary landscape related to them. The way I observed, moved around, recorded and measured the buildings was not the way the local community interacted with these structures. They would certainly not use this methodology in order to understand or interpret the past. Through the survey I was reaffirming and renegotiating the traditional archaeological image of blackhouses within the Ness landscape, based on their material character. I would translate what I saw on the ground into types and categories, from which I would generate a label and a classification. The dynamic building would be recreated and re-imagined as a sketch, a photograph and an outline on a computer screen to be compared to other buildings translated by the same practice. This type of engagement and re-imagining was very different from that of the local community. For them, the ruins of these buildings were part of their contemporary everyday life, not often consciously distinguished as separate places of the past.

Within the townships of Ness, the blackhouses had been treated in various ways: some had been completely dismantled and perhaps reused to build other houses and structures and were therefore unrecognisable; others survived as low walls covered with grass and acted as convenient shelters for sheep; while still others were converted into loom-sheds or were places to store old croft tools or materials which have yet to find a use. These features were not only blackhouses; they were also part of the everyday landscape. The Ness blackhouses were not being preserved in these ways as museums, as an image of the recent past, as they were in Arnol.

However, this is not to imply that the people of Ness were not interested in the past. The opposite is true; most of the people we met were quite happy to talk about the past: how community life had changed, how in the past everyone would come together to help each other on the crofts. Although the ruins of some of these houses are still a part of their everyday contemporary landscape, when they were drawn into thinking about blackhouses this did reflect a different style of life, from the past. Their imagined idea of lived blackhouses, and the associated image of the life that went with it, were seen as part of the bygone era. Few living in Ness now had ever lived in a blackhouse. Many said that they did not want to return to those dwellings, as they could imagine that life in them was harsh, cold and dark. The people of today were happy with their modern conveniences. The direct experience of life in a blackhouse survives as stories rather than from living memory (e.g. Thompson 1984, Ferguson 2003, MacDonald 2004). The material remains of these buildings are not seen as the lived-in blackhouses of the imagined past; these ruins are part of the present landscape, which seamlessly integrates the past within the everyday present.

A story viewed on the *Comunn Eachdraich Nis* webpage in 2010 demonstrates how Ness was not immune to rapid changes in settlement. In 1957, 34 years after he had been forced to emigrate to North America, Donald Macleod returned to Ness to find that only the sea and the natural landscape appeared unchanged. Although members of the diaspora from the island may have been disappointed to see that the homes that they knew were gone, for the communities living in Lewis and Ness the influences of modernisation seemed to override the preservation of the blackhouse. The local community adapted. Generations later, the current inhabitants of Ness we spoke to seemed not to feel they needed to preserve the houses of their ancestors. For them, it was sufficient that the past was alive in their stories and memories, in the footprints of some of the modern homes and in the surrounding landscape. Francis Thompson, a teacher from Stornoway, has suggested in regard to housing in general: 'the Gael has always been an outdoor man. "Home" to him was the great outdoors, and his house was merely a convenient shelter' (Thompson 1984: 49). I would not agree that blackhouses (or for that matter whitehouses or modern houses) should be seen as merely convenient shelters; but it is certainly true that houses have been indistinguishable from everyday experience of the landscape – the Gael's outdoor life. Activities in the landscape such as cutting peat, manuring the field with used thatch and tending livestock all related to and were integral to the blackhouse.

The local community of Ness, now as then, affirmed its identity through everyday practices. In one case, while in the backyard of a croft trying to locate the traces of a blackhouse that was depicted on the 1st edition Ordnance Survey map, the owner – who was hanging laundry at the time – told me that she knew where the house of her grandfather was and she tapped her foot under the washing line. This illustrated the way in which the people of Ness seemed to know that their history was within the landscape, embodied in their everyday practices.

Blackhouses were, as Fenton suggests, embodiments of change and continuity, constantly being rebuilt and recreated as land was re-allotted and crofting systems changed. For some archaeologists, when blackhouses were no longer built, this signalled the end of a tradition in vernacular architecture. Some of the construction materials and techniques utilised in the whitehouses, cottages, bungalows and prefabricated house have, of course, been different from those used in building the blackhouse. Cement, mortar, corrugated iron, and plasterboard came to be favoured over stone, earth, turf and thatch. However, it has been shown that settlement in the Hebridean landscape was essentially about adaptation (Fenton 1978, 2003). Whitehouses were an adaptation to a changing wider world which affected the social and economic setting of the Isles. This process of adaptation was slow and variable; when whitehouses were first built, many were built as extensions to the blackhouses. Now, by contrast, the remnants of blackhouses are extensions of whitehouses and modern houses. Despite the change in the construction techniques used, the homes built today still form part of this tradition, as many are constructed directly over the footprints of the earlier blackhouses.

Anthropological studies of rural life in Lewis (Parman 1990) and in Skye (MacDonald 1997) have illustrated the complex social life created through the daily and seasonal tasks of the crofting system, highlighting the constant renegotiation of identities through the traditions of the past within an ever-changing modern setting. MacDonald's research has highlighted the awareness of the local community of the generally romanticised view held by visitors of their lifestyle, including the physical landscape setting and traditional houses – which in Skye were not blackhouses but whitehouses (MacDonald 1997). For many people in this community, not only does the Gaelic language distinguish them from mainland Scotland but so too do the traditions of rural life and their strong sense of community; these characteristics saw them through the harsh conditions of the past, and they have the potential to see them through the conditions of the present and the future. This past therefore plays a very important role in the present.

It was not part of the field methodology of the NALS project to record the views, memories and stories of the local community. My conversations with a few of the local people were unexpected and not conducted as systematic ethnographic interviews. What these interactions did highlight, however, was the value of recording and presenting the diverse perspectives of the local community in tandem with the fieldwork of an archaeological survey. The results should be used to situate the dwelling of archaeological practice together with the dwelling of the local community in relation to the material culture and structures of the past in the present. Although such a reflexive project was not directly employed in the field during the NALS project, one of the products of the project was a public exhibition, entitled *Ness Remains*, in the local heritage centre. One element of the exhibition displayed photos of the archaeologists in the field and the results of our work alongside pictures of the local community undertaking their everyday activities and the everyday landscapes. All the photos were taken during the 2006 season. Other display cases held artefacts and the tools of archaeological investigation and survey. The exhibition highlighted the role of archaeologists as part of the whole dwelling perspective of Ness.

Conclusions

Archaeological imaginings of blackhouses have been founded on engagements with the materiality of these buildings. The motivations for studying blackhouses have varied over the years and so too have interpretations and understandings of their meaning. When blackhouses first captured the interest of archaeologists, some were still inhabited. At this time, however, they were rapidly being replaced by more 'modern' housing, similar in form and appearance to that built throughout the mainland. Today, no one lives in blackhouses and they survive largely as ruins, if they have not been completely demolished. A distance has grown between living memory and the life of dwelling in these structures.

Over the years archaeological perspectives have changed. Initially blackhouses were studied only in direct comparison to prehistoric structures. Today, however, blackhouses are no longer viewed as 'primitive' buildings within a modern world. Rather, they are increasingly viewed as a valuable focus of research in their own right. Recent studies have positioned blackhouses in relation to their specific nineteenth- and twentieth-century historical, social and political settings and have considered them as dwellings within a wider landscape of everyday life at that time (e.g. Holden 2004).

However, blackhouses are still a part of the twenty-first-century landscape. My experiences of blackhouses in the course of my work as part of the Ness Archaeological Landscape Survey in 2005 (Barrowman 2006, 2007a, 2007b) has shown me that although they are no longer dwellings, the ruins are still a part of the contemporary world. The relationship between the local community and the remains of blackhouses are variable and may appear to some as ambivalent, but these remains are an integrated element of the everyday experiences of the wider landscape. Through day-to-day activities the local community renegotiates its relationships to the past in the present. These relationships are part of the biographies and stories of the blackhouses and, more generally, of the on-going experiences of dwelling within the landscape.

Archaeological practice – recording and interpreting the past in the present – is also a form of dwelling. In the case of blackhouses, archaeologists have engaged with these structures through the practice of fieldwork. The result has been an enduring tradition in the archaeological engagement with blackhouses. Although the practice of archaeological study of blackhouses has endured, as outlined above, some of the approaches and aims of archaeology have changed and thus the interpretation of blackhouses has also changed. Furthermore, the resulting archaeological imaginings of blackhouses are different from the imaginings of those who inhabited them and different again from those of their descendants who dwell in the landscape today.

As Thomas (2004) observes, the study of archaeology is a product of modernity – a subjective practice which reflects a wider philosophical, political and scientific process and which has formed the modern 'Western' way of thinking. A dominant archaeological agenda has been to engage with the material culture of the past in order to understand the past within the present. Current reflexive considerations have highlighted the fact that the archaeological perspective is only one among many. In the future collaborations between archaeologists, anthropologists and oral historians should be encouraged in order to explore how the past is perceived, created and imagined in the present and for the future and how these studies are part of these imaginings (Edgeworth 2006). These reflexive collaborations would aim to situate the images created by archaeological practices alongside those derived from alternative perspectives, and to see them as part of a shared experience.

References

Barrowman, C. 2006. *Ness Archaeological Landscape Survey. Desk-based Assessment 2005: Project 2000.* Unpublished report, Glasgow University Archaeological Research Division.

Barrowman, C. 2007a. *Ness Archaeological Landscape Survey: Field Survey 2006: Project 2217.* Unpublished report, Glasgow University Archaeological Research Division.

Barrowman, C. 2007b. *Ness Archaeological Landscape Survey: Field Survey 2007: Project 2378.* Unpublished report, Glasgow University Archaeological Research Division.

Buchli, V. and Lucas, G. (eds) 2001. *Archaeologies of the Contemporary Past.* London: Routledge.

Chadwick, A. 2003. Post-processualism, Professionalization and Archaeological Methodologies. Towards Reflective and Radical Practice. *Archaeological Dialogues*, 10, 97–117.

Childe, V.G. 1931. *Skara Brae: A Pictish Village in Orkney.* London: Kegan Paul.

Curwen, E.C. 1938. The Hebrides, a Cultural Backwater. *Antiquity*, 12, 261–89.

Dodgshon, R. 1993. West Highland and Hebridean Settlement Prior to Crofting and the Clearances: A Study in Stability or Change? *Proceedings of the Society of Antiquaries of Scotland*, 123, 419–38.

Edgeworth, M. (ed.) 2006. *Ethnographies of Archaeological Practice. Cultural Encounters, Material Transformations*. Lanham: AltaMira.

Fenton, A. 1978. *The Island Blackhouse*. Edinburgh: Her Majesty's Stationary Office.

Fenton, A. 1985. *The Shape of the Past 1. Essays in Scottish Ethnology*. Edinburgh: John Donald.

Fenton, A. 1987. *Country Life in Scotland. Our Rural Past*. Edinburgh: John Donald.

Fenton, A. 2003. Continuity and Change, in *Scottish Life and Society*, edited by G. Stell, J. Shaw and S. Storrier. Volume 3: *Scotland's Buildings*. East Linton: The European Ethnological Research Centre, Tuckwell Press.

Fenton, A. 2005. *The Arnol Blackhouse: Isle of Lewis*. Edinburgh: Historic Scotland. [Revised edition of *The Island Blackhouse* (1978)].

Ferguson, C. 2003. *Children of the Black House*. Edinburgh: Birlinn.

Fraser, S.M. 2000. The Materiality of Desire: Building Alternative Histories for a Hebridean Crofting Community. *Archaeological Journal*, 157, 375–98.

Hance, W. 1951. Crofting Settlements and Housing in the Outer Hebrides. *Annals of the Association of American Geographers*, 41(1), 75–87.

Hodder, I. 2003. Archaeological Reflexivity and the 'Local' Voice. *Anthropological Quarterly*, 76(1), 55–69

Holden, T. 2004. *The Arnol Blackhouses: Research Report*. Edinburgh: Heritage Policy Group, Historic Scotland.

Holden, T., Dalland, M. and Burgess, C. et al. 2001. No. 39 Arnol: The Excavation of a Lewis Blackhouse. *Scottish Archaeological Journal*, 23(1), 15–32.

Ingold, T. 2000. The Temporality of Landscape, in *The Perception of the Environment: Essays in Livelihood, Dwelling and Skill*. London: Routledge.

Jaatinen, S. 1957. *The Human Geography of the Outer Hebrides*. Helsinki: Helsingforsiae.

Lawson, B. 2008. *Lewis. The West Coast in History and Legend*. Edinburgh: Birlinn.

Lorimer, H. 1999. Ways of Seeing the Scottish Highlands: Marginality, Authenticity and the Curious Case of the Hebridean Blackhouse. *Journal of Historical Geography*, 25(4), 517–33.

Lucas, G. 2001. *Critical Approaches to Fieldwork. Contemporary and Historical Archaeological Practice*. London: Routledge.

Kissling, W. 1943. The Character and Purpose of the Hebridean Blackhouse. *Journal of the Royal Anthropological Institute*, LXXIII, 75–100.

MacDonald, D. 2004. *Lewis. A History of the Island*. London: Steve Savage. [First published 1978].

MacDonald, F. 1998. Viewing Highland Scotland: Ideology, Representation and the 'Natural Heritage'. *Area*, 30(3), 237–44.

MacDonald, S. 1997. *Reimagining Culture: Histories, Identities and the Gaelic Renaissance*. Oxford: Berg.

MacDonald, K. 2003. *Peat Fire Memories. Life in Lewis in the Early Twentieth Century*. East Linton: The European Ethnological Research Centre, Tuckwell Press.

MacGregor, C. and Walker, B. 1996. *The Hebridean Blackhouse: A Guide to Materials, Construction and Maintenance*. Historic Scotland Technical Advice Note 5. Edinburgh: Historic Scotland.

MacLeod, J. (ed.) 1999. *A Description of the Western Islands of Scotland circa 1695 by Martin Martin; Including a Voyage to St. Kilda by the Same Author, and a Description of the Occidental i.e. Western Isles of Scotland by Sir Donald Monro*. Edinburgh: Birlinn.

Mitchell, A. 1880. *The Past in the Present. What is Civilisation?* Edinburgh: David Douglas.

Parman, S. 1990. *Scottish Crofters. A Historical Ethnography of a Celtic Village*. Fort Worth: Holt, Rinehart and Winston.

Pennant T. 1790. *A Tour in Scotland and Voyage to the Hebrides, 1772*. [Reprinted in 1979 by the Melven Press, Perth].

Piggott, S. 1966. A Scheme for the Scottish Iron Age, in *The Iron Age in Northern Britain*, edited by A.L.F. Rivet. Edinburgh: Edinburgh University Press, 1–15.

Roussell, A. 1934. *Norse Building Customs in the Scottish Isles*. Copenhagen and London: Copenhagen: Levin and Munksgaard.

Shanks, M. and Tilley, C. 1993. *Reconstructing Archaeology: Theory and Practice*. Cambridge: Cambridge University Press.

Stoklund, B. 1984. Building Traditions in the Northern World, in *The Northern and Western Isles in the Viking World. Survival, Continuity and Change*, edited by A. Fenton and H. Palsson. Edinburgh: John Donald Publishers Ltd.

Tabraham, C. 2006. Interpreting Historic Scotland, in *Heritage Interpretation*, edited by A. Hems and M. Blockley. London: Routledge, 55–69.

Thomas, F.L.W. 1867. On the primitive dwellings and hypogea of the Outer Hebrides. *Proceedings of the Society of Antiquaries of Scotland*, 7, 153–95.

Thomas, J. 2004. *Archaeology and Modernity*. Routledge: London.

Thompson, F. 1984. *Crofting Years*. Edinburgh: Luath Press.

Webster, J. 1999. Resisting traditions, ceramics, identity, and consumer choice in the Outer Hebrides from 1800 to the present. *International Journal of Historical Archaeology*, 3(1), 53–73.

Chapter 4

OrkneyLab:
An Archipelago Experiment in Futures

Laura Watts

A venture capitalist from one of the world's largest venture capital firms was in the islands of Orkney. As soon as I heard (a company director called me to cancel lunch), I knew this was going to be one of those important ethnographic moments, a keystone to my research here.

I sat at my hotdesk in the environmental consultancy where I had spent much of my time over the last four months, and wondered how I might become entangled in the VC's visit. I stared out, as always, over the blue-grey sea of the archipelago, at the low green pasture of the nearby islands, and the silver clouds that crowned the mythic hills of Hoy beyond.

This archipelago off the northern coast of Scotland was too-often scissored off the top of UK maps, and pasted into a box on the side. I had been drawn here by the landscape, as thousands of tourists are every year. Along with teams of archaeologists, they come for one of the world's most intensely monumental landscapes. Everywhere are stone circles, standing stones, passage graves, and stone settlements from the Neolithic to the Vikings and Picts. Past technologies endure in the landscape here, and will endure into the future. And it was the future of these islands and their landscapes that was my work. It was not simply the past, nor simply the present; it was how these islands participated in making their futures that formed my fieldsite.

For when I speak of futures I mean futures as an effect of social and material practice. The 5,000-year-old Ring of Brodgar stone circle, in the Heart of Neolithic Orkney World Heritage Site, was emblematic. Sitting in the warm offices, staring out to sea, I recalled how the circular monument was an orchestration of stone, sea and sky that had been created in the prehistoric past (Richards 1996), was continually changed through on-going archaeological and heritage practice in the present (Bender 1998), and would be experienced as an effect of those practices into the future. The monument was prehistoric, contemporary, and part of the future simultaneously (following Serres 1995: 60). And it was hard work making such futures in excavation, reconstruction, academic publication, and heritage strategy. I found this hard graft that is future-making compelling. Futures are absolutely not some unknown realm over the temporal horizon, they are not floating untethered. They are situated in everyday practice (Haraway 1991), and are therefore inseparable from the landscapes of their making. As an ethnographer of futures, particularly technological futures, I had been drawn to the Orkney archipelago by its sheer technological *longue durée*, and by the extraordinary landscape of 20,000 people living in 20 scattered low-lying islands, in a place where the sun barely sets in summer, and barely lifts to light the waves in winter.

Over the months I had learned that the future of these fragile islands was pressing and urgent for people living here. Energy futures were everyday conversation, and ever-present in my work. They were in the high cost of electricity, and in the all-too real levels of energy poverty, but also in the potential Gigawatts of renewable energy in the North Sea wind, and in the Atlantic waves and tides. The technological *longue durée* that had drawn me here did not begin and end with the prehistory, but was a continuum that merged into the monumental undersea structures of tidal turbines and wave energy generators being installed and tested here. The newspapers, local radio, and word on the street and farm were shot through with energy futures.

And that was why *he* was here, the Venture Capitalist. The story was that he had been carried north by a wily local after a renewable energy conference down south in Scotland. The VC had been bundled in to a car, and driven north until there was nothing but broiling sea and dark cliffs rising over a distant horizon.

I heard voices behind me, and turned. Grant, the wily local as well as director of the environmental consultancy, stood in the doorway. He waved me over and invited me to join him and the VC in their meeting next door.

* * *

And there he sat, listening to Grant as I wrote at speed in my notebook, his ankle resting on his knee, in a frayed black-hooded top, blue jeans, clean white trainers, surf-stubble beard. A venture capital company scout from Silicon Valley and Los Angeles, he blurred the places together in his American west-coast accent. He was looking to recommend a small investment of 10 or 20 million dollars in the islands' burgeoning marine renewable energy industry, or the CleanTech sector, as he named his portfolio interest.

Futures were in the making.

Sea-bright sun lit the room through high windows set in stone. The building had once been a school and was now repurposed as a business centre, but it retained a glorious view out over the sky and sound between the nearby islands.

Grant gave his presentation on the distinctive features of the Orkney renewable energy industry, and the powerful tidal ebb and flow that had been dramatised by the Scottish Executive as the potential Saudi Arabia of marine power. He talked a little about the European Marine Energy Centre (EMEC) who managed the tide and wave energy test sites in the islands, and was based in the building next door. But most of all he talked about Orkney as a unique place to live and work. He talked about the Orkney people, about the entrepreneurial way of working, the teamwork and collaboration inherent to living an island life.

Collaborative business models was one bullet point he repeated, emphasising its uniqueness to Orkney.[1]

Alec the VC shrugged. '*So much of the stuff is generic, applicable to anyone who wants to be an innovator,*' he said. Teamwork, collaboration, the terms were uninteresting to him. They were generic, the same the world over, not at all unique to Orkney in his eyes.

As an ethnographer attentive to situated knowledge, to how knowledge is done differently in different places (Haraway 1991), and to ontological differences in world-making, my ears prickled as he spoke. They were not talking about the same practices of collaboration or teamwork. They were not the same for Grant in Orkney as they were for Alec from Silicon Valley. There was something incommensurable in their translation back and forth. There were two worlds here: Orkney as seen by the Venture Capitalist, and Orkney as seen by the local company director.

'*I think Silicon Valley is important,*' said Alec. '*So what is it about Orkney that is unique that separates it from the rest of the world? ... I want to know the secret behind the marine business.*'

He said he wanted the Orkney story. That's what would sell the marine renewable energy industry to him and to others. He wanted a story of an Orkney with sea-borne Vikings, who formed such a strong part of the heritage here. He wanted a story of a maritime Orkney to justify his maritime energy industry investment.

'*People like stories,*' he said. '*So weave a strong story of a Viking hub. [That you've] been here from day one as a marine hub.*'

And it was in such a story that he hoped to find a company for his small multi-million dollar investment.

Over the course of Grant's presentation, and no doubt from the moment he headed north with his guest, phones had begun to ring around the Orkney business community and an itinerary created. That was why my lunch had been cancelled. Alec was to be shepherded through the day from company to company, on foot through this stone harbour town of Stromness.

You work together to keep each other in business, I had once been told. It was unimaginable that Alec would be monopolised by one organisation, as perhaps might have been the case in other places. A different sense of commitment was involved. Someone had explained to me that, rather than their employer, they felt '*... part of Orkney PLC, Orkney Limited. [I spend] a lot of time promoting the well-being of Orkney, rather than the objectives of [my organisation].*'

But Alec's commitments seemed more diverse. As we talked after the meeting with Grant, his commitments and interests ranged from his freelance business, to the venture capital firm he was contracted to, to a concern with the global environment, to his Hollywood script project.

---

1   Quotations in italics throughout this chapter are taken directly from my ethnographic notes of conversations, taken during my fieldwork in Orkney, May–November 2008.

Figure 4.1 Ferry MV Hamnavoe and the town of Stromness, Orkney
Source: Image courtesy of the author.

Grant outlined the arrangements for Alec's day ahead. As always in Orkney, making time for the landscape was paramount. In my experience, almost no visitor passed through without a brief tour of the islands. Differences between mainland expectations of island life and life as lived in Orkney became present in the visitor. The sense that knowledge is embodied, is made in practice, and is particular to a place, was intrinsic here. Universality got short shrift. Only by being in Orkney could understanding of its particularity occur. As a local politician had explained, '*Come visit us. Unless you've been here you don't know.*'

Grant was adamant that Alec needed to experience Orkney, but he himself had no time. So I offered to trade my services as a local guide for taking ethnographic notes of our conversation.

* * *

So after the walking and the meetings, Alec settled himself into the passenger seat of the car, awaiting my tour of the islands.

It was then I realised that I had become part of 'Orkney PLC'. I felt beholden to the islands, committed to their future. I sensed a rush of possibility, futures forming that had not been there before, futures that I was suddenly bound up with. The Venture Capitalist wanted to see the islands, to see its secrets and to envision its futures. But seeing and vision were exactly what I felt were at stake, since vision is necessarily partial and professional (Goodwin 1994). He was looking for evidence of a marine story that had been here from day one. What Orkney would he see for investment? Would it be an Orkney PLC future, or some other future he reported back to LA?

There was much at stake in my tour of the landscape.

* * *

We drove always in sight of water, up over a low hill, and down in to a basin. The circular vista enclosed a disc of brackish loch rimmed by moorland, and broken in two by the dark line of an isthmus.

We followed the thin road up the isthmus and parked.

In the cool summer air I walked Alec up a pathway of well-trodden grass, and into the long, rising curve of standing stones that was the Ring of Brodgar stone circle. The stones were sharp-edged, bedding planes divided vertically, a geological mitosis that had been on-going since they were dragged and up-ended 5,000 years ago.

There was an excavation on-going, and one of the directors of the archaeological dig was giving an impromptu talk. I propelled the VC forward to listen.

High-visibility jacket flapping, white hard-hat pushed down firmly over his brow, the archaeologist wove the latest evidence before an enrapt audience. Alec soon fell to the thrall of the metal cage surrounding the dig, and the possibility for future pasts that were being sifted and sampled within. The archaeologist wove a story that re-centred technological innovation:

'Stone circles came 400 years later in Wessex [in the South West of England]. Grooved Ware [a type of pottery associated with stone circles] took 500 years to get from here to Wessex. This,' he spread his arms, *'was the centre in the Neolithic, and spread to what is the centre now.'*

Orkney was the origin for a type of monument and pottery that was later replicated in the south of England (Parker Pearson et al. 2007). The Ring of Brodgar came first. Stonehenge in the south-west of England was akin to a copy (following Jones 2007). Orkney was an origin site of a social and technological innovation in prehistory. The archaeologist's story inverted the contemporary relationship between the urbanised south of England as the UK centre of technological innovation, and Orkney as the island periphery.

Origin stories have potency in technology industries. They reproduce a Darwinian view of technological progress, as though one technology evolves out of another in a linear tree of evolution (Haraway 1989). Such origin stories naturalise a particular place as the single source of a particular technology. There has been extensive critique of such simplistic accounts of technological development, from its assumptions of temporal linearity to its absenting of distributed social and political relations (e.g., Schiffer 1991, Strathern 1992, Latour 1996, Downey and Dumit 1998, Law 2002). However, origin stories remain potent, despite such critique. The making of an origin story gives a place power, to those who want to

Figure 4.2 Ring of Brodgar stone circle, Orkney
Source: Image courtesy of the author.

hear. Alec had said that he wanted to hear the marine energy story *from day one*. He was in Orkney because he believed that this was the place where that origin story could be told. He was not interested in whether it was true, but in whether the story would be repeated and would hold over time. He wanted to be convinced that this would become the origin of marine renewable energy in the future, that here was the location the origin myth would fix upon.

The archaeologist's tale of Orkney as a centre and origin for stone circle technology was exactly the move I imagined he wanted to hear. That Orkney had been and therefore may yet be a world-centre of invention was what he was looking for. No matter that the archaeological evidence was complex, the dating was unconfirmed, and the movement of ideas in prehistory was difficult to interpret.

We got back in the car, and Alec was infused with the archaeologist's passion. But he now spoke of Orkney in the past tense, as though by stepping into the stone circle he had stepped back in time. He seemed to be succumbing to an imagined Orkney that was caught in the past, filled up with prehistory, with little space left for futures.

As we drove away from the stone circle, I pointed out five wind turbines turning grey and faint on the horizon. 'That was the test site of the UK's first large scale wind turbine,' I explained, trying to shift his attention to more recent archaeologies.

But he said nothing. The wind industry was not what he had come for.

* * *

We were at odds for a while as I drove east out of the basin, towards the main administrative town of Kirkwall. He told stories of his script development, actress negotiations. Another world.

I parked the car at the harbour front, and left it to be watched over by the red sandstone glare of the cathedral. We boarded the white and blue council-run ferry heading out to the northern isles of the archipelago.

There's a place to stand on the ferry that's outside, but tucked in against the wind behind the passenger lounge. The Venture Capitalist and I stared out over the handful of cars on the open deck below, tasting salt and fumes. The ferry pulled out and rolled past small square fields, white sand beaches, a dapple of sunlit farmsteads.

Half an hour or so into our journey the water began to ripple from beneath the surface. Eddies swirled, and then broke and sheered. We were close to the intense tidal zone that marked one of the EMEC test sites.

We were in luck and one of the tidal energy generators was out of the water, jacked up on a huge yellow platform 20 meters above our heads. Its name, OpenHydro, was stamped on the side of the maintenance platform. Alec pointed at the quick seawater, which rose up in great bulges around the two stout metal legs. The tidal turbine was a vast white iris, an open industrial stargate through which new energy futures passed, and were tested by the demands of the fierce tidal currents.

Alec smiled at me. This was part of what he had come to see. In the metal-flesh, in the water, a full-sized marine energy device connected to the national electricity grid. The future switched to On.

He asked me how many devices could be tested here, and I explained there were five berths.

'*Marine renewables are a long way from the hype,*' he said with disappointment. He had been expecting many more.

The director of EMEC would have perhaps agreed. '*Marine energy is absolutely still in its infancy,*' he had said to me. '*We are where the Wright brothers were after their first flight. We have proven we can do this, but we have not yet mastered our art ... [It's like the first planes] are for sale, but it's a long way from a commercial airline industry.*'

I repeated the Wright Brothers' analogy to Alec.

He shook his head. '*It's too early for investment,*' he said. He was looking for tested systems, for technologies that were market-ready.

We stared out at the open iris of the tidal turbine, now sliding backwards into the horizon as the ferry pushed north. He wanted tested devices, and this was an operational test-site, and yet he wanted something more certain, more solid and saleable.

Marine renewables was an industry in-the-making, and the EMEC test site was where it was being made. Yet I wondered if Alec realised that the test site was more than just the electrical cables and devices. It was part of a network of countless local experts: mariners, engineers, marine biologists, divers, ornithologists, and all those who, I knew through my research, embodied and worked at the unwritten knowledges that were being made here. There were no standards, no processes, no markets or value chain, no books, few reports to read. Only those people to ask. '*It's terrifying how little we know*,' a local academic had said to me.

Alec seemed to feel it was the wrong time. The marine energy test site was too far in the future for him, too early for investment. In a reversal of his sense of the islands being in the past, this part of Orkney was in his future. Not unlike the archaeologist's tale, here the Orkney periphery had become the leading edge of innovation, and the Silicon Valley centre had become the site seeking to replicate that future.

Orkney was a test site for the world's marine energy industry, and had been the test site for the UK's wind energy industry. The islands were rich in experimental futures. But this was not as some isolated *terra nullis* (Rainbird 1999), rather a uniquely connected island laboratory for future-making (Greenhough 2006). Island studies emphasise how maritime islands connect people over apparently large distances to particular places through favourable currents and winds (Baldacchino 2007). Orkney was part of Viking Norway, not nearby Scotland, for 600 years. Islands as connected peripheries are not microcosms. Orkney was not an island laboratory for those living elsewhere. It was a self-determined island laboratory for re-imagining and re-making its own energy futures, which others participated in and gained from (such as the device developers). Orkney was a demonstration of a particular future, a *demo* in Silicon Valley parlance that Alec could come and witness.

I turned away from the glowing blue water rushing along the sides of the boat, and looked down into the car deck below. Beneath the railing were two open-top lorries, their battered containers filled with grey aggregate for concrete. This was the only way concrete, or anything else, would reach the northern islands. The aggregate was a very visible reminder of how islands were not only connected through the sea, but how seascapes make those connections visible. When the weather is too ferocious to sail in, there is no more concrete for builders. When storm force winds damage the telecoms microwave beacons, the phones stop working; on a landmass such 'landline' phone services would be buried cables and largely invisible. The sea is not a flat tarmac road but a shifting, tempestuous, subtle routeway that makes the tenuous character of all connections visible. Only a week before, in a light summer storm, the electricity had gone out over much of the main island. Infrastructures were fragile and therefore highly visible in the Orkney Islands. It was another reason why energy futures were an everyday topic of conversation, not shelved as an environmental one. Here the dependency of ordinary life on electricity generation and transmission was made obvious, and imagining and making new energy futures was a necessity. The social and material relations between landscape and futures were experiential.

It was an approach that permeated the way Orkney businesses engaged in future-making. The environmental consultancy where I was based insisted on talking about environmental interaction rather than impact. The director had said that, '*[we look at] both what the environment does to you, and what you do to the environment*' (Aquatera Ltd. 2008). I was told that as a largely farming community, Orkney people had a strong sense that the '*landscape bites back ... If you abuse the landscape it will lead to significant hardship in the future.*'

The landscape of Orkney bit-back at the way futures were made here. The seascape made infrastructures and connections visible. The ways of living demanded by this distributed island landscape led to an intrinsic understanding that knowledge is different here, that knowledge and therefore futures are situated rather than universally the same. Businesses worked from the premise that the environment interacts with people, decisions, and futures. The landscape and seascape of Orkney were integral parts of their experiments in making futures. If Orkney was an island laboratory, then the landscape was part of the apparatus. As philosopher Karen Barad argues, apparatus has agency in an experiment, it kicks-back, as she puts it, and makes a difference to the knowledge made (Barad 1998, 2007). Here in Orkney, the landscape had agency and altered the way the future was imagined and made.

But would the Venture Capitalist be able to see the agency of the Orkney landscape in the marine energy industry? Would he see the energy futures being tested here as simply the harnessing of natural power, or as co-constituted by the Orkney seascape and its people? Perhaps he might when we reached our destination.

* * *

With a sudden chugging of its engines, the ferry pulled in to the short pier that extruded out of the green rise of the island of Westray. A gaggle of sea-worn cars and the always-immaculate island minibus greeted us as we walked up the metal ramp to set foot on the island.

Alec smiled with sudden enthusiasm. There was a light in his eyes for the landscape, and he strode on ahead.

The engineer-entrepreneur I'd arranged to meet waited for us in his Landrover. We leapt in, three abreast at the front, and set off up the single-track spine through the island. The sea held us in view on both sides and propelled us north-west, through farmland to the northern edge of the island.

We turned, pulled in to a farm, and parked up beside a large cattle byre. Next to the byre, half sunk in the concrete ground and running almost the entire length of the shed, was something akin to a vast Flash Gordon submarine, studded with rivets. It looked like the kind of Space-Age technology that seems indestructible, made for aeons of industrial hard life. Alec walked up to one of the portals at the prow and squinted through the glass, trying to see in.

'*It's an anaerobic digester,*' Colin the engineer explained. He had designed and built the system, and was one of the start-up company directors. One of the abundant sources of energy they had on this fertile island was slurry. The whole system was integrated with the byre, where the cattle were kept during the long winter. Their slurry fell down through the floor and was transported direct into the airless digester, and the resulting methane was turned into biogas for power (Heat and Power Ltd. 2007).

'*The kye [cows] are the workforce,*' said the engineer with a smile.

Alec looked at my expectant face, looked at the byre, at the industrial digester, and then quizzed Colin about the business model.

The engineer explained that the system was unique to the farm where it was installed. Each digester was a collaborative project with the local farmer, who became a shareholder in the company. No two digesters would be the same, Colin said, since no two farms were the same. The company was not about selling digesters, but about developing and installing systems uniquely adapted to their location in Orkney. He was not interested in mass production or scaling up.

'*It's always in research & development,*' he said.

Alec was taken aback. I imagined he was wondering how such a company would roll out its technology to the world. In conversation he had talked about Silicon Valley solutions being rolled out in Africa. His futures were global, and globally the same. The Orkney engineer's futures were local, and locally distinct.

Colin replied to the unspoken question.

'*The solution is not right for urban,*' he said. '*You can't have trucks of slurry going in and out of a city. You've always got to ask, what's the geography?*'

I wondered what Alec saw as the stable unit of investment here, since the technology was designed to be fluid and adaptable, with the farm and the farmer, the landscape and people, as integral components in its design. There was no 'immutable mobile', to use Bruno Latour's term (Latour 1987). The digester was not simply a social and technical object, but also an environmental one. Its characteristics were particular to its location; change the location, and the digester would change in its design. It was a 'mutable mobile' and made no claims for universal applicability (de Laet and Mol 2000). Rather than a manufactured device that might be personalised, it was a sophisticated design that incorporated all the particular relations at a unique location into a unique device. It operated not only as a technical demonstration, but as a social and environmental one. Colin was not demonstrating a technology that could be replicated and moved, he was demonstrating a device with social relations and the landscape built-in.

Alec asked more closely about the shareholders, and Colin did not blink as he replied. The project was about supporting shareholders located in the island of Westray, and for those in Orkney. It was about making money to keep their island alive with possibility for the future; they were a growing population of 600 people, but de-population was still a serious concern. It was about addressing energy poverty on the island, reducing farm fuel costs, and reaching the island goal of becoming 100 per cent energy sustainable by 2012. Making money for unknown shareholders from around the globe was not where the heart of the company was. He was working with the island, not with the whole world. As an engineer he worked and tinkered with specific landscapes and people as components in the digester, not in an instrumental way but in a practice of ongoing care (Mol 2006).

'*Orkney is a place that acts through people,*' he said.

I had a smile on my face as the engineer's enthusiasm glittered beneath his modesty. This Flash Gordon tank of island energy, this Westray Anaerobic Digester, was another Orkney test site, another part of the island laboratory demonstrating and making possible its future. The landscape of Orkney had agency and acted, not in some theoretical or metaphorical way, but in material practice, through the experience of bodies. Colin felt the islands acting through him.

There was still more to see of the anaerobic digester, and we followed the engineer around to the other side of the byre. Parked up was a large white, slightly rusting, refrigeration container that held the pumping equipment for the system. Colin explained that the container had been part of the fishing industry here, but once things were on the island they were hard to get rid of so you made use of them.

Again the islands made infrastructure visible, in this case waste. There was no landfill to bury things out of sight, everything moved on and off the island by boat. You re-used and consumed with care, because things were difficult and expensive to get on and off the island. Re-use was part of how people in Orkney imagined, designed and made the 'new'. The re-use of *bruck*, as it was known, was every day with its own slot in the local radio breakfast show. An Orcadian had explained to me: '*As islanders we make do. If you needed a spare part, you always knew someone who could make it – from tin, woodworking. We're practical. That's island living. You tied it together with string.*'

Alec was staring out to sea. I did not know what he saw, but I suspected it was not an exciting future for CleanTech. This demo was not for his urban and suburban world of Silicon Valley. Before us was an old, rusting refrigeration container, hand-crafted metal pipes, rivets, and a well-used cattle byre. Demos of new technologies and prototypes in Silicon Valley looked very different, but both had a similar effect: as enactments of a future, as rehearsals, demonstrations made a future possible (Suchman et al. 2002). But Alec did not seem to see this demo, nor could he participate in enacting its future.

Parts of the digester were re-used and re-purposed, but their reconfiguration and integration with the Orkney landscape was new. This was cutting edge innovation. Its fluidity as an object and its embedded design was part of what made it innovative. The components might look old and rusting, but it *was* a new technology, and part of the new high-tech industry of biofuel. But there was no shining new object to admire, there was no profit to be made for CleanTech investors from outside Orkney, and so this innovation was invisible to Alec. It was a new-ness that he could not see.

**Figure 4.3 Anaerobic digester built by Heat & Power Limited,
           Westray, Orkney**
Source: Image courtesy of the author.

Colin drove us back to the pier with the sun setting behind us. Alec was happy to have seen another island in the archipelago, but it was disassociated from his business interests. For him, there had been no relevance to the story of the marine renewable energy industry here.

* * *

On-board the ferry, we were drawn southward into the dusk, distant grey shorelines gliding past. I wanted the VC to see the fading landscape as part of the future he was looking for, integral to the island laboratory and its marine energy test site.

My phone bleeped with a text message. I saw with astonishment that it was time-stamped from the year 2020. But the message was not for me, it was for Alec.

I gave him the phone and let him read:

> I can see the sea lit with a hundred orange stars, each one a buoy marking a marine energy test device in the depths below. Orkney has gone from testing five, to testing a hundred. From two test sites with five berths, to tens of test sites all around the archipelago. It has become the place for developers to test not only their devices, but their ideas. Here they can work with people who know how to make marine energy happen on a shoe-string, in a place whose powerful

waters kick-back and teach them hard lessons about marine energy. Old familiar designs, long deployed and earning their keep elsewhere, come back here to be adapted for deployment in new locations, or tinkered with to care for their sea-embattled bodies.

Each orange light marks a device plugged in to the national grid, a candle for the future. As the tides turn, the electricity powers the islands, and beyond. It has made fuel poverty here almost a thing of the past. This liminal laboratory has also made the UK's and the EU's 2020 target for renewable energy generation possible. This future was made by the people of Orkney, and by Orkney itself.

The message had taken fragments of my ethnographic evidence and reconstructed them into a future Orkney. I recognised parts of the technology roadmaps, decisions, hopes and ideas I had documented over the months. The message had done what I could not in the ethnographic present. It had reconstructed a future Orkney for Alec to see, not as fiction but as empirical imaginary.

But Alec handed the phone back to me without a word.

* * *

We returned to Stromness, into a purple sunset over the Atlantic. Alec would be leaving on the next boat, and I wondered if he had found the secret Orkney he had desired. What futures or origins had he seen?

As we parked back at the old school I asked a pointed question. Was there an opportunity for investment in marine renewables here?

He looked hard at me. '*VCs should not be making the decisions on what technologies will save the world*,' he said. '*They should make money for those that do.*' His investors were large corporations and universities, whom he accepted as the predominant developers of world-saving technology.

'*If they [the VC company] invested in Orkney, I don't know what they would invest in*,' he said with a shrug.

He looked away. Out of the passenger window was the metal sign at the entrance of the European Marine Energy Centre. Both EMEC and the environmental consultancy where we had begun the day employed around 10 people full-time. Yet upon these small businesses at the geographic periphery rested the responsibility for a new industry.

'*They all come here [to Orkney]. Think it is happening here. And they are a bit surprised at the old school and ten people*,' the EMEC director had said.

But now I felt I understood why this marine energy future was being made here and not elsewhere. And why the Venture Capitalist saw nothing for investment. Scale and timing were not quite the investment issue, it was the object itself. It was not 'how large' or 'when' but 'what' the VC could see to invest in.

Alec had been looking for a company with particular markers that constituted financial success for him. However, wealth was not a significant marker of enterprise success in Orkney. The distributed and distant archipelago landscape resisted the simple economics of cost-effectiveness. Instead, organisations and their services grew through interaction and integration with Orkney as a unique place. The landscape, which always meant both people and place, the natural and the cultural, was an acknowledged agent in enterprise success. Alec was looking for a company as an object, but successful companies in Orkney had boundaries that blurred with the local landscape. The Westray anaerobic digester company was integral to Westray, the island and its community. EMEC was not just two test sites and ten people, it was inseparable from its seascape and the hundreds of other Orkney people around the archipelago who embodied and practiced the unwritten knowledge of its working.

As usual, it had taken someone in Orkney to help me understand. The director of the environmental consultancy, Grant, had explained that, '*a business comes out of a collective symbiosis within the community.*'

Alec was no doubt extremely astute in his assessments. It was not that he was inattentive or obtuse but that his professional vision and practice as a Venture Capitalist established an Orkney that was very different to mine or Grant's. Staring at the EMEC sign, he was perhaps wondering how so much international hype could surround so few people. But the disproportion was perhaps because EMEC as a commercial organisation was only part of a far larger and more heterogeneous entity. Alec might see the contractual relationship between the people involved, but he could not see the symbiotic relationship, and the mutual practice of care for the fragile body of Orkney that bound them together. The boundary of the organisation was not EMEC but the much more distinct archipelago and its geography, history, dialect, identity, and self-determination. It was a care for Orkney PLC, as it had been named, a care for the future well-being of Orkney. It was this care that had led to the urgent re-imaginings of energy futures for the islands, and the beginnings of marine renewable energy here; the care that enacted the island as laboratory.

I was frustrated at my inability to translate this for Alec. How to make this Orkney laboratory with its distributed companies, people, places, and landscapes, visible as an object of investment to a VC?

The incommensurate versions of *collaboration* that had existed between Grant and Alec at the start of the day heralded my problem. Collaboration in Orkney was the practice of care for the islands and their communities. It was symbiotic, and involved blurring the boundaries to create an archipelago-wide organisation, which still retained strong internal incoherence and disagreement, of course. For Alec, by contrast, collaboration was a way of working that was generic to good business practice, but did not tend to make company boundaries dissolve and reform in radical ways; to include a symbiotic relationship with the landscape, for example.

It was time for Alec to catch the boat, and I offered to walk him through the town to the ferry terminal. Perhaps it would give me time to explain this archipelago organisation that was the potential origin and investment site for Orkney marine renewables.

* * *

Gusts of wind caught us as we walked through the narrow lanes of the town. A mizzle of light rain swirled beneath the streetlights, and I zipped up my waterproof and pulled on my gloves.

Just as we turned into the harbour, faces to the sea of ink and islands beyond, my mobile phone beeped. It was another text message, sent from the year 2020 again. Another message for Alec:

> You can just see the forest of lights from the new container port out there. Tomorrow, the First Minister will sail over to switch on a tidal-powered data farm for the investment industry, a demo made in a few months from a disused container and an old tidal turbine.

> There are still crowds of business tourists passing through, looking to see how Orkney became OrkneyLab, to understand how it started as the laboratory for the world marine energy industry. Tour guides explain that the test sites were never just a technology demonstration. They demo-ed a new business, a collaboration between local landscape, community, and technology.

> Just behind you, those rectangles of light from that steel and glass building up the hill, that's one of the OrkneyLab campuses. It is home to scientists, technologists, artists, and university students in residence. You have to come to Orkney to know Orkney, so the residencies are for companies and individuals to live and work here, to become part of the place – and for the place to become part of them. There are residencies on each of the 20 inhabited islands, all with different landscapes and so different demonstrations of the future.

> OrkneyLab is not an experiment in global futures, but an experiment in making global futures local.

Again the message had taken my ethnographic evidence and reconstructed it into a future for the Venture Capitalist. The method was similar to an archaeological reconstruction. As an archaeologist reconstructs the past from fragments of evidence, so the messenger had reconstructed the future from fragments of evidence (for more on this method, see Watts 2007; 2008). The message had once more done what I could not. It had reconstructed an empirical future in which the archipelago organisation had a more explicit and visible social and material form. And the message had named the entity: OrkneyLab.

Alec passed the phone back to me with a raised eyebrow.

We were at the ferry terminal, and the end of my tour. I asked the Venture Capitalist if he would be back. There had been moments when the islands had touched him, I knew. But he was coy. He could be back sometime. He hoped to come back. But he didn't know. It depended on how his report was received.

We exchanged business cards, and Alec gave a single wave as he walked away. I did not hear of him again.

* * *

My footsteps re-traced their steps back through the flagstone streets, following the tight wall of grey houses, shoulders to me and the sea. As I walked, my footsteps traced through months of ethnography. For this was not an attempt to describe a whole and complete experience. Rather this day had been formed from parts of my ethnography connected together; for ethnography can only ever be partial connections, parts connected into whole accounts that are not part of any pre-existing whole (Strathern 1991). This day with the Venture Capitalist had been a collage of moments and experiences from my ethnography, juxtaposed to create a fieldsite (Clifford 1988, Gupta and Ferguson 1997). I was now walking through those moments as I walked through the rain, weaving them into a narrative which I could empirically account for in fragments.

I had woven my ethnographic evidence with a particular literary style, a narrative, to do my work of making the landscape visible. But as Tim Ingold has argued, 'telling a story … is not like unfurling a tapestry to cover up the world, it is rather a way of guiding the attention of listeners or readers into it' (Ingold 2000: 190). I had been a guide, I hoped, to the archipelago experiment in futures that was Orkney.

My footsteps had taken me down to a short pier between two houses. I breathed in the salt-air, and listened to the engines of the boat and the lapping of water.

Tide was in.

Acknowledgements

With thanks to everyone I spoke with in Orkney, and special thanks to everyone at Aquatera Ltd. who made me feel so welcome. This chapter is woven out of on-going conversations with Lucy Suchman and Endre Dányi as part of The Leverhulme Trust research project, *Relocating Innovation: Places and material practices of future-making* (grant reference F/00 185/U).

References

Aquatera Ltd. 2008. *Introduction to Aquatera*. [Online]. Available at: http://www. aquatera.co.uk/documents/IntroductiontoAquatera_2.pdf [accessed: 1/11/08].
Baldacchino, G. 2007. Introducing a World of Islands, in *A World of Islands: An Island Studies Reader*, edited by G. Baldacchino. Charlottetown PE, Canada: Institute of Island Studies, University of Prince Edward Island, 1–29.

Barad, K. 1998. Getting Real: Technoscientific Practices and the Materialization of Reality. *Differences: A Journal of Feminist Cultural Studies*, 10(2), 87–128.

Barad, K. 2007. *Meeting the Universe Halfway: Quantum Physics and the Entanglement of Matter and Meaning.* Durham, NC: Duke University Press.

Bender, B. 1998. *Stonehenge: Making Space.* Oxford: Berg.

Clifford, J. 1988. On Ethnographic Surrealism, in *The Predicament of Culture: Twentieth-Century Ethnography, Literature, and Art*, edited by J. Clifford. Cambridge, MA and London: Harvard University Press.

De Laet, M. and Mol, A. 2000. The Zimbabwe Bush Pump: Mechanics of a Fluid Technology. *Social Studies of Science*, 30, 225–63.

Downey, G.L. and Dumit, J. 1998. *Cyborgs and Citadels: Anthropological Interventions in Emerging Sciences and Technologies.* Santa Fe: School and American Research Press.

Goodwin, C. 1994. Professional vision. *American Anthropologist*, 96(3), 606–33.

Greenhough, B. 2006. Tales of an Island-Laboratory: Defining the Field in Geography and Science Studies. *Transactions of the Institute of British Geographers*, 31(2), 224–37.

Gupta, A. and Ferguson, J. 1997. Discipline and Practice: 'The Field' as Site, Method, and Location in Anthropology, in *Anthropological Locations: Boundaries and Grounds of a Field Science*, edited by A. Gupta and J. Ferguson. Berkeley: University of California Press.

Haraway, D. 1989. *Primate Visions: Gender, Race and Nature in the World of Modern Science.* London: Routledge.

Haraway, D. 1991. Situated Knowledges: The Science Question in Feminism and the Privilege of Partial Perspective, in *Simians, Cyborgs and Women: The Re-Invention of Nature*, by D. Haraway. London: Free Association Books, 183–201.

Heat & Power Ltd. 2007. *Heat and Power – Introduction.* [Online]. Available at: http://www.heatandpower.ltd.uk/Introduction.htm [accessed: 10/4/08].

Ingold, T. 2000. The Temporality of the Landscape, in *The Perception of the Environment: Essays in Livelihood, Dwelling and Skill*, by T. Ingold. London: Routledge, 189–208.

Jones, A. 2007. *Memory and Material Culture.* Cambridge: Cambridge University Press.

Latour, B. 1987. *Science in Action: How to Follow Scientists and Engineers through Society.* Cambridge, MA: Harvard University Press.

Latour, B. 1996. *Aramis or the Love of Technology.* London: Harvard University Press.

Law, J. 2002. *Aircraft Stories: Decentering the Object in Technoscience.* London: Duke University Press.

Mol, A. 2006. Proving or Improving: On Health Care Research as a Form of Self-Reflection. *Qualitative Health Research*, 16(3), 405–14.

Parker Pearson, M., Cleal, R. and Marshall, P. et al. 2007. The Age of Stonehenge. *Antiquity*, 81(313), 617–39.

Rainbird, P. 1999. Islands Out of Time: Towards a Critique of Island Archaeology. *Journal of Mediterranean Archaeology*, 12(2), 216–34.

Richards, C. 1996. Monuments as Landscape: Creating the Centre of the World in Late Neolithic Orkney. *World Archaeology*, 28(2), 190–208.

Schiffer, M.B. 1991. *The Portable Radio in American Life.* Tuscon and London: University of Arizona Press.

Serres, M. 1995. *Conversations on Science, Culture and Time: Michel Serres with Bruno Latour.* Ann Arbor, MI: University of Michigan Press.

Strathern, M. 1991. *Partial Connections.* Lanham, MD: Rowman and Littlefield and AltaMira.

Strathern, M. 1992. *Reproducing the Future: Essays on Anthropology, Kinship and the New Reproductive Technologies.* Manchester: Manchester University Press.

Suchman, L., Trigg, R. and Blomberg, J. 2002. Working Artefacts: Ethnomethods of the Prototype. *British Journal of Sociology*, 53(2), 163–79.

Watts, L. 2007. *A Future Archaeology of the Mobile Telecoms Industry.* Unpublished thesis. Centre for Science Studies, Department of Sociology, Lancaster University.

Watts, L. 2008. The Future is Boring: Stories from the Landscapes of the Mobile Telecoms Industry. *21st Century Society: Journal of the Academy of Social Sciences*, 3(2), 187–98.

Chapter 5

Imagining Aridity: Human–Environment Interactions in the Acacus Mountains, South-West Libya

Stefano Biagetti and Jasper Morgan Chalcraft

Introduction

In this chapter we discuss two key topics related to understanding the human condition in extremely arid lands, namely the interaction of people and environment, and the relevance of the study of the present for the comprehension of the past. We consider the case of the Kel Tadrart Tuareg, a small pastoral lineage currently dwelling in the Acacus Mountains, a massif situated in south-western Libya (Figure 5.1). The ethnoarchaeological investigations at the core of the chapter are part of a broader project: the study of the past of a large region, with emphasis on the late phases (e.g., from 10,000 years before present onwards) of prehistoric occupation and on subsequent historical phases. The project has highlighted the major role that animal husbandry has played within the societies that have dwelt in the area since the adoption of domesticates some 7,000 years ago. The *Italian Libyan Archaeological Mission in the Acacus and Messak* has been working in south-west Libya since 1955, adopting an interdisciplinary perspective which focuses upon the investigation of the cultural trajectories and the palaeoenvironmental reconstruction of the Pleistocene and Holocene of the area. Under the direction of Mori (1955–1996) and Liverani (1997–2003), copious data have been collected about the prehistory and the history of the region, contributing to a broad understanding of the development of human occupation in the presently drier Sahara. Furthermore, the study of the rock art panels (mainly 'Neolithic', that is 7,000–3,500 years ago) was important in leading to the inclusion of Tadrart Acacus in UNESCO's World Heritage List in 1985.

Under the current direction of Savino di Lernia (since 2004), the project now also encompasses the study of the present: the current inhabitants of the area. From its inception, archaeological research has focused upon human–environment interactions, thanks to the detailed reconstructions of the climatic fluctuations that have occurred over the last 10,000 years. With these human adaptations to climatic oscillations extending from the Holocene to the present, and combined with a long tradition of research in the southwest Fezzan, the central Sahara represents a particularly interesting place for the study of the ecological and social landscapes

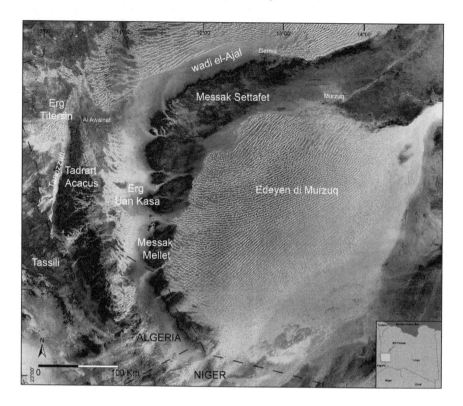

**Figure 5.1 The area licensed to The Italian Libyan Archaeological Mission in
the Acacus and Messak (central Sahara)**

Source: Image courtesy of the archive of The Italian Libyan Archaeological Mission in the
Acacus and Messak (central Sahara).

of contiguous human groups (Brooks et al. 2005). It is from the vantage point
of this great temporal depth, and with a remarkable archaeological record, that
we approach an understanding of the current relationships that the few remaining
herdsmen have with 'their' landscape (Figure 5.2), the mountains and pastures of
the Tadrart Acacus and the surrounding area.

This entire area falls under the prescriptive understandings of western
climatology and geography, as well as established stereotypes regarding the world's
largest desert. One of these is aridity, defined by the *Oxford English Dictionary* as
an 'arid state or quality, parched or withered condition, lack of moisture, dryness,
barrenness'. However, we will argue that aridity might be in the mind (see di Lernia
2006a: 6), and we want to see how useful this concept actually is: what bearing
does it have on current subsistence strategies, on perceptions of the environment
that Kel Tadrart call home, on the techniques and ideas that might have driven and
developed previous societies living in the area? For us, investigating the validity of

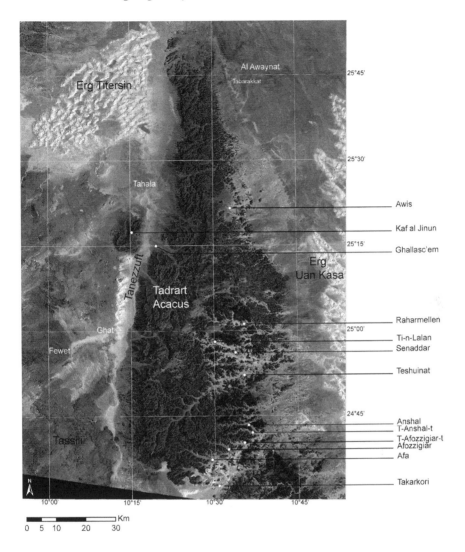

Figure 5.2 The Tadrart Acacus

Source: Image courtesy of the archive of The Italian Libyan Archaeological Mission in the Acacus and Messak (central Sahara).

aridity as a meaningful concept in the central Sahara means bringing together the scientific data on the environment, topography, hydrography and other measurable features of the area with the embodied experiences and livelihood strategies of those who currently live there. In our perspective, these are not necessarily mutually exclusive. Rather, it is between them, between the imagined worlds they describe, that those lived realities that bear most closely on the ways the area's past inhabitants interacted with their environment are most clearly revealed. There are problems, of course, but matching the holes in the ethnographic record are those in the scientific data; notably, in this case, on rainfall, which local people describe as falling erratically and occasionally over their area. There exists a certain incommensurability between rainfall patterns, their local perception, and their scientific measurement. Climate here can be local, unmeasured by science, but remembered, and evident in the ethnoarchaeological record, in shelters, dung, rock art, and in on-going grazing strategies.

Our challenge to move beyond 'aridity' is straightforward: if contemporary pastoralists inhabiting what is technically speaking a hyper-arid area neither perceive nor imagine it as such, then it is unlikely that their historic and prehistoric predecessors perceived it any differently. In other words, we cannot assume that just because western science judges an environment to be arid, such a negative perception of climate and environment – defined in terms of what it lacks – would have driven the choices that made the area viable and amenable for its various human populations. This is another way of saying that 'cultural' reasons may override environmental determinism, that the adaptive strategies of contemporary pastoralists are underwritten not so much by a sense of the 'harshness' of the environment (as it appears to western eyes) as by a culturally inflected mode of perception that is attuned to local variations and to the possibilities they afford. Of course, we would not go so far as to question the realities of what is undoubtedly a place *where water matters*. Our objection to the concept of 'aridity' lies in its lack of nuance: it is a clumsy concept, since topography, cultural adaptation and other factors clearly mean that aridity matters more in some parts of the Sahara than others (see di Lernia and Palombini 2002, for different responses to aridity in southwest Libya during the Holocene). Knowledge of this variation would have mattered to mobile groups, and thus their ability to exploit it perhaps made mobility their key resource (Tafuri et al. 2006). Significantly, it also matters who you are, as the appalling loss of life through dehydration currently suffered by sub-Saharan migrants entering Libya from Algeria on foot only a few kilometres west of the Acacus makes painfully clear. We need to add a social dimension to 'aridity', both as an echo and as a recontextualisation of Marcel Mauss' classic 1906 *Seasonal Variations of the Eskimo* (see Bravo's reassessment in Bravo 2006): if we are interested in human-environment interaction in the central Sahara, then we have to look at aridity as a social phenomenon. To do so is to confront head-on the incommensurabilities between western and local ideas.

Ethnoarchaeology and the Sahara

Given the ethnoarchaeological nature of the project, and its relevance to archaeological investigations, it is worth briefly outlining the main issues involved in the archaeology of mobile groups, and the role that the observation of the present can play in that type of research. The mobile hunter-gatherers and pastoralists of the past have traditionally presented a challenge to archaeologists working on the identification and interpretation of temporary campsites. Rather than running through the development of approaches to non-sedentary communities of the past, it suffices to stress what studies published to date have amply confirmed, namely that an 'archaeology of mobility' is well-established with 'specific and well-defined methods, which take into account the low density of artefacts and concentrate on regional studies' (Wendrich and Barnard 2008: 1). However 'ethnoarchaeology', which is one of the methods we wish to take into account here, is not a specific and well-defined approach. This discipline has traditionally held a problematic position within the anthropological sciences. Whether considered to be merely an approach or to be a 'science' in its own right, ethnoarchaeology resists any single or exact definition; nevertheless it can generally be described as the study of living cultures for archaeological purposes. Arguably, the widespread use – and misuse – of ethnographic analogy has made a significant contribution to archaeology worldwide, highlighting the potentialities and pitfalls of ethnoarchaeologically driven strategies for the interpretation of the past (see David and Kramer 2001 for a recent overview). Yet the aforementioned issues have not given rise to a systematic and explicit discourse around ethnoarchaeology and its procedures. Instead, they have generated confusion and dissatisfaction. Indeed, ethnoarchaeology remains marginal, so much so that in the 2009 conference of the Association of Social Anthropologists, the theme of which was the 'relationship between archaeology and anthropology', not one of the 41 panels was dedicated to ethnoarchaeology.

Despite these problems, ethnoarchaeology has made crucial contributions to understanding pastoralism in the past. In arid and semi-arid zones of Africa and the Near East several scholars[1] have demonstrated how pastoral sites can be found and investigated by way of ethnoarchaeological indications, adopting various approaches and techniques. Unfortunately, few similar projects have been undertaken in the Sahara in the last few decades. Many reasons, such as low population densities and fragile, frequently explosive political contexts, have contributed to this. Furthermore, Saharan communities, often nomadic and lightly equipped, were a low priority for scholars who needed to record complex *chaînes opératoires*. Saharan communities seemed to reveal few attractive elements to those interested in the symbolic facets of human behaviour (e.g., Hodder 1982). Adherence to Islam on the part of certain societies also led to their exclusion from study. Eventually, work on the formation processes for archaeological sites (*sensu* Schiffer 1987) collided with the debate about the alleged invisibility – or difficulty in identification – of nomadic campsites (e.g., MacDonald 1999, di Lernia 2001, Lane in press). All these things have made the Sahara seem an Islamicised, residual, elusive, contaminated context and thus almost worthless for archaeological investigation (see Biagetti 2009).

---

1 For example, David 1971, Robbins 1973, Gifford 1978, Hole 1979, Smith 1980, Cribb 1991, Gallay 1991, Avni 1992, Banning and Kohler-Rollefson 1992, Bradley 1992, Biagetti and di Lernia 2003, Shahack-Gross et al. 2003, Shahack-Gross et al. 2008.

In our view, however, the Sahara is exactly the place where our western-derived interpretative tools and categories can be challenged and sharpened. Brooks and colleagues (Brooks et al. 2005: 258) have suggested that the Sahara can be viewed as a laboratory of human response to environmental change, 'given the overwhelming nature of the climatic changes that have affected the region throughout the relatively archaeologically accessible Holocene'. Thus, current approaches in Saharan archaeology emphasise human-environment interaction, which is recognised to have affected the development of cultural trajectories over the last 10,000 years. Generally speaking, scholars (e.g. Hassan ed. 2002) agree that severe and abrupt dry spells occurred in the Holocene, and that they had a severe impact on human groups, both the societies of late foragers (10th–8th millennia BP) and the herdsmen of the long Pastoral Neolithic (8th–3rd millennia BP). Different perspectives exist on the responses on the part of groups in the past. As di Lernia recently argued (2006a), some scholars view the arid spells as having been the catalyst for the diffusion of pastoralism in the Sahara whilst others suggest that those same spells led to its contraction. Besides the obvious need for more refined data on the archaeology and palaeoecology of the area, the careful study of data from contemporary societies inhabiting these allegedly 'marginal' environments should help to reveal some of the solutions, perspectives and adaptations that have made these environments suitable for human habitation. Many pastoral groups are to be found in what are classified as arid and semi-arid lands: in steppes, savannahs, and deserts. Yet in these lands, pastoral societies (and states) have flourished in antiquity and still 'survive' in the present.

The Environment

The study area is located in the southwest corner of Libya, bordering Algeria, in the region of the Fezzan. It is roughly delimited by the coordinates of 24°30'– 26°N latitude and 10°–11°E longitude. The main physiographic element in the area is the Tadrart Acacus massif, comprising a dissected mountain range mainly composed of sandstone. The massif runs approximately 150km North-South and 50km East-West at its maximum (see Figures 5.1 and 5.2), with an altitude ranging from 800 to 1,300 meters above sea level. The Tadrart Acacus is bordered by the *wadi* (a dried river valley) Tanezzuft to its west. This *wadi* runs along the international border and divides the Tadrart Acacus from the plateau of Tassili n'Ajjer in Algeria. At the north-west summit, the mountain is edged by the *erg* (dune field) of Titersine (600km^2). The *erg* of Uan Kasa (3,500km^2) is located east of the massif. Just a few small villages are to be found along *wadi* Tanezzuft, where the 'town' of Ghat is located. On the other side of the massif, the town of Al-Awaynat is set close to the northeast extremity of the Tadrart Acacus.

The geomorphology of the Tadrart Acacus has been described in detail elsewhere (Marcolongo 1987, Cremaschi and Frezzotti 1992, Cremaschi 1998). Most importantly, the longitudinal orientation of the Acacus massif lends its eastern and western sides very different characteristics. The steep western side, with a vertical slope set along a fault-line, is pretty inaccessible, except for some steep passageways that were used a good deal in the past but are nowadays of only minor importance, because they cannot be used by motor vehicles. Conversely, the eastern edge tends to slope off, with several flat structural surfaces, dipping eastward, forming so-called 'structural terraces'. Present-day human occupation occurs along the flat alluvial valleys that run along the bottom of the *wadi* and along their banks. These dried river valleys cut deeply into the Acacus (Figure 5.3), attesting to ancient fluvial activity. The large valley floors furnish characteristics that are in principle favourable for resource regeneration. In particular, vegetal coverage should be more developed in the large valleys, creating suitable conditions for human occupation. To the east of the Tadrart Acacus, a transition belt separates the massif from the dunes of the *erg* Uan Kasa. Here, geological strata forming a sequence of *cuestas* merging toward the east provide favourable conditions for the capture and persistence of groundwater for the formation of phreatic aquifers (a water table) close to the surface.

The climate of the area is technically arid. Rain frequency is uneven and precipitation does not occur every year, consequently there is no proper alternation between rainy and dry seasons. Some data are available for the nearest oases of

Figure 5.3 Wadi Teshuinat and the Kel Tadrart campsite TES_07/1
Source: Image courtesy of Stefano Biagetti.

Ghat and Al-Awaynat: in both oases an average of 10mm per annum is recorded, although the recording itself has been erratic. Generally speaking, the figures clearly indicate that almost completely dry years can and have occurred in the course of the last two decades. However, the collection of these data has been so erratic that it is impossible to reconstruct the rainfall pattern with confidence, making it difficult to match precise precipitation levels with the oral information we recorded. The *wadis* are presently dried up, even if they may still sometimes contain ephemeral water after rain.

Despite this, permanent plant cover can actually be recorded all year round, allowing for the presence of both humans and animals. Even when no rain has occurred throughout the twelve months, residual waters stored at shallow depths allow vegetation to survive in severe conditions. Descriptions of the flora of the Tadrart Acacus sub-region are quite poor. Mercuri (2008) summarises the situation, stating that *wadi* vegetation and Saharo-montane vegetation, typical of the Saharan Transitional zone (White 1983), are prevalent. In the *wadi* Teshuinat – one of the main valleys of the Acacus – permanent communities of *Acacia–Panicum* and *Acacia–Panicum–Zilla* (Schmidt 2003: 122–3) are well developed, though their consistency varies from year to year due to the inconstant rain. Hygrophilous vegetation concentrates around the *gueltas* which are widespread in the area. A *guelta* is a rock pool where rain water collects: generally speaking, the *gueltas* in the Acacus are very different in size and water capacity, and most importantly, they represent a key feature of the Acacus landscape for local communities.

Sub-surface water plays a major role in resource availability for most inland Saharan settlements. Modern technology has increased the exploitation of ground water in some areas of the Fezzan, where pumping has allowed the irrigation of fields. This intensive use of water raises several issues about its sustainability over time, as recently stressed by Brooks et al. (2005). Of particular importance to our project are the two wells that the government bored in the early 1980s in the intermediate area between the *erg* Uan Kasa and the eastern ranges of the Acacus massif: at present, the wells of Eminanneia and Taluaut assure a regular supply of water for the people inhabiting the mountains.

The Kel Tadrart of the Acacus Mountains

The fieldwork on which this study is based was undertaken in January and September–October 2007. This was preceded, however, by many years of archaeological work in the area and built on close relationships established with local people. The Tadrart Acacus is the landscape of small pastoral communities of Tuareg who refer to themselves as Kel Tadrart of the Kel Ajjer group. Kel Tadrart practise livestock husbandry, owning mainly goats and sheep: small ruminants constitute the basis of their economy. This stock is essential for self-subsistence and as a source of income. Many Kel Tadrart stated that camels are less frequently owned than in the past, though they are still herded and allowed to graze freely.

Donkeys are valued as beasts of burden, and are extremely useful for transporting water from the *gueltas* to the settlements. Dogs help in herding activities but only a few chickens, kept for the eggs, were observed. The twelve households recorded in the Tadrart Acacus belong to the same lineage, with the elders being brothers or first cousins. At the time of fieldwork only one household was recorded outside of the mountains, 30 km west of the Northern Acacus, displaced there in 2005 after the substantial rains of that year. The strong family ties are constantly refreshed by visits and reciprocal favours.

The number of Kel Tadrart inhabiting the Acacus massif is low (see Table 5.1). Their campsites are to be found along dry river valleys throughout the Acacus. Outside of the mountains, a larger number of them can be found, mainly in the 'village' of Tabarakkat (alternatively known as 'Oubarakkat'), located three km south of Awaynat. There, the government has been building concrete houses for all the Kel Tadrart since the early 1980s, in the hope of encouraging them to leave the mountains and settle in the vicinity of the oasis. According to non-Kel Tadrart informants, the overall number of Kel Tadrart in the Acacus, Tabarakkat, and in the small oases of Tahala is approximately 300 people. This figure is probably on the high side. At the time of fieldwork 54 persons were recorded throughout the massif, and as noted above all belong to the same lineage, and are closely related. The density of inhabitants per square km is extremely low (0.012). Typically for pastoralist groups, these figures should not be considered 'fixed', as the number of inhabitants can vary over time, depending on social and environmental contingencies. All ages are represented, even if young adults

Table 5.1 The Kel Tadrart campsites and their inhabitants

Site	Child (0–10)	Youngster (11–17)	Young adult (18–25)	Adult (26–49)	Elder (>50)	Total
ALO_07/1	–	1	–	2	1	4
IMH_07/1	–	–	1	1	1	3
IMH_07/2	1	1	1	1	1	5
IMH_07/3	–	–	–	1	1	2
IMH_07/4	3	–	–	1	1	5
IMM_07/1	3	1	1	2	–	7
RAH_07/1	–	–	–	1	1	2
SUG_07/1	3	–	–	1	1	5
SUG_07/2	2	–	–	2	–	4
TES_07/1	–	–	2	–	2	4
TIB_07/1	1	1	–	1	1	4
TIH_07/1	4	–	–	2	2	8
Total	17	4	5	15	12	54

(around the age of 30) are slightly under-represented. Young people tend to move to villages in search of work, especially following the rapid increase in tourism and the high demand for Tuareg guides or workers in tourism facilities. Some families may send their children to relatives in settled villages, to attend school. The Qaddafi-era Libyan government encouraged the Kel Tadrart to join the army and to serve in the checkpoints and outposts of the area (currently of increased importance given trans-Saharan economic migration), because of their knowledge of places and the desert way of life. The dominant household type among the Kel Tadrart is the nuclear family household, composed on average of 4.5 persons. Each household is an independent economic unit that achieves viability mainly through the sale of its own resources, namely their livestock and its by-products, and, as previously mentioned, through the labour power of its male members. No significant differences in wealth have been recognised so far among the Kel Tadrart.

In the Acacus, the Kel Tadrart lineage is represented by 12 settlements, corresponding to 12 households. Their settlements (see Figure 5.4) are the main sites for almost all the households. The campsites are the focus of daily activities and comprise different structures, each inhabited by a nuclear family. The only geomorphological map available (Marcolongo 1987) indicates some locations where the regeneration of vegetation can occur more rapidly, due to the capacity of the large valley floors and, to a lesser extent, pediment soils to retain water. The higher parts of the massif ('second terraces') are yet to be fully explored and may feature, in principle, some patchy and ephemeral grazing. However, the large valley floors do indeed attract a large proportion of the Acacus' dwellers, where other drainage and soil choices exist. The majority of sites are located upon or in close contact with the most favourable soils. Three cases are exceptions: RAH_07/1 and SUG_07/1 and 2. While RAH_07/1 is actually located only 2.5km from the 'green' area, the other two sites (i.e. RAH_07/1 and SUG_07/1) are quite distant from good soils. However, these two sites are set in the immediate surroundings (within 1km) of a well, and in this case water availability surely plays a major role in the choice of location. In fact, the other crucial factor to be considered is access to water, either from wells or from *gueltas* (rock-pools).

Recourse and access to water is obviously a crucial issue in such a marginal environment. Presently, three permanent wells are normally available throughout the year: *bir* Sughd, *bir* Taluaut, and *bir* Eminanneia. These provide a constant supply of water for the inhabitants of the Acacus as well as for the many tourists and travellers who cross the area. *bir* Sughd is the only non-mechanised well, exploiting shallow subterranean waters. The others exploit deep fossil water by means of mechanical pumps, and were established in the early 1980s. These wells are not necessarily close to the settlements. Only in Sughd are two sites very close to a well (see also Figure 5.4).

In the other cases a variable distance has to be covered (12km minimum to 73km maximum). This implies that the flocks cannot normally be brought to the wells as part of their daily grazing (no more than 10km back and forth from

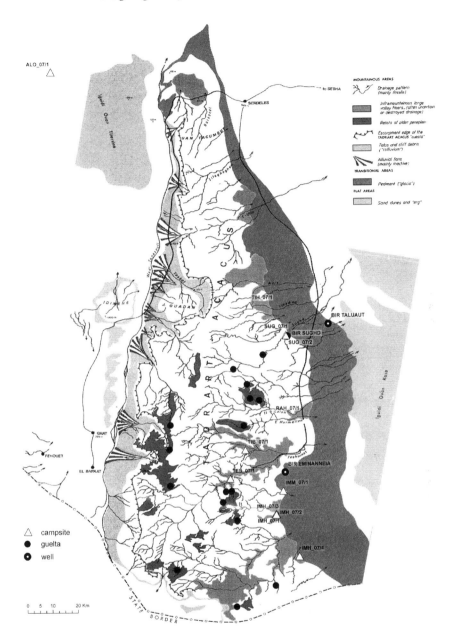

Figure 5.4 The Kel Tadrart campsites, the gueltas, and the wells placed upon the geomorphological map by Marcolongo (1987)

Source: Image courtesy of Bruno Marcolongo.

Table 5.2 Distance between the Kel Tadrart campsites and the well in the Acacus Mountains

Site	bir Taluaut	bir Eminanneia	bir Sughd
ALO_07/1	n.a.	n.a.	n.a.
IMH_07/1	12	73	62
IMH_07/2	12	73	62
IMH_07/3	12	73	62
IMH_07/4	25	73	62
IMM_07/1	58	7	50
RAH_07/1	30	16	24
SUG_07/1	12	38	1
SUG_07/2	12	38	1
TES_07/1	15	50	42
TIB_07/1	43	13	37
TIH_07/1	22	49	13

the campsites); rather, some water is brought to the settlements, though often not without considerable effort (due to the nature of the routes). No data are yet available about other 'traditional' wells like *bir* Sughd. Occasional abandoned wells have been spotted throughout the massif, though we will focus upon the *gueltas* which have traditionally supplied water for the Kel Tadrart and to which – in most cases – the flocks can be brought. The *gueltas* are often set on the first structural terrace, so that accessibility can be conditioned by the morphology of the terrain. A *guelta's* water capacity is almost impossible to evaluate precisely, given the variability of the water level. However, some rocky pools are assumed to be almost permanently full of water, while others are more ephemeral (see also di Lernia et al. 2012). Their fullness is entirely dependent on rainfall, and on individual rates of evaporation which are affected by the micro-climatic niches in which they are located (orientation, degree of shade, rock morphology, etc.). Generally speaking, the main *gueltas* are said to retain water for around three years. It is quite rare for three dry years to occur in a row, so that these *gueltas* are considered to provide a dependable water supply.

It is worth considering the intra-annual degree of mobility (Table 5.3), as diverse patterns can be outlined. Only the household living at site ALO_07/1 undertook a regular (strictly seasonal) transhumance journey, every summer. Only two households claim to be fully sedentary. They are, noticeably, the household of the *amghar* (TES_07/1), a respected local leader for the Kel Tadrart Tuareg, although now playing no more than an informal role in maintaining the moral community; and that of his son (IMM_07/1), formally entrusted by the Libyan government with some official duties. The rest of the sample stated that they could move 'where rain occurred' when the pasture is low in the vicinity of their

Table 5.3 Mobility

Site	Regular transhumance	Opportunistic displacement	Fully sedentary
ALO_07/1	√		
IMH_07/1		√	
IMH_07/2		√	
IMH_07/3		√	
IMH_07/4		√	
IMM_07/1			√
RAH_07/1		√	
SUG_07/1		√	
SUG_07/2		√	
TES_07/1			√
TIB_07/1		√	
TIH_07/1		√	

Source: Interviews and direct observations.

settlement. Some of them have secondary settlements; others do not and can count upon their relatives in that locality for accommodation.

The most striking thing is that almost all of the Kel Tadrart asserted that they generally move towards *wadi* Teshuinat, which is recognised as the favoured place in the Acacus. It is true that this *wadi* is one of the richest in grass (see also Figure 5.4), but other reasons can be identified for its importance as well. It is likely that this *wadi* holds a place, and maybe a key place, in Kel Tadrart identity and memory, and it is not by chance that the settlement of the Kel Tadrart's *amghar* is located there. In other words, even when there is pasture in the surroundings of their current locations people choose to head for this area, and this is not just for ecological reasons. Other areas of the Acacus are, in fact, also provisioned with good pastures (Figure 5.4), but they were not – at the time of our fieldwork – considered as suitable alternatives. On the basis of the few ethnohistorical sources available, we can build better understandings of the current situation, and shed light on the special role of *wadi* Teshuinat.

The study has highlighted some variability in land use, based on consideration of the several factors that can affect pastoral lifestyle in the area. Our interpretations remain partial, as not all the data collected have yet been analysed. Nevertheless, some key points can be emphasised. Different strategic choices are particularly noticeable within the sample, regarding location in relation to resources and the type of mobility pursued throughout the year. From a genuinely ethnoarchaeological viewpoint we need to question the reliability of any interpretation of past societies based on fixed models, since – especially in marginal environments – behaviour can be fairly dynamic and include considerable variation. In fact, variability is apparent at the micro-level, that is when people live in the same 'region' and belong to the same lineage as well. In our sample, we stress that there has been a trend towards increasing sedentism, which has been favoured by local institutions. We agree with Lane (in press) when he suggests that this process 'may be unique in terms of its historical and cultural specificity but not necessarily unique in a more generic sense to regional pastoralist practices'.

Following this perspective, it is worth taking into account the few sources related to the early-twentieth century. In fact, ethnohistorical accounts (Gigliarelli 1932, Scarin 1937) can be helpful in tracing back the historical dimension of cultural dynamics in the Tadrart Acacus. An Italian officer (Gigliarelli 1932) reported that the Kel Tadrart of the Acacus – mentioned here with their current ethnonym for the first time – and their slaves numbered 78 in 1932, and between them had 337 ovicaprids and 27 camels. This report stresses that the connection with the Wadi Tanezzuft occurred regularly, giving the chance for the Kel Tadrart to be in contact with the decreasing but still active trans-Saharan commercial fluxes occurring along the *wadi* Tanezzuft, descending from the massif by means of the mountain passageways, one of them being located just above the oasis of Ghat. This pattern of mobility and trade in the colonial era is confirmed by the memories of Kel Tadrart adults, and particularly by the elders we interviewed, who gave us detailed accounts of their past nomadic lifestyle and the long-lasting movements of transhumance that occurred when they were young. In the light of this, we argue that the Wadi Teshuinat might well have played the role of a key 'link' in the past, cutting through the massif from east to west and ending close to Ghat, which can be reached after a few kilometres of mountain path – providing a large natural supply of water – after the end of the valley.

It is, then, no coincidence that the settlement of the Kel Tadrart's *amghar* is found here, in the Wadi Teshuinat, a dried river which maintains a symbolic as well as an economic importance in the minds of Kel Tadrart. Memories of past caravans and journeys to Ghat and surroundings through the Acacus are still alive among the Kel Tadrart, who continue to profess an attachment to the area of Ghat and the *wadi* Tanezzuft, even though the trajectories of their pastoralist livelihoods no longer take them across it. Other reasons, however, may take them to the area, albeit – and tellingly – not by way of their previous routes.

Inconclusive Remarks

To conclude, we argue that the two territorial patterns of the Kel Tadrart which can be observed in the Acacus over the last thirty years are likely to have developed from earlier trends: (i) some of the Kel Tadrart left the massif and settled in the village of Tabarakkat, close to the oasis of Al Awaynat; (ii) others stayed in the Acacus, modulating their movements to a 'smaller' environment, shaping their lifestyles to a new set of dynamics. The Kel Tadrart dwelling in the Acacus gradually shifted their focus to the oasis of Awaynat where many of them were already settled, reorienting their trade. As a result, passageways in the western slope of the Acacus were gradually abandoned. This process was prompted by the adoption of cars, which can reach Awaynat quite easily but cannot cross the western passageways. This north-south oriented pattern has replaced the east-west one, and it may provoke further changes in the social (and individual) memory of the Kel Tadrart whose connection with the southern and western oases along the *wadi* Tanezzuft are nowadays lost or insignificant from a merely economic viewpoint. It is likely that those members of the Kel Tadrart lineage who made the choice of living in the mountain are re-elaborating their identity, reinvigorating it by reinforcing their ties with the mountain itself, and with the *wadi* Teshuinat in particular. Viewed in this way, it is no surprise that many of them stated that they were born 'here', where 'here' is a more or less extended conception of land that may also include, for instance, the village of Tabarakkat, described as 'the desert' by one of its new Kel Tadrart inhabitants. Memories of past trade routes are still alive and inscribed in the rock walls of the passageways, whilst the new directions of trade do not leave visible traces but car tracks in the flat areas bordering the eastern Acacus. An informed ethnoarchaeology (*sensu lato*) thus helps us to grasp the key aspects of pastoralism in arid lands, where strictly deterministic and normative perspectives are often far too easily adopted.

We must also recognise the limitations of our own approach. Whilst we know enough of local ideas of the environment and the significant variation in subsistence patterns and strategies in and around the Tadrart Acacus to question the environmental determinism that the concept of aridity entails, our research is on-going, and the interview format through which we have gauged this variation needs further correlation against archaeological survey, as well as more participatory observation of actual herding practices over longer periods. Nevertheless, the diverse settlement patterns, flexible grazing strategies, and use of *gueltas* and modern wells, as well as the existence of sedentary Kel Tadrart in 'urban' spaces who still keep flocks of ovicaprids and yet see themselves as living in the mountains, strongly suggest that in today's Tadrart Acacus at least, aridity does not equal abandonment. The implication is rather that needs and wants can be modified to suit the environment.

We also recognise further limitations in applying these observations to the archaeological record where there is good evidence that increasing aridity is linked to social change (Brooks 2006, di Lernia 2006), and especially to the mobility of populations (Tafuri et al. 2006). Should archaeologists therefore reject this ethnoarchaeological data from the lives of contemporary Saharan herdsmen as irrelevant to their models for the area's prehistoric societies? To do so, one would have to be sure that the socio-economic and political realities of contemporary Saharan populations are categorically different from the socially constructed contexts within which prehistoric populations acted. One would have to be certain that those parts of the social world not available to us in the archaeological record – but which ethnoarchaeology can directly engage with – were neither important nor decisive. We suggest that no matter how convincing the palaeo-climatological data, without access to prehistoric worldviews (ideological, political, environmental, etc.) and taking into account the heterogeneous contemporary use of the Acacus mountains during what is currently a hyper-arid period, the notion of aridity must be handled with care. Taking the idea of aridity as the leitmotif of social change and increasing complexity in prehistoric societies risks masking those key symbolic, conceptual and ideological aspects of human agency that material culture and faunal remains can only vaguely hint at. If even anthropologists have reason to doubt their generalised certainties regarding contemporary pastoralists (Bogerhoff Mulder et al. 2010, for example, unseat the idea that most pastoralist societies are egalitarian), then modelling prehistoric populations requires caution.

Tellingly, all of the varied pasture and water-source uses, diverse settlement patterns and livelihood strategies discussed above are linked by the broad understanding amongst Kel Tadrart that this is *not* – to return to the *Oxford English Dictionary*'s definition of aridity – a parched, withered or barren area. To describe it as bountiful would be to overstate local perceptions, but most of our informants described years of plenty in the past, and of the many Tamasheq words for different species of grasses and fodder, several were identified as existing in and around the Acacus. What this small and as yet incomplete ethnoarchaeological investigation tells us, then, is simple: if we are to take aridity as the driving force of Saharan prehistory, then we must be aware that data we do not have on the lived experiences of the area's prehistoric inhabitants could potentially lead to the identification of different dynamics, different catalysts, different push and pull factors. In other words, and in spite of the seductive symbolism of the area's rock art, we are still far from understanding how human-environment interaction in the Tadrart Acacus was perceived in prehistory, and therefore what factors drove it.

If we must have a key environmental trope for the central Sahara, it sits somewhere between western science's obsession with aridity and Kel Tadrart livelihoods: namely *changeability*. This is an environment characterised by change, of morphology (from dune fields, to tall peaks, plains, etc.), of water (aquifers, *gueltas*, bore-holes, palaeo-lakes and rivers, rain, remembered rain, vegetation-rich *wadis*), and of the livelihood strategies of its inhabitants. Aridity, by contrast, is a concept that modifies the idea of dry lands to Euro-American needs and wants: a need for alterity, for colonisation and settlement (in the case of America's 'West'), for capturing and envisaging the world through categorising it. The Kel Tadrart's dynamic use of this part of the central Sahara demonstrates that imagining aridity in areas where water matters limits our possible understandings of how humans have interacted with this environment.

References

Avni, G. 1992. Survey of Deserted Bedouin Campsites in the Negev Highlands and its Implications for Archaeological Research, in *Pastoralism in the Levant:*

Archaeological Materials in Anthropological Perspective, edited by O. Bar-Yosef and A. Khazanov. Madison: WI Prehistory Press, 241–54.

Banning, E.B. and Köhler-Rollefson, I. 1992. Ethnographic Lessons for the Pastoral Past: Camp Locations and Material Remains Near Beidha, Southern Jordan, in *Pastoralism in the Levant: Archaeological Materials in Anthropological Perspective*, edited by O. Bar-Yosef and A. Khazanov. Madison: WI Prehistory Press, 181–204.

Biagetti, S. 2009. Etnoarcheologia: Pensieri e prospettive dal Sahara. *Origini*, XXX: 285–94.

Biagetti, S. and di Lernia S. 2003. Vers un modèle ethnographique-écologique d'une société pastorale préhistorique. *Sahara*, 14, 7–30.

Bogerhoff Mulder, M., Fazzio, I. and Irons, W. et al. 2010. Pastoralism and Wealth Inequality: Revisiting an Old Question. *Current Anthropology*, 51(1), 35–48.

Bradley, R. 1992. Nomads in the Archaeological Record. *Meroitica*, 13.

Bravo, M.T. 2006. Against Determinism: A Reassessment of Marcel Mauss's Essay on Seasonal Variations. *Études/Inuit/Studies*, 30(2), 33–49.

Brooks, N. 2004. Beyond Collapse: The Role of Climatic Desiccation in the Emergence of Complex Societies in the Middle Holocene, in *Environmental Catastrophes in Mauritania, the Desert and the Coast. Abstract Volume and Field Guide.* First Joint Meeting of ICSU Dark Nature and IGCP 490, Mauritania, 4–18 January 2004, edited by S. Leroy and P. Costa, 26–30.

Brooks, N. 2006. Cultural Responses to Aridity in the Middle Holocene and Increased Social Complexity. *Quarternary International*, 151(1), 29–49.

Brooks, N., Chiapello, I. and di Lernia, S. et al. 2005. The Climate–Environment–Society Nexus in the Sahara from Prehistoric Times to the Present Day. *The Journal of North African Studies*, 10(3–4), 253–92.

Cremaschi, M. 1998. Late Quaternary Geological Evidence for Environmental Changes in South-Western Fezzan (Libyan Sahara), in *Wadi Teshuinat. Palaeoenvironment and Prehistory in South-Western Fezzan (Libyan Sahara)*, edited by M. Cremaschi and S. di Lernia. Milano: Quaderni di Geodinamica Alpina e del Quaternario, 7, 13–48.

Cremaschi, M. and Frezzotti, M. 1992. La geomorfologia del Tadrart Acacus (Fezzan, Libia). I lineamenti ancestrali e la morfogenesi tardo quaternaria, in *Arte e Cultura del Sahara Preistorico*, edited by M. Lupacciolu. Quasar, Rome, 31–9.

Cribb, R. 1991. *Nomads in Archaeology*. Cambridge: Cambridge University Press.

di Lernia, S. 2001. Visibilità dei depositi pastorali in ambienti aridi: Problemi e percorsi operativi. *Atti del I Convegno Nazionale di Etnoarcheologia. Archeologia Postmedievale*, 4. Firenze: All'Insegna Del Giglio, 141–50.

di Lernia, S. 2006a. Cultural Landscape and Local Knowledge: A New Vision of Saharan Archaeology. *Libyan Studies*, 37, 5–20.

di Lernia, S. 2006b. Building Monuments, Creating Identity: Cattle Cult as a Social Response to Environmental Changes in the Holocene Sahara. *Quarternary International*, 151(1), 50–62.

di Lernia, S., Massamba N'Siala, I. and Zerboni, A. 2012. 'Saharan Waterscapes'. Traditional Knowledge and Historical Depth of Water Management in the Acacus Mts (SW Libya), in *Changing Deserts: Integrating Environments, People and Challenges*, edited by L. Mol and T. Sternberg. Cambridge: White Horse, 101–28.

di Lernia, S. and Palombini, A. 2002. Desertification, Sustainability, and Archaeology: Indications from the Past for an African Future. *Origini*, XXIV, 303–34.

David, N. 1971. The Fulani Compound and the Archaeologist. *World Archaeology*, 3, 111–31.

David, N. and Kramer, C. (eds) 2001. *Ethnoarchaeology in Action*. Cambridge: Cambridge University Press.

Gallay, A. 1991. Organisation spatiale des campements touaregs du Sahara central, in *Itinéraires ethnoarchéologiques, 1. Documents du Département d'Anthropologie et d'Écologie de l'Université*, 18. Genève: Département d'Anthropologie et d'Écologie de l'Université, 31–151.

Gifford, D.P. 1978. Ethnoarchaeological Observations of Natural Processes Affecting Cultural Materials, in *Explanation in Ethnoarchaeology*, edited by R.A. Gould. Albuquerque: University of New Mexico Press, 77–101.

Gigliarelli, U. 1932. *Il Fezzan*. Tripoli: Tipo-litografia del R.C.T.C. della Tripolitania.

Hassan, F.A. (ed.) 2002. *Droughts, Food and Culture. Ecological Change and Food Security in Africa's Later Prehistory*. New York: Kluwer Academic and Plenum Publishers.

Hirsch, E. and O'Hanlon, M. (eds) 1995. *The Anthropology of Landscape: Perspectives on Space and Place*. Oxford: Clarendon Press.

Hodder, I. 1982. *Symbols in Action*. Cambridge: Cambridge University Press.

Hole, F. 1979. Rediscovering the Past in the Present: Ethnoarchaeology in Luristan, Iran, in *Ethnoarchaeology: Implications of Ethnography for Archaeology*, edited by C. Kramer. New York: Columbia University Press, 192–218.

Lane, P.J. forthcoming. Archaeologies of East African Pastoralist Landscape: Places and Paths of Memory, in *Path versus Place: Reconfiguring Nomads to Fit the State*, edited by V. Broch-Due. Uppsala: Nordiska Afrikainstituet.

Marcolongo, B. 1987. Natural Resources and Palaeoenvironment in the Tadrart Acacus: The Non-Climatic Factors Determining Human Occupation, in *Tadrart Acacus. Archaeology and Environment in the Libyan Sahara*, edited by B.E. Barich. Oxford: BAR International Series, 269–82.

MacDonald, K.C. 1999. Invisible Pastoralists: An Inquiry into the Origins of Nomadic Pastoralism in the West African Sahel, in *Prehistory of Food: Appetites for Change*, edited by C. Gosden and J. Hather. London: Routledge, 333–49.

Mercuri, A.M. 2008. Human Influence, Plant Landscape, Evolution and Climate Inferences from the Archaeobotanical Records of the Wadi Teshuinat Area (Libyan Sahara). *Journal of Arid Environments*, 72, 1950–67.

Robbins, L.H. 1973. Turkana Material Culture Viewed from an Archaeological Perspective. *World Archaeology*, 5, 209–14.

Scarin, E. 1937. Nomadi e seminomadi del Fezzan, in *Il Sahara italiano. Fezzan e oasi di Gat*, edited by Reale Società Geografica Italiana. Roma: Parte Prima, 518–90.

Schiffer, M.B. 1987. *Formation Processes of the Archaeological Record*. Albuquerque: University of New Mexico Press.

Schmidt, P.R. 2003. Development of a Fuzzy Expert System for Detailed Land Cover Mapping in the Dra Catchment (Morocco) Using High Resolution Satellite Images. Elektronische Dissertationen der Mathematisch-Naturwissenschaftlichen Bonn: Fakultät der Universität. [Online]. Available at: <http://hss.ulb.uni-bonn.de/2003/0209/0209-1.pdf>.

Shahack-Gross, R., Marshall, F. and Weiner S. 2003. Geo-ethnoarchaeology of Pastoral Sites: The Identification of Livestock Enclosures in Abandoned Maasai Settlements. *Journal of Archaeological Science*, 30(4), 439–59.

Shahack-Gross, R., Simons A. and Ambrose S.H. 2008. Identification of Pastoral Sites Using Stable Nitrogen and Carbon Isotopes from Bulk Sediment Samples: A Case Study in Modern and Archaeological Pastoral Settlements in Kenya. *Journal of Archaeological Science*, 35(4), 983–90.

Smith, S. 1980. The Environmental Adaptation of Nomads in the West Africa Sahel: A Key to Understanding Prehistoric Pastoralists, in *The Sahara and the Nile: Quaternary Environments and Prehistoric Occupation in Northern Africa*, edited by M. Williams and H. Faure. Rotterdam: A.A. Balkema, 467–87.

Tafuri, M.A., Bentley, R.A., Manzi, G. and di Lernia, S. 2006. Mobility and Kinship in the Prehistoric Sahara: Strontium Isotope Analysis of Holocene Human Skeletons from the Acacus Mts. (Southwestern Libya). *Journal of Anthropological Archaeology*, 25, 390–402.

Wendrich, W. and Barnard, H. 2008. The Archaeology of Mobility: Definitions and Research Approaches, in *The Archaeology of Mobility: Old World and New World Nomadism*, edited by H. Barnard and W. Wendrich. Los Angeles: Cotsen Institute of Archaeology, 1–21.

White, F. 1983. *The Vegetation of Africa*. Paris: UNESCO.

Chapter 6

Meaningful Resources and Resource-full Meanings: Spatial and Political Imaginaries in Southern Belize

Sophie Haines

Introduction

This chapter is part of research that aims toward a better understanding of the present conflicts and impasses occurring in relation to land use, development, rights and representations in southern Belize. Historical cycles of development and protest are well-documented in the region (Wilk 1991, Harrison et al. 2004, Wainwright 2008); I hope this investigation may reveal some of the factors contributing to these patterns, and identify potential areas for fruitful dialogue.

The study highlights the complexity and multivocality of ecological debates in the current political environment, and investigates the importance of environments and their representations for understandings and articulations of citizenship and development. Struggles over land and resources in the region have been well-studied; I attempt to broaden the scope of research by exploring the implications of ever-changing and ever-contentious land relations for a complex and by no means monolithic Maya population, and also for other ethnic groups of rural Toledo district, for example the principally Mestizo population of Mahogany Bank village.

Land and its political potency are familiar subjects for social scientists working in the Americas. The 1970s saw a focus on structuralist analyses based on dependency/world-systems frameworks (Frank 1969, Wallerstein 1974–1989), yet a subsequent resurgence of interest in these subjects appears more situated within post-structuralist social theory, drawing together wide-ranging perspectives in search of more nuanced understandings of processes rather than conditions (Robbins 2004, Biersack 2006). Similar analyses are being applied across the globe, often gathered under the broad and multifaceted umbrella of 'political ecology'.[1] The context-dependence of social, political, economic and ecological

---

1   A field that originally grew out of a Marxist critique of cultural ecology, and has itself faced criticism for being both too broad or context-dependent, or too reliant on *a priori* political assumptions. A 'second-generation' of political ecology is attempting to address these criticisms (Robbins 2004, Biersack 2006).

relationships may make the task of developing understandings seem out of reach; however, this open-mindedness in theory and methodology can illuminate novel connections and comparisons.

Following a now familiar critique of Eurocentric, Cartesian, vision-privileging conceptions of 'landscape', and having spent an extended period of time observing, discussing and participating in interactions with many aspects of people's surroundings, I argue that the spatial context of political engagement in rural Toledo is a dynamic lived-in environment where processes, events and relationships are performed and negotiated through daily practices and episodic events (Heidegger 1971, Ingold 1992, 2000, Hornborg and Kurkiala 1998). The way people interact with environments is intrinsically connected to the way they experience political and economic change; their engagements simultaneously have a bearing on the forms and effects of these processes. It thus seems apposite to approach politicised environmental predicaments from a perspective which acknowledges both micro-level phenomenological experiences (Merleau-Ponty 1962) and broader political economy. Bourdieu's theory of practice (1977) goes some way toward a framework of this kind, yet ethnographic applications and analyses in the field of citizenship and natural resource politics are few and far between: political ecology has been slow to embrace interpretive approaches while phenomenological and interpretive anthropology has also struggled with representing political relations.[2] As Sivaramakrishnan argues, exploration of micro-level experiences and stories is a valuable methodology which has often been overlooked:

> ... *development* – as is it imagined, practised and re-created – is best described as stories that can change in their telling, as they are pieced together in contingently coherent narratives. Development's stories are rife with a micropolitics often obscured by the consistency or more orderly progression implied by the terms *discourse* or *narrative*. (Sivaramakrishnan 2000: 432)

The use of the term 'imaginary' in relating spatial and political experiences is not unproblematic. To some, it may imply that experiences and perceptions are mere abstract figments. This is not my intention. I use the term instead in an attempt to evoke the potentiality of ideas about space, environment, and politics, in a way that relates strongly to memory, past experience and knowledge, yet allows for these to be made real in the present, and projected creatively into possible futures; an interaction of the concrete and abstract that is potentially very productive, rooted in experience and practice as well as discourse. As Derek Gregory explains: 'imaginative geographies are never "merely" representations because they have

---

2   Though see studies in Biersack and Greenberg (2006), Croll and Parkin (1992), Hornborg and Kurkiala (1998), and Sivaramakrishnan and Agrawal (2003) for valuable contributions.

practical, performative force' (2001: 107). Relevant here is the characterisation by Watts and Peet of 'environmental imaginaries' as transformative:

> ... there is an active interaction between practice and idealization in which imaginaries are constantly rebuilt and refigured, accumulate and change, during practical activities which imagination has previously framed. Yet the word "imaginary" is meant in the full sense of creativity – the projection of thought into the scarcely known – so that it is a vital source of transformational, as well as merely reproductive, dynamics: the imaginary links natural conditions with the construction of new social forms. (Watts and Peet 1996: 268)

In this chapter I attempt to mesh experiential notions of environments with an appreciation of their practical and discursive powers and reflections, and to explore a hitherto underexploited point of reference between politics, ecology and phenomenology. I hope this will prove fruitful in better understanding the complex relationships and processes currently being enacted and negotiated in Toledo – and in many other locales – where livelihoods, ecological niches, tangible and intangible heritage and human rights are at stake. As Wilk explains; 'If Amerindian history has taught us (and the Kekchi and Mopan) anything, it is that land, and the control of land, is vital to cultural and economic survival' (1991: 236). Far from 'essential' in a static, deterministic way, land and environment play often ambiguous roles in the unfurling of histories. I will outline how they can be conceived of as meaning and resource simultaneously, using observations of vernacular discourse and practice to explore engagements of people, environments, and spatial imaginaries, and examine how certain frontiers are perceived, interacted with, created, negotiated, imagined and re-imagined by inhabitants of some of southern Belize's rural villages.

In sum, I evaluate some of the implications and limitations of conventional dichotomies – such as mythical versus legal land, and identity versus strategy – questioning physical, imagined and epistemological frontiers. A better understanding of relevant contexts and relationships may help to avoid the repeated failures of development projects, by opening up discursive spaces through which local people can engage with decision-making for socially and ecologically appropriate initiatives.

Context: Land, Citizenship and Development in Toledo

Having gained independence from Britain in 1981, Belize is a new and diverse nation-state, home to a broad array of ethnicities and cultures including Creole, Garífuna, Mestizo, Mopan and Q'eqchi'[3] Maya, South Asian, Chinese, Lebanese,

---

3 Alternative spellings: Kekchi; K'ekchi'; Ketchi. The orthographies within follow as closely as possible those recommended by the *Academia de las Lenguas Mayas de*

Mennonite and others. Although part of mainland Central America, Belize also has many links with the Caribbean; these myriad affiliations and roots are reflected in a wide variety of cultural, political and economic expressions and practices among the approximately 311,500 inhabitants of the 22,965km^2 country (Abstract of Statistics: Belize: 5). Belize has a British-style parliamentary system with two main parties; the leadership changed in a general election held in February 2008.

I carried out fieldwork in three rural settlements in the southernmost district of Toledo, which borders Guatemala to the west and south.[4] The market town of Punta Gorda lies on the coast at the foot of the Southern Highway, which has recently been paved (albeit partially). There is no official immigration post along Toledo's western border, though the frontier is frequently traversed by both Belizeans and Guatemalans on foot, by bicycle and by horse or mule. Toledo has the country's highest measured levels of poverty (GoB and IDB 2000: 27, Harrison et al. 2004: 4), and is commonly referred to as the 'forgotten district' due to physical, institutional and political isolation in colonial and contemporary times. A number of governmental and non-governmental initiatives have been implemented in an attempt to rectify this and address obstacles to economic development and poverty alleviation, with varying degrees of success. The general consensus is that most projects have failed (Wilk 1991: 66, 84, GoB and IDB 2000, van Ausdal 2001, Harrison et al. 2004, Wainwright 2008: 203–12).

Outside Punta Gorda, the district's residents live in villages of 1,500 people or fewer, situated either along the highway, or inland towards the forested Maya Mountains. These latter are accessible by dirt roads or by boat in the case of more remote villages (or more extreme weather conditions). The majority of Toledo's rural population comprises Mopan- or Q'eqchi'-speaking Maya, though the town and more easterly settlements are also inhabited by Garinagu, Creoles, Mestizos, South Asians, Chinese and Mennonites.[5] Apart from some individual parcels and 77,000 acres of Maya reservation (GoB and IDB 2000: 76), most of the land used by the villages is officially national land. In the non-reservation villages with which I became familiar, this tends to function as *de facto* reservation, with community

---

Guatemala for Mopan and Q'eqchi' (see England and Elliott 1990: i–viii). In the text the following abbreviations are used in translations: M. = Mopan; Q. = Q'eqchi'; Sp. = Spanish.

4   San Carlos (Mopan), Santa Paloma (Q'eqchi'), and Mahogany Bank (Mestizo, some Q'eqchi'); names of villages and individuals have been changed to protect anonymity. The administrative district of Toledo was established in 1882; I use the name heuristically to refer to the area encompassing the villages in which I studied. The district boundaries do not seem particularly meaningful in practice or discourse for many residents, although they do have political-economic implications, for example the electoral wards of Toledo West and East determine which area representative must be consulted on development issues.

5   According to the 2000 census, people of Maya ethnicity represented 65.4 per cent of Toledo's total population (74.4 per cent of its rural population). At country level the Maya populations represented 10.6 per cent of the whole (Abstract of Statistics: Belize 2007: 26).

leaders taking responsibility for governing its distribution and use. This way of life is increasingly threatened by commercial land speculation.

Interactions of space, time and history are crucial within Belize's anxious multicultural nationalism: effectively *imagining* a Belizean community (Anderson 1983) remains problematic. The crux of the conflict often appears to lie between Belize as Caribbean and Belize as Latin American; recent increases in migration of Spanish-speakers from Guatemala, El Salvador and Honduras have added to this tension. Unlike many other Latin American countries, Belize's nationalism rests on 'unity in diversity' rather than *mestizaje*; this has important implications for the political imagination of different ethnic and linguistic groups.

The legacy of colonisation in Belize has contributed to the ambiguities of contemporary nationalism, land tenure and borders. Britain and Spain argued for many years about the status of British settlement on the margins of Spanish-controlled territory, and sovereignty was finally agreed subject to a road being constructed to link Guatemala to the coast through what is now Belize (*The Belize Issue* 1978: 15–16). As this has not yet materialised, Belizean territorial integrity is still not accepted by Guatemala; the on-going conflict involves Belize, Guatemala, Britain, the Organization of American States and now, potentially, the International Court of Justice.

Within British Honduras and colonial Belize,[6] land laws – especially for the remote south – were apathetically administered. Indigenous peoples were excluded (if they were acknowledged at all) in favour of extractive industries (timber and sugar). The Belizean government inherited a confused and out-of-date land policy at independence, and this provides the backdrop for contemporary struggles and negotiations (Wilk 1991: 55–6, Bolland 2003, Wainwright 2008: 47–8).

Several projects, debates and law suits are being implemented and discussed at the present time; these include a landmark case brought by Maya organisations against the Government of Belize in 2007, which successfully demonstrated communal village land rights in two communities.[7] Current infrastructure development introduces new opportunities and accessibilities, and ways of overcoming old obstacles; conversely it can also create new risks and insecurities, which need to be assessed and negotiated as part of an on-going dynamic of sociocultural, economic and ecological adaptation. It is imperative to acknowledge that land and development conflicts in Toledo are by no means new occurrences (Bolland and Shoman 1977, Wilk 1991, Bolland 2003, Wainwright 2008), but

---

6   The name of the colony was officially changed in 1973, eight years prior to full independence.

7   An outline of the case's progress, including claim forms and affidavits (by local people and international experts in anthropology and archaeology), is available at the website of the Indigenous People's Law and Policy (IPLP) programme of the University of Arizona <http://www.law.arizona.edu/depts/iplp/advocacy/maya_belize/index.cfm?page=advoc>. At the time of writing, the details and implications of the case are still being debated, following a change of government in 2008.

with the Southern Highway paving almost complete, contracts signed for a new feeder road into the Pan American Highway, and debates over land use, ownership and value reaching the courts, now is a vital time to explore the impacts as they happen.

Territory and Autochthony

Potent and visible examples of intersections of time and space, meaning and resource, are located in Classic period Mayan architecture in the district (for example the sites of Lubaantun, Nim Li Punit, Pusilha' and Uxbenka). These ruins invoke Mayan autochthony, by providing a concrete link of place and ancestry (though these terms themselves are not unproblematic). They consequently furnish evocative evidence in indigenous land claims, which encompass demands for resources, farmlands, rights and territory, and involve complex and controversial ideas of heritage and descent. The physicality of architecture can fix otherwise intangible connections of past and present. The ruins may thus be meeting points for the imaginaries of many groups and individuals – farmers, activists, archaeologists, governments and others seeking to learn or gain other affordances

Figure 6.1 Structure at the site of Lubaantun
Source: Image courtesy of the author.

from them. Their presence can be interpreted as an index through which cultural-historical and political-economic meanings become embodied. As a result the management of these sites by states, private companies, non-governmental organisations (NGOs) or communities is highly contested.[8]

The afore-named sites have been recognised and explored, yet travels and conversations throughout the district also reveal many unassuming rocky mounds in fields, forested areas and hillsides. These may well be remnants of pre-colonial settlements, as local people and visiting archaeologists explained to me. While walking through *milpa* fields, my local hosts and guides would point out collections of protruding rocks, proclaiming 'that is for the old Mayas' [M. *uch ben mayas, uch ben indios*]. These sites of varying size and visibility are incorporated in the lived-in environment – clambered on, circumambulated, planted, chopped and burned around, driven over and discussed. The memories they hold provoke reflection on the physical and spiritual traces of the area's ancient inhabitants. These conversations are held not only by Maya; I also heard them in Mahogany Bank among Mestizo people who, despite holding some negative views of Maya resource management, also spoke of their own 'Indian blood' and the strength of ancient Maya intellects, bodies and faith.

Other features of the environment conjure relationships with the ancient past. Some caves and remote parts of the forest are widely reported (by both Maya and Mestizo residents) to be the dwelling-places of the *uch ben mayas*, the 'old Mayas'. These encounters-in-place are experienced through a variety of senses, for example the sounds of drumming and the 'feeling' that they are coming near you. One male village elder in San Carlos described how

> ... in the month of December you can hear those ancient Mayas in their Maya cities, where the archaeological sites are, you can find them in the mountains, you can hear them playing drums, you can hear them singing, you can hear like some sort of *marimba*, different sounds they do in the jungle ... many people used to say they are spiritual now so they are not really human beings like us ... that is the reason you can just hear them, like they are coming near you, but you can't see them. And then when they are getting near you, you will get frightened, and you will run! Because you already have in mind that they are spiritual, you will have a feeling that they are not human beings. That is why we are afraid of them.

I also heard similar stories in Mahogany Bank, reported by Mestizo farmers. Not only are invisible spirits said to inhabit certain places (often caves and mountains)

---

8   The political and cultural potency of archaeological sites is a well-recognised, documented and utilised idea in many parts of the world and Belize, within the so-called '*Mundo Maya*', is no exception. Many events/organisations have chosen Xunantunich in Belize and Tikal in Guatemala as venues for trips, meetings and ceremonies celebrating Mayan cultural heritage.

– filling lone hunters with a fear almost as great as that associated with a run-in with illegal Guatemalan *xateros* [Sp. xaté leaf collectors] – but there are also stories of 'wild Indians' still living in the bush, having eluded colonial and postcolonial regimes (Wilk 2007: paragraphs 18–24, Wainwright 2008: 61).

This proximity of ancient and contemporary, tangible and intangible, is evocative and powerful. It is also politically potent. As Medina (1999) explains, the state's position in the 'native debate' is contradictory: while denying continuous occupation and attendant territorial rights for present-day Maya, it has actively pursued the economic benefits of 'cultural tourism', relying heavily on exactly those connections between ancient and living Maya in Belize that its stance on the land rights issue disputes.[9]

A connected sense of injustice emerged in conversations with local Maya. I visited the Classic period site of Nim Li Punit [Q. big hat] with some friends, including Miguel, a Q'eqchi' speaker from San Gerardo village. Miguel works for a local NGO, and also holds a Belize Tourism Board guiding licence. Visiting the site after hours, he told us stories of 'his people' and their strength and intelligence in constructing monuments and trade and defence strategies, as we wandered through the partially reconstructed palaces, plazas and ball court, surrounded by the axial *Ceiba pentandra* [M. *ya'axche'*] of ancient Maya cosmology, and the rubber trees (*Castilla elastica*) used to produce balls for the famous Maya game. He became absorbed and emotional as we wandered around the otherwise deserted site. Afterwards, he spoke of the injustice he felt, citing the familiar phrase, 'we are the forgotten district', saying that the government makes its money from his people's temples yet Toledo's residents see neither money nor development.

Herein lies a paradox not only for the state but for local people (Maya and others), and for anthropologists, archaeologists and others seeking to engage with these issues. In accentuating the relationships of land, territoriality, ancient histories and cultures, there is a danger of essentialising 'Maya culture', neglecting the concerns of local non-Maya groups and overlooking the dynamic roles of flexibility and change (Watanabe 1995, Hervik and Kahn 2006). Sometimes, the ability of rural populations to claim access to decision-making relies upon their classification as 'indigenous' or 'traditional',[10] or even 'poor', but paradoxically these categories can concurrently exclude them from active engagement through lack of access to economic, institutional and rhetorical resources. It could be argued that a degree of 'strategic essentialism' (Spivak 1990) is employed by indigenous movements themselves, as a way of presenting a united front and a legible cause. The concept however is fraught with politically-problematic misconceptions, highlighted by Spivak herself among others (Danius et al. 1993: 34, Kobayashi 1994: 77, Fischer

---

9   See also Watanabe (1995: 35) on *indeginismo* in Mexico and Guatemala.

10   For a local example, see Wainwright's (2008: 250–57) account of the Maya Atlas (TMCC 1997), in which he analyses what was included and excluded in this text, produced by Maya organizations and UC Berkeley geographers in 1997 to support the land claims at the time.

1999). As the examples given here and in other studies demonstrate, this is too simplistic an explanation to account for the complexities of experience, identity, knowledge, memory and rights.

Sensory Engagement and the Vernacular Environment

Toledo's forests, streams, mountains, caves, rivers, fields, swamps and valleys provide not only wild foods and the means to cultivate one's own sustenance, but also ways to generate income, resources for constructing dwellings, materials for tools, furniture, crafts and medicines, and sites to which visitors can be guided by entrepreneurial locals. Although for some households and household clusters[11] (especially in the more accessible villages) varying forms of cash cropping and paid employment are contributing to household economies, a subsistence base of maize [M. *ixi'im*, Q. *ixim*] and beans [M. *bu'ul*, Q. *kenk*] remains an important buffer against the risk and insecurity of wage work, as well as being a continuation of what may be deemed 'tradition' by both outsiders and farmers themselves (Wilk 1991: 141, 157–8).[12] Self-identification as a farmer [M. *kolileen*, Q. *aj awinal*] is often strong, and great pride is taken in the knowledge and ability to self-sustain. Men and women, children and the elderly engage with farming and gathering activities spanning many resources and ecosystems. Agriculture is also important in Mahogany Bank, although due to the area's ecology and rather pervasive disapproval of swidden farming, fishing is central for livelihoods, while rice, taro and cassava are more popular than corn and beans.

Many farms are only accessible on foot or horseback, requiring an approximate average of three hours travel each day along farm tracks which turn from squelching muddy ravines to ankle-turningly rugged paths, treacherously pitted with hoof prints, at the end of the wet season. Where they are still performed, rituals relating to burning, planting and harvesting are enacted in place in the fields.[13] Farming activities are labour-intensive and carried out by hand, with sticks [M., Q. *che'*] and machetes [M. *maskaa'*, Q. *ch'iich*]. Bodily sensation and damage from insect bites, irritant foliage, rocks, blister-inducing use of tools, carrying loads by tump-

---

11   See Gregory (1984: 18) and Wilk (1991: 185–7) for descriptions of household organization and 'clustering'.

12   Wilk (1991) and Grandia (2006) provide details of agricultural practices and resource use among Q'eqchi' Maya; many of the same practices are employed by Mopan Maya inhabitants of the region. Although acting as a buffer in some cases, Meillassoux (1981) has argued that subsistence production among populations undergoing proletarianisation may in fact subsidise low wages and exploitation.

13   Protestant churches have contributed strongly to the neglect of many such rituals in the villages in which I worked. Some farmers still burn copal incense and make offerings to spirits to ensure successful harvest; many of these practices are syncretic and also involve Christian prayers.

Figure 6.2 Walking in the *milpa*
Source: Image courtesy of the author.

line, snakes, scorpions, heat exhaustion, mud-filled boots and slipping machete blades are regular occurrences, embodying to varying degrees and durations the tasks of work and effects of the environment, and providing a contrast to the more pleasant experiences of tasting fresh fruits, observing flora and fauna, taking a rest in the shade or a cool wash in the creek.

In addition to subsistence- and cash-cropping, people in rural Toledo carry out hunting, fishing, and gathering, mostly for food and occasionally to sell. They travel by foot, bicycle, motorcycle, mule, dory, skiff, truck and bus within and between villages, along rocky roads, paved highways, overgrown trails and muddy riverbeds, in order to buy and sell goods, to attend school or university, to find and carry out work in many sectors, to visit friends and family, and to attend religious functions and political events. These movements are not always contained within national borders.

Vernacular references to spatial features and temporal processes reveal aspects of social and political life, often through sensory experiences. Sitting in the kitchen of my host's house in San Carlos with Fidelia – the mother of the family – we chatted about village life and its advantages and disadvantages. She told me how she loved her village [M. *kaj*]: although sometimes her husband wanted to pursue employment in a different district, she insisted on staying.[14] The sense of belonging to place, kin and community was strong: 'I love my village,' she explained, 'because it is cool.'

This emerged as one of the most common descriptions of village life in several communities. Fidelia had been speaking to me in English at this time; it later became apparent that in Mopan too, 'cool' [M. *siis olal*] expresses tranquillity as well as climate. Not only is San Carlos served well by refreshing mountain breezes and two clean rivers, it is also said to be relatively undisturbed by the perceived violence, expense and stress of the market town, swampier settlements, border villages, Belize City, and, most pointedly, Guatemala.

This association recalls the 'moral climatology' (Livingstone 1991), cited by Gregory (2001: 100) as part of a 'moral economy of nature' within colonial and postcolonial discourses on race and the tropics, connecting heat with lassitude and disease. In this context too these comparisons evoke and shape senses of place, identity and morality:[15]

> When you are cool you can't say nothing [can't complain] … you are cool in your house, in your home … and when you are hungry, when you are thirsty, you can go in your kitchen and get it. But when somebody come and kill you, or thief you … you are worrying about that – why they come and do that for us? You don't want to eat or drink again because you are thinking about that, you are worrying about that. But when nothing happen you can't say nothing. (Fidelia, San Carlos)

> I have my daughter in Belize [City], but I don't like to stay there much – it is too hot and dangerous, too much killing. (Marcelo, San Carlos)

---

14 Although often less vocal than men in public decision-making, and also vulnerable to domestic abuse (McClusky 2001), many women do play active roles in household decision-making – choices over whether to move from the home village were common examples of this.

15 The balance of hot and cold has great significance for many Meso-Amerindian groups, especially concerning issues of health, as Fink (1987: 400–405) explains with specific reference to the Mopan Maya of Toledo.

Coolness and tranquillity are fragile, vulnerable to land expropriation, illegal immigrants (most commonly identified as 'Spanish' Guatemalans) and the influence of drugs, alcohol and gang violence. People are affected by episodic political events: Fidelia and others in San Carlos spoke of the 'heat' [M. *chuk'uj*] of election campaigns – periods of frayed tempers and threats to delicate peace. In Mahogany Bank village, *tranquilidad* and 'quiet' are explicitly aligned with the crystallisation of the community around one evangelical church. Services and prayer meetings [Sp. *cultos*] are focal, and residents see the village as a moral haven, away from the *corrupción* of Punta Gorda and places further afield.

Rivers and creeks [M. *ja'*, Q. *ha'*] are the centre of many regular activities such as bathing [M. *ichkiil*, Q. *atsink*] and laundering [M. *po'o'oj*, Q. *okeech puchuk t'ikr*]. They help to make the village *siis olal* [M.], or *ke'* [Q. cool], and evoke ideals of cleanliness. The presence of rivers was central in the choice of sites for San Carlos and Mahogany Bank. Although Santa Paloma and San Carlos both have non-metered potable water (installed by the government's Social Investment Fund), most families choose still to bathe and wash in the creeks.

Questions about the establishment of settlements and changes that have happened in living memory almost always elicit commentary on changing forestscapes, experienced through many senses. References to 'high bush' [M. *nuk che'*, Q. *k'iche'*], and 'low bush' [M. *wahmiil*, Q. *koq'pim*] measure changes in land use and suitability over time, and evoke the long- and short-term impacts of migration, agricultural cycles, seasons and natural disasters. A visible, meaningful and resource-full frontier, the high bush is now relatively distant from the residential areas of many villages. Distances travelled to find resources, sounds of howler monkeys, colour and clarity of creeks, and visibility through the forest inform people's perceptions of ecological change; they are phenomenological realisations of environmental effects, experienced in these ways before being made officially visible through quantitative reports and assessments.

The bush is also a locus of trepidation. Although stated beliefs in such beings are in decline, for the most part due to evangelical Protestantism, stories of spirits and mythic creatures persist among Maya and other groups, with perhaps the most charismatic character (excepting the ghostly *indios* already mentioned) being Tata Duende – 'Father Duende', a small man-like spirit which protects the forest and which is a familiar figure in Mesoamerican and Caribbean folklore. It seems that the people most likely to encounter Duende are the *kula'anil winik* [M. drunken men]. In addition to supernatural threats I was warned that there are the *kula'anil* themselves to worry about, as well as jaguars, snakes [M. *kan*, Q. *kan tz'i*], crocodiles, organ traffickers and *xateros*. Fears associated with the forest often relate to fears of illegal immigrants, the contested border and land loss – evoked by contemporary events, informed by the past, and projected into the future.

In both Mopan and Q'eqchi', the words for land [M. *lu'um*, Q. *cho'och*] also mean soil, earth and ground. Fertile terrain is 'pretty', 'clean', 'healthy', 'fresh' [M. *kich'pan*, Q. *cha'ibil*]. In Santa Paloma and San Carlos, a major advantage of establishing and living in the community was the good soil. In Santa Paloma, one elderly farmer explained in Q'eqchi' that locating a favourable village site was 'like finding a beautiful girl that you want to take care of'. While the high forests are indeed resources for livelihoods and identities in many ways, aesthetic references to cleared or chopped land as *kich'pan* and *cha'ibil* also suggest appreciation of the managed and ordered agricultural environment.

In the familiar rhetoric of the Forest Department (FD) and many NGOs concerned with conservation and development, villagers' shifting swidden farming practices are to blame for apparent degradation, reflecting Hardin's (in)famous 'tragedy of the commons' (Hardin 1968, Ostrom et al. 1999) and the trope of the 'Maya Collapse'. These powerful narratives have been taken on by many actors (including local farmers and village co-operatives); however they often make assumptions regarding the definition of degradation (Lambin et al. 2001: 264, Robbins 2004: 129–48), and can overlook the potential sustainability of local practices (Ostrom et al. 1999, Spurney and Cavender 2000), the political-economic influences of dominant social structures (Blaikie and Brookfield 1987), and the impact of natural disasters, for example Hurricane Iris which destroyed swathes of Toledo's forest and farmland in 2001.[16] It is nevertheless inadvisable to reify and romanticise 'traditional ecological knowledge' as a static primordial system (Bebbington 1996, Burnham 2000: 40, Robbins 2004: 191–97, Wainwright 2008: 67–98). A detailed discussion of this politics of sustainability is beyond the scope of this chapter, though it is significant to note how the very idea of 'sustainability', in terms of potential futures, interacts with past and present spatial and political imaginaries.

Contemporary development processes are spatial, tactile, visual and aural experiences. One man in Mahogany Bank told me that when a road was opened through the dense forest to the village, people chose to move their homes across the river to be near the new route, 'because they say the light is coming'. Wilk has also reported Q'eqchi' references to roadside areas as 'bright' (2006: 162). The sensory allusion is polysemic. Roadbuilding brings light by breaking forest canopy and enabling the sun's rays to penetrate, while in some cases it may also be hailed as a precursor to the extension of electricity along routes to more remote settlements (many interlocutors referred to electricity in English simply as 'the light'). Improved access to electricity, hospitals and high schools contributes to this sense of opportunity through formal education, vocational skills and business, though the need for cash to pay associated bills is recognised as a potential challenge.

In spite of the current absence of mains electricity in Santa Paloma, San Carlos and Mahogany Bank, fluorescent lights and loud music often punctuate the dark evenings. DIY systems of car batteries, converters, inverters, battery chargers, solar panels and kerosene generators are used to run televisions, DVD players, radios, laptop computers, refrigerators and church PA systems. These power

---

16   As well as jeopardising livelihoods and ecosystems this provided a way in to the forest for foreign logging companies, through salvage licences.

configurations and devices are by no means available (or desirable) to all, but regardless of ownership they have effects for all residents, who will be privy to nearby church services or *punta-* and *reggaeton*-soundtracked graduation parties, who will be able to buy ice-cold drinks from the shops, and whose children may have access to a laptop computer at the primary school. Rural residents make a wide variety of choices regarding their use and incorporation of technologies and consumer goods (Wilk 2006).

In San Carlos, access to cash has increased the number of cement block houses with zinc roofs [M. *tz'inkleh naj*] replacing timber and thatch buildings [M. *tutz'il naj*]. The sensory experiences of these buildings are significant, and reflect a range of choices and desires. As well as their different visual appearance, it is noticeable that one does not have to stoop beneath overhanging thatch to enter, nor can one experience the cooling breezes which pass through thatch and timbers on even the hottest days. In addition to increasing the heat of the rooms, zinc roofs are acoustically dramatic, most noticeably during the rains when it can be impossible to hold a conversation.

For these reasons of noise and ever-important temperature as well as cost, several families with the means to build cement-and-zinc houses have eschewed the opportunity.[17] Sitting on the porch of the two-year-old house in which I was living (cement floor and pillars, timber walls and thatch roof), I discussed changes in the village with Roberto, a long-term San Carlos resident. He talked of how the building materials were changing, but only gradually:

> I think we have to stay like this, no? Because if we totally change we will feel the heat. Because when the sun is coming on the zinc roof it make a different feeling for us … the way I see like Dangriga, Belize City, it's pretty hot there even in the night, but like this building here is nice, you no have to use fan.

Since Hurricane Iris in 2001, however, many families have decided to at least build walls or supports from cement blocks if at all possible. These choices also have implications for social cohesion and moral economies: house thatching is a communal task which can involve up to thirty men and their families, engaging in either reciprocal labour or cash payment in some circumstances.[18] Concrete, cement and zinc constructions nearly always involve hiring men from outside the village, who require cash payment.

17　Other reasons include reluctance to display wealth conspicuously, for fear of direct or indirect (through witchcraft) retribution, as I was made aware of during fieldwork, and as Wilk (2006: 162–3) also reports.

18　For example, one of the sons in my host family works for the Belize Defence Force (BDF) and is regularly away from the village on lengthy work cycles. His frequent absence means he is likely to be unavailable to reciprocate labour, so when his new house needed thatching he paid a team of men in cash for their work. His outside employment both necessitated and facilitated this arrangement.

**Figure 6.3 Village view showing thatch, zinc, timber and
cement building materials**
Source: Image courtesy of the author.

During election campaigns, otherwise elusive politicians become visible
and vocal in the villages, and projects may be started, restarted, or abandoned.
Their stuttering progress leaves physical traces that are often cited as examples of
the current and historical political climate, the ebb and flow of state penetration
and withdrawal, and the problems of patronage and factionalism. While many
people in the villages welcome the opportunities and services afforded by certain
development projects (including roadbuilding and electricity provision), there
is a great deal of apprehension regarding the security of land as a vital basis
for livelihoods. For some settlers, these fears evoke difficult memories of land
expropriation in Guatemala; for those without personal memories the anxiety of
potential land and rights loss is informed by an awareness of the recent histories
of neighbouring nations.

Imagining Frontiers

Due to the potency of the experiences and relations described above, ownership
and management of environments, particularly those comprising fertile farmlands,

archaeological sites and other sacred or beautiful places, are extremely controversial, especially where boundaries are unclear, and individuals and communities vie with each other and with local, national and international institutions for the rights to manage and benefit from them.

I visited a waterfall near San Carlos one day with my host Diego and his young daughter and niece who wanted to swim. We enjoyed the hour-long hike through the humid jungle, passing *milpa* fields, fallow lands and creeks to reach the spot where we explored undisturbed for the afternoon. I later spoke to another village farmer and guide, Geronimo, about the area. In 1985 a British soldier posted at Salamanca camp had requested a guide to the waterfall and suggested establishing a business. Over the next few years Geronimo and two fellow residents communicated with the FD and the Nature Conservancy (NC), trying to negotiate permits to guide in the neighbouring forest reserve, and applying for grant money. Ultimately the FD was reluctant to grant the appropriate permissions,[19] and although the NC apparently approved the grant, no money materialised.

Geronimo and his partners had, however, obtained a demarcated government lease on the national land surrounding the waterfall, in a stated attempt to conserve the beauty of the area and simultaneously gain advantage in the guiding market. Due to a combination of factors, including political confusion over the lease, land requirements and a lack of tourists, it emerged that the area had been cleared and burned for *milpa*, though it never became clear by whom. Geronimo told me that others in the village had disagreed with the lease: 'Yes, we get that, but people never respect it for us ... once they see something they cut it and they no respect it.' Rumours and accusations spread around the village, though the full story never emerged.

The dispute illuminates the interactions of the economic, cultural and environmental value of such places, indicating intra- as well as inter-community alliances and inequalities over access to, and bounding of, environmental features. Alongside the examples of ruins given above, it helps to demonstrate how places are imagined in different ways: as sacred places; landmarks in the forest; areas for potential income; sites of stories, myths and Maya heritage; agricultural land; 'biodiversity hotspots'; areas for academic investigation or aesthetic appreciation; the property of individuals, groups, communities or states.

Communities themselves – perhaps especially those inhabiting forests – are notoriously slippery entities to define, as Sharpe (1998) and Burnham (2000) have highlighted in West-African contexts. In Toledo, certain geographic and historical logics do make 'villages' meaningful units, and practices such as group labour, face-to-face interactions and modes of local governance characterise performed and imagined community. These communities are adaptive, with flexible membership that expands and contracts. They are performed rather than prescribed, and it is these social and ecological interactions that create and maintain significant

---

19   Steinberg (1998: 413) reports the government was often more enthusiastic about supplying licenses to logging companies.

attachments (Barth 1969, Gregory 1984). As many ethnographers of the Maya have noted, ever since Redfield in the 1930s, it is vital to also take into account the fragmentations within these supposed units, and the strong links beyond them – for example based on party politics, generation, gender, language, employment, resource use, kin, education and trade (Redfield and Villa Rojas 1962, see also Wilk 1991: 41–2, 73–4). The elusive definition can be problematic for legal property determination, and for 'community development' projects (for example forestry or tourism initiatives).

Grasping 'communities' has also been an issue for Indigenous rights debates. Following a now-revised campaign for an extensive 'Maya homeland', the current claims involve defining communities as geographically delimited, in order to gain legal recognition and facilitate village land control. If viewed through the crude dualistic lens of commons versus bounded property, this, as well as the individual parcelling promoted by the state and some foreign-funded development projects (van Ausdal 2001, Campbell and Anaya 2008), can seem at variance with the fluidity of communities, the extent and overlap of resource use patterns, and the conventional wisdom that the Maya conception of land is mythic and boundless. As mentioned above, local people's resource use practices and conceptions of land are sophisticated and adaptive. Changes in resource use patterns and choices, social organisation, land value and security are a nexus of globalised and localised political economies, relationships, ecologies and decisions, which standard dichotomies (global/local, common/private property, legal/mythical) seem poorly equipped to explain.

The increasing urgency of land security issues emphasises these dilemmas. Lines between communities – annually or biannually re-negotiated and marked by machete by village leaders – are now facing permanent demarcation using GPS technology and concrete posts; this is a new process with different implications for inter- and intra- village relations, interactions, and resource distribution. A multitude of agenda-driven maps is being produced, and tensions have arisen over the location of borders (especially where neighbouring communities are not seeking to bound their land), determining the parties to whom control will be devolved, and dealing with accusations of 'Balkanization' disseminated through media and popular discourse. Recognising the temporal and political aspects of imagining and demarcating frontiers, Grandia writes that 'their mapping is deeply political – because descriptions and projections of the contours of a frontier ultimately are discussions about the future' (2006: 24).

The bureaucratisation of, and consequently *through*, space (Gregory 1994: 401, drawing on Lefebvre 1991, see also Scott 1998) relates to the ability to negotiate rights and resources with powerful actors. This is not only the case for the Maya rights claimants: Mahogany Bank independently called on a local NGO to assist them in producing a village map with a trained cartographer, GPS, and the co-operation of neighbouring communities. Formalising the boundaries was an attempt to retain control over village land in the face of threats from a Mennonite logger. Although several of the Mestizo and Q'eqchi' residents of Mahogany

Bank expressed favour for the acquisition of private leases for their farms, it was decided that demarcating wider community territory was an important way to safeguard land and conserve forest collectively for the future.[20] The concession debate is on-going.

In Santa Paloma, the boundary between (*de facto*) village land and the neighbouring forest reserve is unclear and controversial, and interacts with national tenure and protected areas legislation, and also with international security and immigration issues surrounding the Guatemalan frontier. In this area the national border is contested and permeable: an anxious space that conjures both fear and opportunity, realised more in its crossing and negotiation than in any physical markers on the ground.

These dilemmas relate to farmers' urgent quandaries regarding communal versus individual security. Private leasing of land can appear to be the only viable way to gain economic security, by providing collateral for loans for cacao seedlings, house-building, high school fees and so on. However, there are obvious risks involved in using land as collateral, depending on cash crops at the expense of a subsistence base, and removing land from a village's communal pool. The process of lease administration itself is rife with uncertainty, clientelism and exploitation: in San Carlos and Mahogany Bank, where leasing has become rather popular as a way to seek security, many of my interlocutors explained depressingly familiar frustrations over bureaucratic failures, unfulfilled promises, missing documents, armed confrontations and crooked middlemen. The proposed border road that would link Toledo with the Pan American Highway in Guatemala is poised to alter these relations further, by changing the patterns and processes of state and capital penetration into the area, shifting the value of the land, and transforming the nature of the already contested national border.

These examples illustrate some of the varied approaches and responses to frontiers and boundaries that are to be found in this context. Adopting legalistic structures may dilute movements, legitimising and exacerbating existing inequalities – especially for those whose cultural as well as physical distance from the state may be one of their key political assets (Scott 1998, Davis 1999). Opening up land to state or commercial expropriation via knowledge gleaned through surveying is risky, especially as infrastructure is developed in the region. However, refusal or inability to make these adaptations may exclude groups from decision-making processes altogether. Conventional notions of domination and resistance attribute ultimate power to dominant structures at the expense of acknowledging local people's creativity and agency. The perceived dichotomy

---

20 Having an *alcalde* as well as a chairman is significant. I was told by residents in Mahogany Bank and activists in Punta Gorda that this enables the village to call upon the *Ten Points of Agreement* between the MLA/Toledo Maya Cultural Council and the Government of Belize (GoB and Maya Peoples of Southern Belize 2000). The agreement stipulates that consultations must be held and honoured when concessions or leases are requested in village lands.

of mythical versus legal land underlies the political impasse in many situations; it disregards the expansive multivocality and context-dependence of spatial and political imaginations and strategies.

Discussion: Environment as Meaning and Resource

People imagine and re-imagine spaces, places, frontiers and histories through their own experiences, and through complex and expansive discourses – also including the representations that emerge from conservation and development NGOs, state departments, archaeological or anthropological projects, politicians, indigenous movements, and local, national, and international media. These discourses have polyvalent[21] implications for the communities and areas they attempt to characterise. Outcomes are real, though not always intended (Ferguson 1994).

Spatial gradients relative to Punta Gorda are articulated by rural and urban residents, and by NGO and public sector workers. The further from town the village, the closer it is to Guatemala – a site of fear and danger in popular and nationalist discourses. Terms such as 'back-a-bush' and 'way to the back' denote distance and also imply a development gradient: those villages are viewed from towns and highway-side villages as relatively alien, primitive, uncivilised and dangerous, and these perceptions have implications for the negotiation of citizenship and rights.

The ambiguity of state presence is highly significant. As already mentioned, in popular parlance, Toledo retains the onerous epithet of the 'forgotten district' – geographically distant from the political and economic centres and poorly understood (leading to poorly-planned and administered projects). The neglect is lamented by rural residents, who complain that the government does not provide promised basic services; yet when the state does make its presence felt it is often in ways which attract criticism or fear from many of the district's residents. Exasperation with political manipulation, dread of disenfranchisement and expropriation of lands, and anxiety about the outcomes of the proposed border highway all contribute to this.

The above accounts demonstrate how examining land and environment as sources and repositories of meanings as well as valuable economic, ecological and political resources can illuminate political relations in Toledo. Literature on sociopolitical action has often focused on either the role of resource mobilisation *or* that of identity, and as such has failed to facilitate comprehensive understandings that acknowledge the importance of both concurrently (Cohen 1985, Foweraker 1995, Alvarez et al. 1998, Davis 1999, Gledhill 2000). With history and language,

---

21 See Wainwright's use of this term to mean 'motivated by multiple distinct and conflicting tendencies' (2008: 155, 187). I understand the distinction between polyvalence and ambivalence to be a temporal one: ambivalence suggests shifting values, while polyvalence implies simultaneity.

land is a potent actual and theoretical interface of identity *and* strategy: a vital material resource; a font of meaning; a potential source of political legitimacy and voice; a vital component of the political imaginary. Neither resource nor meaning is prior – they are mutually constitutive and simultaneous.

Perceived incommensurability between legal and mythical conceptions of land (Scott 1998, Abramson and Theodossopoulos 2000) can lead to political impasse. While there may be hegemonic pitfalls when indigenous groups use formalised discourses in order to engage politically, such dichotomies (mythical/ legal, identity/strategy, global/local, commons/enclosures) can themselves be misleading and unproductive, as they do not account for the myriad historical and spatial contexts of their employment. Demarcation of boundaries is both feared and desired, depending on the context.

The ambivalences of power and knowledge mean that there is neither a simple, linear movement from mythic/boundless land towards formal/alienable property, nor a reified gulf between them, and there is power to be located and appropriated both in engagement with official discourses and in secrecy and elusiveness. It is interesting to observe that supposedly formal state strategies contain perhaps more than their fair share of illegibility: states as much as categories such as 'the Maya people' or 'rural Belizeans' are not monolithic, bounded entities (Abrams 1988). It is important not to underestimate the flexibility and creativity demonstrated by a wide range of groups and individuals in political, economic, social and ecological adaptation.

I therefore propose that we should continue to acknowledge and critically develop not only a political approach to ecology, but also a phenomenological and holistic ecological approach to exploring political processes, emphasising experience, relationality, interdependence, adaptation/maladaptation, and the *longue durée*, without overlooking the real outcomes and significance of specific events and power relations within historical structures. This may prove useful in analysing the contingent and relational factors of decision-making processes, facilitating negotiation between (and within) interested groups, and bringing a potential for better understanding of meaningful resources *and* resource-full meanings, in the past, present and future.

Acknowledgements

Thanks are due to all my hosts and interlocutors in Belize, to my supervisors Professor Nanneke Redclift and Dr Barrie Sharpe, and to the Human Ecology Research Group at University College London. This work was supported by the Economic and Social Research Council [grant number PTA-031-2005-00034].

References

Abrams, P. 1988. Notes on the Difficulty of Studying the State. *Journal of Historical Sociology*, 1(1), 58–89.

Abramson, A. and Theodossopoulos, D. 2000. *Land, Law and Environment: Mythical Land, Legal Boundaries*. London: Pluto Press.

Abstract of Statistics: Belize. 2007. Belmopan: Statistical Institute of Belize.

Anderson, B. 1983. *Imagined Communities: Reflections on the Origin and Spread of Nationalism*. London: Verso.

Alvarez, S., Dagnino, E. and Escobar, A. 1998. *Cultures of Politics/Politics of Cultures: Re-visioning Latin American Social Movements.* Boulder: Westview Press.

Barth, F. 1969. *Ethnic Groups and Boundaries: The Social Organization of Cultural Difference*. Boston: Little.

Bebbington, A. 1996. Movements, Modernizations and Markets: Indigenous Organizations and Agrarian Strategies in Ecuador, in *Liberation Ecologies: Environment, Development, Social Movements*, edited by R. Peet and M. Watts. London and New York: Routledge, 86–109.

Biersack, A. 2006. Reimagining Political Ecology: Culture/Power/History/Nature, in *Reimagining Political Ecology*, edited by A. Biersack and J.B. Greenberg. Durham: Duke University Press, 3–40.

Biersack, A. and Greenberg, J.B. 2006. *Reimagining Political Ecology*. Durham: Duke University Press.

Blaikie, P. and Brookfield, H. 1987. *Land Degradation and Society*. London: Routledge.

Bolland, O.N. 2003. *Colonialism and Resistance in Belize: Essays in Historical Sociology*. 3rd edn. Benque Viejo del Carmen: Cubola Productions.

Bolland, O.N. and Shoman, A. 1977. *Land in Belize 1765–1871*. Kingston: Institute of Social and Economic Research.

Bourdieu, P. 1977. *Outline of a Theory of Practice*. Cambridge: Cambridge University Press.

Burnham, P. 2000. Whose Forest? Whose Myth? Conceptualisations of Community Forests in Cameroon, in *Land, Law, Environment: Mythical Land, Legal Boundaries*, edited by A. Abramson and D. Theodossopoulos. London: Pluto Press, 31–77.

Campbell, M. and Anaya, S.J. 2008. The Case of the Maya Villages of Belize: Reversing the Trend of Government Neglect to Secure Indigenous Land Rights. *Human Rights Law Review*, 8(2), 377–99.

Cohen, J. 1985. Strategy or Identity: New Theoretical Paradigms and Contemporary Social Movements. *Social Research*, 52(4), 184–7.

Croll, E. and Parkin, D. 1992. *Bush Base – Forest Farm: Culture, Environment, and Development*. London: Routledge.

Danius, S., Jonsson, S. and Spivak, G.C. 1993. An Interview with Gayatri Chakravorty Spivak. *Boundary 2*, 20(2), 24–50.

Davis, D. 1999. The Power of Distance: Re-theorizing Social Movements in Latin America. *Theory and Society*, 28, 585–638.

England, N.C. and Elliott, S.R. 1990. *Lecturas Sobre la Linguistica Maya*. Guatemala: Centro de Investigaciones Regionales de Mesoamerica.

Ferguson, J. 1994. *The Anti-Politics Machine: 'Development', Depoliticization, and Bureaucratic Power in Lesotho*. Minneapolis: University of Minnesota Press.

Fink, A.E. 1987. Shadow and Substance: A Mopan Maya View of Human Existence. *The Canadian Journal of Native Studies*, 7(2), 399–414.

Fischer, E.F. 1999. Cultural Logic and Maya Identity: Rethinking Constructivism and Essentialism. *Current Anthropology*, 40(4), 473–99.

Foweraker, J. 1995. *Theorizing Social Movements*. Boulder: Pluto Press.

Frank, A.G. 1969. *Capitalism and Underdevelopment in Latin America: Historical Studies of Chile and Brazil*. New York: Monthly Review Press.

Gledhill, J. 2000. *Power and its Disguises: Anthropological Perspectives on Politics*. London: Pluto Press.

GoB and IDB. 2000. *Environmental and Social Technical Assistance Project: Regional Development Plan for Southern Belize*. Belmopan: Government of Belize.

GoB and Maya Peoples of Southern Belize. 2000. *Ten Points of Agreement*. [Online: IPLP Maya Villages Document Library]. Available at: <http://www.law.arizona.edu/depts/iplp/advocacy/maya_belize/documents/TENPOINTS OFAGREEMENT.pdf> [accessed: 13/08/2009].

Grandia, L. 2006. *Unsettling: Land Dispossession and Enduring Inequity for the Q'eqchi' Maya in the Guatemalan and Belizean Frontier Colonization Process*. PhD Dissertation, University of California-Berkeley.

Gregory, D. 1994. *Geographical Imaginations*. Cambridge, MA: Blackwell.

Gregory, D. 2001. (Post)colonialism and the Production of Nature, in *Social Nature: Theory, Practice and Politics*, edited by N. Castree and B. Braun. Oxford: Blackwell, 84–111.

Gregory, J. 1984. *The Mopan: Culture and Ethnicity in a Changing Belizean Community*. Columbia: University of Missouri.

Hardin, G. 1968. The Tragedy of the Commons. *Science*, 162(3859), 1243–8.

Harrison, J., Castaneda, A. and Castillo, P. et al. 2004. *Toledo: A Study in Elusive Development*. Belmopan: Government of Belize and United Kingdom Department for International Development.

Heidegger, M. 1971. *Poetry, Language, Thought*. New York: Harper and Row.

Hervik, P. and Kahn, H. 2006. Scholarly Surrealism: The Persistence of Mayanness. *Critique of Anthropology*, 26(2), 209–32.

Hornborg, A. and Kurkiala, M. 1998. *Voices of the Land: Identity and Ecology in the Margins*. Lund: Lund University Press.

Ingold, T. 1992. Culture and the Perception of the Environment, in *Bush Base – Forest Farm: Culture, Environment and Development*, edited by E. Croll and D. Parkin. London: Routledge, 39–56.

Ingold, T. 2000. *The Perception of the Environment: Essays on Livelihood, Dwelling and Skill*. London: Routledge.

Kobayashi, A. 1994. Coloring the Field: Gender, 'Race', and the Politics of Fieldwork. *The Professional Geographer*, 46(1), 73–80.

Lambin, E.F., Turner, B.L. and Geist, H.J. et al. 2001. The Causes of Land-use and Land-cover Change: Moving Beyond the Myths. *Global Environmental Change*, 11, 261–9.

Lefebvre, H. 1991. *The Production of Space*. Oxford: Blackwell.

Livingstone, D.N. 1991. The Moral Discourse of Climate: Historical Considerations on Race, Place and Virtue. *Journal of Historical Geography*, 17(4), 413–34.

McClusky, L. 2001. *Here, Our Culture is Hard: Stories of Domestic Violence from a Mayan Community in Belize*. Austin: University of Texas Press.

Medina, L.K. 1999. History, Culture and Place-making: 'Native' Status and Maya Identity in Belize. *Journal of Latin American Anthropology*, 4(1), 133–65.

Meillassoux, C. 1981. *Maidens, Meal, and Money: Capitalism and the Domestic Community*. Cambridge: Cambridge University Press.

Merleau-Ponty, M. 1962. *Phenomenology of Perception*, translated by C. Smith. New York: Humanities Press.

Ostrom, E., Burger, J. and Field, C.B. et al. 1999. Revisiting the Commons: Local Lessons, Global Challenges. *Science*, 284(5412), 278–82.

Redfield, R. and Villa Rojas, A. 1962[1934]. *Chan Kom: A Maya Village*. Chicago: University of Chicago Press.

Robbins, P. 2004. *Political Ecology: A Critical Introduction*. Oxford: Blackwell.

Scott, J.C. 1998. *Seeing Like a State: How Certain Schemes to Improve the Human Condition Have Failed*. New Haven: Yale University Press.

Sharpe, B. 1998. 'First the Forest': Conservation, 'Community' and 'Participation' in South-west Cameroon. *Africa*, 68(1), 25–45.

Sivaramakrishnan, K. 2000. Crafting the Public Sphere in the Forests of West Bengal: Democracy, Development, and Political Action. *American Ethnologist*, 27(2), 431–61.

Sivaramakrishnan, K. and Agrawal, A. 2003. *Regional Modernities: The Cultural Politics of Development in India*. Stanford: Stanford University Press.

Spivak, G.C. 1990. *The Postcolonial Critic: Interviews, Strategies, Dialogues*. New York: Routledge.

Spurney, J. and Cavender, J. 2000. Effects of Milpa and Conventional Agriculture on Soil Organic Matter, Structure and Mycorrhizal Activity in Belize. *Caribbean Geography*, 11(1), 20–34.

Steinberg, M.K. 1998. Political Ecology and Cultural Change: Impacts on Swidden-fallow Agroforestry Practices Among the Mopan Maya in Southern Belize. *The Professional Geographer*, 50(4), 407–17.

The Belize Issue. 1978. London: Latin America Bureau.

TMCC. 1997. *Maya Atlas: The Struggle to Preserve Maya Land in Southern Belize*. Berkeley: North Atlantic Books.

van Ausdal, S. 2001. Development and Discourse among the Maya of Southern Belize. *Development and Change*, 32, 577–606.

Wainwright, J. 2008. *Decolonizing Development: Colonial Power and the Maya*. Malden, MA: Blackwell.

Wallerstein, I.M. 1974–1989. *The Modern World-System*. 3 vols. San Diego: Academic.

Watanabe, J.M. 1995. Unimagining the Maya: Anthropologists, Others, and the Inescapable Hubris of Authorship. *Bulletin of Latin American Research*, 14(1), 25–45.

Watts, M. and Peet, R. 1996. Conclusion: Towards a Theory of Liberation Ecology, in *Liberation Ecologies: Environment, Development, Social Movements*, edited by R. Peet and M. Watts. London and New York: Routledge.

Wilk, R. 1991. *Household Ecology: Economic Change and Domestic Life among the Kekchi Maya in Belize*. Tuscon: University of Arizona Press.

Wilk, R. 2006. 'But the young men don't want to farm anymore': Political Ecology and Consumer Culture in Belize, in *Reimagining Political Ecology*, edited by A. Biersack and J.B. Greenberg. Durham: Duke University Press.

Wilk, R. 2007. *First affidavit of Richard R. Wilk: Manuel Coy (on behalf of the Maya village of Conejo) and Others v Attorney-General of Belize and Another. Claim No. 172 of 2007*. [Online: IPLP Maya Villages Document Library]. Available at: <http://www.law.arizona.edu/depts/iplp/advocacy/maya_belize/documents/FirstAffidavitofRichardWilk.pdf> [accessed: 13/08/2009].

Chapter 7

Imagining and Consuming the Coast: Anthropology, Archaeology, 'Heritage' and 'Conservation' on the Gower in South Wales

Kaori O'Connor

In the anthropology of Britain, much has been written about imagined and experienced landscapes, less about seascapes, and very little indeed about the shifting 'scapes' of the coast. Yet it is in these restless places between land and sea, zones of transition and transformation, that peoples' involvement with place may first have become systematically knowing and productive, a relationship that continues today, hidden in plain sight. Writing against the prevailing discourse of 'conservation', this anthropological study draws upon archaeology and history in order to move beyond 'temporally shallow frames' (Ohnuki-Tierney 1995), and to contextualise an on-going study of people, places, products and practices of coastal South Wales which are threatened by legislation that seeks to impose what Bender called 'the socially empty vistas of modern conservative sensibilities' (1998: 131). The study proceeds from two propositions. The first is that the most important relationship between persons and landscape – or any other sort of 'scape' – is not being in it, but having it be in you. In other words, it is consuming its resources, responsibly. The second is that, from the point of view of the environment and of 'heritage', what people ignore is as important as what they 'see'. These two propositions are explored through two coastal foods – shellfish and seaweed – in an approach that combines ethnography and history for, as Horden and Purcell write (2000: 471), 'ethnography has to be grounded in history to be of any exemplary value'.

That anthropology has largely overlooked the coast of Britain may be because, in legal and in social terms, the shore has become largely invisible. Over the past two centuries, the narrative of the British coast has been one of almost unrelieved loss. The maritime merchant fleet, coastal shipping, ferries and steamers, inshore fisheries, boat-building, the industries they served and the trades and communities they supported during the industrial heyday of Britain have all but vanished. One exception has been the seaside resorts that first appeared in Britain in the early eighteenth century (Borsay 2008), flourishing under the patronage of generations of holidaying factory workers who, in the early period, often shared the same stretches of sand and sea with inshore fishermen, lobster potters and shellfish collectors. Today, parts of the coast that were populous until quite recently have been cleared by continuing labour migration, while other stretches have been so built over that the shore can no longer be seen. Between the two, both literally and figuratively, are the peculiar terrains of 'renewal'. Areas of the coast once blighted by intensive industrialisation have been remediated and transformed; the tracts once given over to foundries, furnaces, factories, works, mills, docks and depots are now redeveloped or simply cleared and left vacant. Confronted by coasts where so many features have been altered or removed and past lifeways forgotten, beaches which are often deserted outside the short holiday season, and once-busy waters on which few working boats are now seen, there seems little to attract anthropological attention. However, there is more to these apparently empty coasts than at first meets the eye.

Until recently, the British coast was also disregarded by policy-makers and planners, but growing realisation that land and sea are total ecosystems, as well as belated concern about terrestrial degradation and the sustainability of deep sea fish stocks, have led to a radical shift in official perspective. Previously, for historical reasons that will become clear, the coast of Britain was a patchwork of jurisdictions, bylaws and widely differing forms of practice, covered by some seventy different statutes and regulations, and administered by a bewildering array of local, regional and national bodies, both formal and informal.

The need for a comprehensive and coordinated national coastal policy finally found expression in a proposed Marine and Coastal Access Bill which sought to provide, among other things, for the contending interests of the protection of threatened marine species and habitats, the tightening up and centralising of fisheries management and shellfish licensing and the granting of unprecedented public access to the coast all around Britain. The successful implementation of the Bill would depend on ICZM – Integrated Coastal Zone Management – the 'scientific' managing of the relationship between protected landscapes and adjacent marine zones (MCZs). ICZMs are supposed to involve 'the adoption of an integrated or joined up approach towards the many different interests in both the land and marine components of the coast' (Integrated Coastal Zone Management (ICZM) 2009). However, legislative progress of the Bill through Parliament was slow because virtually every clause was hotly debated by competing coastal interests, regions and agencies, supported by increasingly factionalised public debate. The Bill polarised the interests of heritage and development, and revived the debate about private property and public rights. Ironically, so much time went by after the Bill was first envisioned that it was overtaken by devolution. Just as legislation that treated the coast and sea of Britain as a whole was finally on the verge of enactment, the body that was to have been jointly administered and managed has now been dismembered into three separate jurisdictions – England, Scotland and Wales. Whatever their differences, the three devolved 'nations' are united by the conviction, among their respective coastal communities, that the proposed Bill sacrificed socioeconomic considerations to the concerns of the environmental conservation lobby, disregarding the sustainable management and harvest of marine food resources in favour of exclusionary 'protection'.

This chapter arises from on-going fieldwork in the least known of these coastal constituencies – the shellfish industry. The primary fieldwork site is on the South Wales coast, along a stretch that contains two extensive estuarine complexes, an award-winning zone of industrial reclamation and a designated Area of Outstanding Natural Beauty, but the study addresses issues common to all British shellfish communities, and many further afield. Shellfish gathering – the collection of molluscs such as oysters, cockles and mussels and crustaceans like shrimp and lobster, along with the collection of seaweed and other marine plants – is one of the oldest of human foraging activities. The British Isles are rich in shellfish resources, but the industry, its activities and products are little known to the public, and are perceived by it – if at all – as an old-fashioned and marginal trade, of negligible social, economic or nutritional importance. It therefore comes as a surprise to most people to learn that shellfish make a larger contribution to the UK economy than sea fish. In 2008, the value of shellfish landings in the UK was £263.6 million, compared to £179.8 million for demersal fish such as cod and haddock and £82.9 million for pelagic fish such as mackerel (Marine Programme Plan 2009/2010). Further, and contrary to a widely held belief, molluscs do not raise cholesterol levels in humans. Low in fat and high in minerals, they can make an important contribution to a healthy diet.

Yet despite the shellfish industry being the only marine growth sector in the UK with projected benefits for the national health as well as the economy, it is the industry that sees itself most threatened by the impending Marine and Coastal Access Bill. The establishment of marine conservation zones (MCZs) where no harvesting of marine resources would be allowed is a major concern within the shellfisheries, which argue that their activities within territorial waters are compatible with sustainability and conservation objectives. While accepting that some fishery activities may be modified and that the closure of some grounds may be necessary, they state reasonably that 'the protection afforded must be balanced and proportionate, restricted in scale and location for specific purpose and determined by the broader consensual conservation interest and not minority activists' (SAGB 2008: 2). They also argue that there is no reason why shellfish activities cannot coexist with recreational and other users of coastal marine parks; that 'shellfish waters' need special designations to safeguard their quality; and that shellfisheries – still without official recognition –should be given special designations that reflect and protect their social and rural importance.

There are geographical differences, variations of practice between types of shellfish, and diverse events and issues that have formed local opinion, but *au fond* the embattled position of the contemporary shellfish industry as a whole arises not so much from the activities of fishers as from the highly contested nature of the coasts where they ply their trade. In England 'and in all parts of the world where the English legal tradition has been received', as Simpson (1994: 120) puts it, the coast has long been a liminal zone trapped between 'law' and 'custom'. This arises from Roman law, which meant different things in different historical periods, leading to contradictory later interpretations (Schiller 1994) that continue to bedevil legal and social practice relating to the coast today, and to inform popular perceptions of the coastal environment.

The Marine and Coastal Access Bill unavoidably entails involving anthropological research in coastal areas with the law, and conducting ethnography within and outside it (Harris 1996). The relationship between anthropology and law has not always been easy. As Nader (2002: 1) put it, 'in the 1960s, the possibility of anthropologists teaching in law schools would have been anathema in most law school faculties'. The relationship between anthropologists and lawyers has often been antagonistic not least, as Harris notes, because the concern of the anthropology of law 'has been to demystify law; to show how rules are not, and cannot always be, obeyed, how laws are self-contradictory, how the practice of law differs from the ideal ... to get away from a stultifying concern with rules as such in order to focus on how those rules were implemented or not, how real-life situations escaped the apparent clarity of rules' (Harris 1996: 4–5). When anthropologists were primarily concerned with faraway cultures, this critical engagement with the law was less apparent outside the profession, and anthropological expertise in issues arising from globalisation and pluralisation has since earned a degree of appreciation from lawyers. However, the more anthropologists work 'at home', the more they are unavoidably drawn back into the contest between local custom and national law, between values and practices, and between the different imagined realities and taken-for-granted customary understandings at work in contemporary legal systems.

The passage and implementation of the Marine and Coastal Access Bill is a unique opportunity for the anthropological analysis of the relationship between people and the legal process in a 'western' context. It is a rare confluence of events that presents an unprecedented opportunity to study an attempt to legislate perception on the micro and macro levels. In one Act, it is proposed to define the 'coast', something which has so far eluded consensual definition; to alter past and present lifeways; to create and manage zones that will transform the environment and ecological dynamics; and to resolve once and for all the ambiguities between law and custom, not only in national and devolved arenas, but also on a European level. Ethnographically, as and after the new legislation comes into effect, the fieldwork would involve studying the coastal communities as they are in the present; their attempts to influence legislation during the 'consultation process'; changes in coastal communities and in their practices; and changes in the coast itself.

As the legislative process is on-going, what is presented here is material – both historical and contemporary – to contextualise the ethnographic work. Relating to coasts generally and to the South Wales coast in particular, it demonstrates how anthropology, archaeology and history can work together 'at home'; it throws light on the roots of the contending imaginaries that are currently contesting the coast; and it contributes a context-rich account of linked human and environmental heritage over time (Harvey 2001).

The Coast in Law and Custom

'Bridging the gap between land and sea' was a catchphrase much used by working parties involved in the early stages of ICZM strategy development. It is a seemingly innocuous phrase in which many of the problems now confronting the British coast and its shellfish industry are embedded. The linked oppositions of this imaginary – land/sea, rich/poor, civilised/wild and agriculture/hunting-and-gathering – are considered to have their origins in the ancient Mediterranean world, in Graeco-Roman culture which later became so influential across Western Europe (Purcell 2001). In Graeco-Roman literature and art, the coast was the place where the stability and morality of the land was confronted by the corrupting allure of sea-borne trade and conquest (Horden and Purcell 2000: 278), while its denizens, the fishermen, were seen as the very embodiment of otherness.

The contrast between the land and sea was enshrined in Roman law. When set out in the sixth century *Digest of Justinian* (Fenn 1925, 1926), the law stated that while land was subject to the right of possession, 'by the law of nature the following things are common to all men; air, running water, the sea, and therefore the shore of the sea' (Abdy and Walker 1876, in Niven 1978: 161). The coast or foreshore was deemed by the early Romans to be part of the sea, and was measured upwards, from the water to the highest point of the highest tide (Sobecki 2008). To this zone and its products, as well as to the sea beyond, all had common access. Navigable rivers and harbours, and the right to moor boats there, were also considered common to all, even though the banks of both might be owned.

Gradually, the clarity of this concept was eroded. The notion of 'guardianship' or 'stewardship' of waterways, shore and sea crept in – glossed as 'the jurisdiction of Caesar'. Then the notion of ownership intruded, as expressed in a later legal opinion on the text of the *Digest* that 'the shores over which the Roman people has dominion I consider to belong to the Roman people' (Mommsen and Kreuger 1985, in Sobecki 2008: 141). This is the flawed foundation upon which law pertaining to coastal and marine matters developed (*Yale Law Journal* 1969–70: 762). Already containing the contradiction between public right and private ownership, it led Vinogradoff (1923: 751) to observe that in this case the use of Roman bricks for the construction of an English edifice was not entirely satisfactory, a conclusion with which all parties interested in the coast have subsequently agreed. Roman law, where it continued to apply after the end of the empire, was differently interpreted and practised across early medieval Europe, but in Britain and generally, public ownership of the coast, waterways and tidal areas gave way to private ownership by local powers and feudatories, who began among other things 'to claim that the right to fish was their personal property and required that all their fishermen be licensed for a fee' (*Yale Law Journal* 1969–70: 764). As this happened, in a further departure from Roman practice, the coast, seabed and riverbeds came to be considered extensions of the land rather than of the sea and therefore subject to ownership, and the coast began to be measured from the land down, not from the water up, and to the line of the median tide, not the highest.

Finally, with the arrival of the Normans in Britain in 1066 and the establishment of centralised authority, rights in the coast, seabed and riverbeds previously claimed by individuals or local interests, as well as those yet unclaimed, were appropriated by the Crown, which led to the possibility of further confusion as to whether 'Crown' meant the state or the private person of the monarch. After the conquest, the Crown either confirmed existing private rights, or granted new ones, as a means of building political and economic support. Growing dissatisfaction with what was seen as abuse led, in 1215, to the undertaking in Magna Carta that the Crown would grant no more private rights to inshore tidal fisheries, so in coastal and tidal stretches for which private rights had not already been granted, 'the ancient public right might be said to have been reinstated' (Neher, Arnason and Mollet 1989: 17) while the rights and property that remained vested in the Crown after Magna Carta, and which were not subsequently alienated or modified by legislation, are administered by the Crown Estates to this day.

As a result of the foregoing history and the laws arising from it, Britain has a complex, confused and contradictory body of coastal and marine jurisdictions and policy, 'pulled in one direction toward common ownership by a tradition as old as the Roman Empire, and in another by precepts of common law and private enterprise requiring that virtually everything have an owner' (Stevens 1980–81: 195). This is the legal background against which the contested coast and its imaginaries must be understood.

Today, in England and Wales – Scotland and the Orkneys have different laws that govern their coasts – only a narrow strip in the middle of the intertidal zone is legally classified as the foreshore. Private property land rights extend into the upper tidal area, while beyond the narrow strip lies the lower intertidal area, which is now designated as seabed (McGlashan et al. 2005: 188). The powers of local planning authorities and terrestrial conservation designations such as 'Sites of Special Scientific Interest' stop at the seaward edge of the foreshore boundary where, under the Marine and Coastal Access Bill, it is planned that they will join up with yet-to-be-established Marine Conservation Zones (MCZs), 'which will be protected from extraction and deposition of living and non-living resources and all other damaging and disturbing activities' (MCZ Project Wales/Countryside Council for Wales 2011). This is what is meant by 'closing the gap between land and sea' – thus, at least in statutory law, making the 'coast', as a place in its own right, non-existent.

The Coast in Archaeology and Anthropology

By contrast, the coast is becoming ever more vital and visible in anthropology and archaeology generally. Within the former, a renewed interest in oceans, islands and coasts has significantly altered previous understandings of, among other things, 'the antiquity of coastal adaptations and marine migrations; variations in marine or coastal productivity; cultural contacts and historical processes; human impacts and historical ecology in island and coastal ecosystems; and the conservation and management of island and coastal sites' (Erlandson and Fitzpatrick 2006: 5). Coastal resources, it is now clear, have been more diverse, and have sustained human life over longer periods, than previously thought (Dillehay 1999, Macaulay et al. 2001, Torben et al. 2001, Erlandson et al. 2007), challenging established models in which marine foods were considered undependable and therefore inadequate and inferior to terrestrial ones (Jones 1991), hunter-gatherer lifestyles inferior to those of agriculturalists, and gatherers inferior to hunters, this last including the gendered opposition of woman-the-gatherer versus man-the-hunter (Cobb 2005).

Archaeological data are underlining the presence in the past of significant populations of coastal people akin to Renouf's (1984) 'hunter-fishers', exploiting both the coast and the hinterlands. The most favoured coastal areas for settlement have been estuarine zones of rich resources and high productivity, which provided 'maritime' travel corridors deep into the interior, facilitating complex social interaction and varied provisioning (Fitzpatrick et al. 2007), as well as estuaries near to kelp and other seaweed beds which were especially desirable because of the habitat they provided for molluscs, fish and mammals. Recent archaeological research has acknowledged not only the importance of marine resources in the diet of early humans, but also the proportion of shellfish in this diet. Previously considered a 'lowly' form of food compared to fish, it is becoming clear that particularly in estuarine areas, the gathering of shellfish is the most efficient food procurement activity, especially for people with limited foraging mobility, such as women and children (Jones 1991). Thus the idea of coastal marginality is being reversed. Instead of the earlier view that peoples from the inland may only have resorted to the coast in times of scarcity, it now appears that coasts have often been the primary settlement zone, from which people forayed into the interior (Glassow and Wilcoxon 1988). Underwater and coastal archaeology is increasingly revealing the extent to which previously occupied coastal sites have been destroyed or obscured by sea level changes, erosion and sedimentation.

This archaeological revaluation of the significance of coasts is paralleled by recent work in social ecology and anthropology developed by Nancy Turner and others, proceeding from the premise that the key to social and ecological resilience is diversity, which is often found to be at its greatest at social and cultural 'edges' such as coasts. From this are derived propositions to inform further research into coastal culture: firstly, that human communities benefit from association with and exploitation of ecological edges; secondly, that cultural edges are characterised by a beneficial diversification of social behaviour and knowledge; and thirdly that:

> Societies seek to expand their use of cultural and ecological edges ... Thus instead of being an accident of nature or of social geography, they are purposely

created and maintained by people in their attempts to promote social-ecological resilience. (Turner, Davidson-Hunt and O'Flaherty 2003: 442)

These propositions are further developed in the concept of 'cultural keystone species', defined as 'plants and animals that form the contextual underpinnings of a culture as reflected in their fundamental roles in diet, as materials, or in medicine', and are so central to a people's lifeways and identity that they can be considered 'cultural icons' (Garibaldi and Turner 2004: 1). This parallels the concept of ecological keystone species, meaning a species that is crucial to the structure and functioning of an ecosystem (Crisancho and Vining 2004). When linked, these concepts consolidate a casting of the coast as a dynamic zone of interaction, beneficial both to humans and to the environment: an optimised or constructed terrain linked not to contemplation but to use and especially to the production, collection and consumption of food.

Foods have become a specialised topic of interdisciplinary study, and those that are considered both symbol and sustenance often go by the name of 'heritage foods'. The term resonates with the discourse of *terroir* in which certain foods are believed to take on the unique physical qualities of the locality where they were grown, gathered or made, as well as the metaphysical essence of events, values, practices and forebears grounded in the 'ancestral soil'. Their antiquity and authenticity are implicit and believed in, whether or not they are grounded in history. Heritage foods make identity, locality, ethnicity and nationhood material (O'Connor 2006, 2009, 2013); dictate production and consumption; illuminate human interaction with the environment over time; and are an ideal medium for

Figure 7.1 Eloquent food: Laver from the Gower Peninsula in Welsh language packaging which reads 'Cooked seaweed. Fresh, pure and ready to eat'

Note: The packaging shows a plate of cooked laver and, above it, a plate of cockles.
Source: Image courtesy of Selwyn's Seafoods.

linked social, ecological and environmental analysis. As forms of material culture, they also link archaeology and anthropology. In the study of coastal South Wales, the focus is on cockles (*Cardium edule*) and edible laver seaweed (*porphyra*) as the primary cultural keystone species.

Gower Histories and Heritage on the South Wales Coast: A 'Persistent Place'

Wales has some 750 miles (1,250km) of coastline consisting of rocky headlands, sweeping bays, sheltered coves, expansive dunes, salt marshes, beaches of sand and of shingle, swift streams or creeks called *pwll*, mud flats, and broad riverine estuaries like the Conwy which empties into Cardigan Bay in the north, and the Burry Estuary that flows into Carmarthen Bay in the south. Some 30 per cent of the Welsh coastline has now been designated 'Heritage Coast' by the Countryside Council for Wales, an arm of the Welsh Assembly Government that aims, in its words, to 'achieve an equitable balance between the social, environmental, and economic needs of Wales' (WCMP – Wales Coastal and Maritime Partnership 2008: 2). The designation does not have any legal status at present although planners are supposed to take account of it, and there is a marine equivalent, with about 70 per cent of the Welsh coast designated as 'European Marine Sites'. One of the most important of these land and sea complexes is the Carmarthen Bay and Estuaries European Marine Site. All along the Welsh coast, although not always visible to the naked eye, is evidence of human activity and systematic interaction with the coastal environment over thousands of years (Davidson 2002). However, neither the specifications of the Carmarthen Bay land site nor the various sea conservation schemes appear to include humans working and interacting with the coast today as an element in coastal diversity, or as a social, environmental or economic asset. The mutualism of person and environment (Ingold 1992), as mediated by culture and history, is entirely absent.

Located within the Carmarthen Bay conservation area in South Wales, the Gower Peninsula exemplifies many of the complexities and contradictions in coastal conservation, as well as the interplay of contending imaginaries. Tourism is seen as an important present and future contributor to the Welsh economy and 'the Gower (*Gwyr*)', as it is known locally, is a prime visitor attraction, described in promotional material and on websites in terms similar to these, from a website promoting local tourism:

> Carmarthen Bay and Gower is one of the most beautiful areas, not only in Wales but in the whole of the United Kingdom. A land of Cliffs, Golden Beaches, Rivers and Streams, Vikings, Romans, Druids, Celts, Merlin, Arthur, Woodland, Castles and Dragons, Fire and Water, Mists, Winds, Rain, Sun, Magic, Mystery, Poetry, Dylan Thomas and Secret Places still waiting to be found. (Gower and Carmarthen Bay website)

Fanciful but not wholly without foundation, this description gives some idea of the Gower's multifaceted past, heritage and appeal. A small peninsula twelve miles long and six miles across at its widest point, the Gower was in 1956 the first place in Britain to be designated as an Area of Outstanding Natural Beauty (AONB), chosen for its classic coastline and outstanding natural environment. The Gower's complex geology has resulted in a wide variety of scenery and natural habitats, and the peninsula as a whole now contains three National Nature Reserves, two Local Nature Reserves, numerous Sites of Special Scientific Interest and the Burry Inlet Special Protection Area (SPA).

In addition to its beauty, the Gower is a place of exceptional archaeological and historic interest, with 83 scheduled monuments and monument sites dating from the Upper Palaeolithic onwards, most notably the Paviland Caves on the Gower's south coast. Discovered in 1823, they contained the earliest modern human remains yet found in Britain, with a (contested) date of c. 29,000 BP (Aldhouse-Green and Pettit 1998, Jacobi and Higham 2008). The Paviland person, once known as the 'Red Lady' but now known to be male, was long considered exemplary of early man-the-hunter, sustained on a purely terrestrial diet of roasted bison, mammoth and other flesh (Sollas 1913). However, in line with the aforementioned revaluation of the coast, isotope analysis now indicates that the diet of the person buried at Paviland (Milner et al. 2003) consisted of up to 20 per cent aquatic protein (fish, molluscs, seabirds) which, with later evidence (Schulting and Richards 2002), establishes the early presence of a semi-nomadic hunter-fisher culture inhabiting and systematically exploiting the Gower coast.

In addition, the ancient internment in Goat's Hole cave at Paviland is recognised as the earliest ceremonial burial yet discovered in Western Europe. Aldhouse-Green interprets the archaeological record as evidence that the cave was a sacred site (Jacobi and Higham 2008: 901) over time, a 'persistent place'. Persistent places, as Schlanger (1992: 97) puts it, 'are neither strictly sites (that is, concentrations of cultural materials) nor simply features of a landscape. Instead they represent the conjunction of particular human behaviours on a particular landscape'. Referring to sites that are used repeatedly but intermittently during the long-term occupation of a region, the concept is attractive because it embraces the physical and the metaphysical, and counteracts the widespread tendency to regard any occupation or use that is not continuous as unimportant. Indeed, it suggests that persistent occupation may be more valuable than continuous habitation in understanding the dynamics of human interaction with the environment over time, and also explains why the periodic non-use of places must be seen as cyclical rather than developmental.

Persistent places also resonate with the coast as cultural edge and with the concept of cultural keystone species. Putting them together, a picture is formed of the Gower coast as persistent place and cultural edge, home to cultural keystone species, prime among them shellfish and seaweed. The importance of aquatic resources to the inhabitants of the South Wales coast is evident from the presence of shell middens all along the shore, and fish weirs (O'Sullivan 2003) in the seas

**Figure 7.2 Persistent people and persistent places: Ashley Jones, member of
a family associated with Welsh seafood for generations, picking
seaweed in the Burry Estuary, Gower**
Source: Image courtesy of Selwyn's Seafoods.

and estuaries, dating back to the Neolithic period and continuing into historic times. During the Roman period, which saw the construction of the fort at Leucarum – present day Loughor, where the Loughor River runs into Carmarthen Bay at the northeast corner of the Gower – Roman soldiers demonstrated a marked partiality to shellfish. Oysters were the most favoured, with mussels, limpets, whelks and cockles also eaten.

Consumption was heaviest at locations near the sea, but shellfish were also sent inland over considerable distances (R.W. Davies 1971). There are few written references to fishing and shellfish collecting in early medieval Wales (Lewis 1903). However, from the material remains it is clear that, like the fishermen in the *Anglo-Saxon Chronicles*, inhabitants of the South Wales coast continued to resort to the estuaries and seashore for 'eels and pike, minnows and burbots, trout and lampreys ... herring and salmon, dolphins and sturgeon, oysters and crabs, mussels, winkles, cockles, flounders, soles, lobsters and many such things' (Crossley-Holland 1982: 223) in the post-Roman period.

The Gower enjoys a relatively mild climate and good soil; these desirable features and its distinctive geographical configuration meant that the Gower was recognised as a 'commote' or administrative district in its own right (Draisey 2002) soon after the Roman withdrawal, and was subsequently fought over almost continually for some 500 years. This is the period that has subsequently been cast as a kind of golden age, an 'Arthurian' *longue durée* in which later notions of heroic Welsh identity and independence are so deeply rooted. As Wendy Davies has noted, early medieval studies of Wales are characterised by the absence of critical social history (W. Davies 2004: 197). Filling this lacuna, Davies shows post-Roman Wales to have been a mosaic of small, independent political units that from the fifth century established the power to rule, transmitted this power dynastically, and within a few generations fell prey to lineage segmentation, with the numerous descendants of a common distant ancestor competing with each other for political control (W. Davies 1990: 38). This resulted in an unstable polity with a tendency to factionalism and regionalism that made the survival and development of the Welsh kingdoms, let alone a unified kingdom, highly problematic, irrespective of the arrival in Wales of the Normans (W. Davies 1990).

Under the Normans, Gower became a Marcher lordship, a unique institution arising from the English Crown's need to keep the borders under control. In return for loyalty and support, the Crown established strong lords on lands in the Welsh borders, within which these lords had total jurisdiction without recourse to the King. Like many Marcher lordships Gower was divided into two – the 'English' Gower or Gower *Anglicana* and the 'Welsh' Gower, or Gower *Wallicana* (Draisey 2002). The difference, as one historian put it, was that 'the wild and comparatively worthless or wooded land was *Wallicana,* while the more easily settled land of greater agricultural value was *Anglicana*' (Nicholl 1936: 167). Gower *Wallicana* comprised the easternmost section of the north Gower coast along the Burry Estuary including present-day Penclawdd, and then the upland territory on the mainland extending nearly to Ammanford. Here the Welsh people of Gower lived in scattered farmsteads combining stock-raising on a small scale in rough pastures with farming in small fields in the typical Welsh fashion. In *Wallicana* the Welsh language was spoken, and Welsh land tenure and other law was allowed to apply, so long as Welsh inhabitants rendered the necessary fees and services to their Norman overlords. In *Anglicana*, which comprised the rest of the peninsula, English was spoken and English law applied. In order to increase the non-Welsh element in the population and also to enable their holdings to be worked productively, successive Lords of Gower actively promoted immigration especially from Somerset, Devon and Dorset just across the Bristol Channel. These newcomers settled into *Anglicana*, speaking English, building villages in the English manner and developing an agrarian economy along English lines supplemented by livestock rearing. Thus, two cultural, social, legal, linguistic and economic landscapes developed on the Gower, and although the Acts of 1535 and 1542 were meant to establish English law uniformly across Wales, Welsh customary practice continued alongside English usage for centuries thereafter.

Fishing villages dotted the shore of *Anglicana* and *Wallicana,* with fishing supplementing seasonal agricultural work (Jenkins 1972, Steane and Foreman 1988). Oysters, mussels and cockles were widely collected (John 1995: 6) while seaweed, which grew abundantly around the Gower, was gathered; some sorts were used like manure, to improve the soil for new agrarian crops (Emery 1956), and other kinds were eaten, especially *porphyra* (laver). Certainly by the medieval period if not much earlier, distinctive figures had emerged on the Welsh coast as elsewhere in Britain – the shellfish women. Often assisted by children, they foraged for shellfish on the coasts and sold them on the shore or at markets, travelling inland for considerable distances with their wares. There were a number of renowned cockle collecting beds in the South Wales estuaries, notably at Penclawdd on the north Gower coast. But to whom did the shellfish the women collected, and the shore they traversed on the way to the collecting grounds, belong?

In 1764 when the manorial system was in decline and Welsh and English practices had coexisted in some confusion for several centuries, Gabriel Powell, seneschal of Glamorgan, undertook a survey of the Gower on behalf of the then Lord of Gower. He found that the peninsula was a patchwork of complicated tenancies, unauthorised enclosures, disputed boundaries, contested inheritances, forgotten titles, surreptitious encroachment on common land, and – most importantly – contested 'rights'. As Powell stated, the Lord of Gower was, 'by immemorial custom confirmed by the Statute of Wales as well as by the Charter of the 5th James the First', entitled to (among other things) wreckage found floating at sea, goods washed ashore, wreckage or goods lying on the sea bed, treasure trove and rights in certain products of the sea (Morris 2000: 78–9). As Seneschal, it was Powell's duty to ensure that the Lord received all that was due to him, and in systematically recording local Gower practice he preserved a network of local custom which does not appear in statutory law, but which continues to influence local perception and beliefs about entitlements and ownership today. Certain of the rights of the Lord of the Gower, held by right of the Crown, were passed on to lesser lords who held manor lands from the Lord, and were then passed on in turn by the manorial lords to their tenants. The tenants of Bishopston Manor, for example, claimed the long-established right to 'gather and carry away sea weed and sand from the sea shore' (Morris 2000: 204). The inhabitants of Pennard and Oystermouth claimed the right to net fish inshore and collect lobsters and crabs, on payment of six pence annually to the lord, and for the latter to use the sands for oystering activities, and virtually every coastal manor had similar claims to the use of the coast. In the eighteenth century, as the sentiment against ancient feudal privilege rose, tenants – especially those whose families had long been Gower residents – began to disregard manorial restrictions and came to believe and then act as though they had independent entitlement to these rights, further obscuring an already grey area.

By the late eighteenth century, the profitability of mixed farming in Gower had declined, while the industrialisation of South Wales was beginning. The dramatic effect can be seen at the town of Llanelli, just north of the Gower. In 1689, Llanelli was a small fishing village with a few hundred inhabitants. By 1729 it was 'a pretty good town, well traded into for sea coal', but by 1800 it had become 'a miserably dirty place, filled with miners and sailors' (Matthews 2003: 458–9). By 1837, when it was described as the ugly exemplar of 'all that was grand and beautiful in nature, ruined by man's sordid quest for gain' (Roscoe 1837: 222), Llanelli was well on its way to becoming 'Tinopolis', the tinplate

Figure 7.3 Gorse and golden sands: Three Cliffs Bay, Gower Peninsula
Source: Image courtesy of the of City and County of Swansea.

manufacturing capital of the world, producing 50 per cent of the world's tinplate in tall-chimneyed factories that stretched along the bay. Just south of the Gower, Swansea specialised in copper, becoming known as 'Copperopolis', presenting an appearance similar to that of Llanelli, on a larger scale. Ships queued in Swansea's docks and trains in its goods yards, for cargoes of coal and copper, iron and tin forged amid fumes, smoke, dust and constant noise. Between 1801 and 1851, the population of Glamorgan, the county in which the Gower and Swansea lie, increased from 70,879 to 231,849, drawing people off the land in the Gower, from elsewhere in Wales and from further afield, transforming the makeup of the population of Llanelli and Cardiff. That 60 per cent of the population lives in the coastal zone of South Wales today is the direct result of industry and substantial labour migration during the industrial period.

It can be no accident that the first Area of Outstanding Natural Beauty in Britain was established within sight of 'Tinopolis' and 'Copperopolis'. Wales was one of the earliest and most industrialised nations in the world, and one of the first to grapple with the challenges to identity, nationality and heritage that came with modernity and industrialisation, in which the 1930s can now be seen as a key period. In 1932, the writer H.V. Morton encountered the cockle women of Gower, whom he first espied sitting with their wares in Swansea market, 'looking as though they were waiting for Rembrandt to come and paint them':

> They come from a heavenly protuberance on the Welsh coast known as the Gower Peninsula and their daily search for cockles is one of the most remarkable sights in Wales. The flat sands stretch for miles with the sea wind over them, and

small salt streams, which become fordable when the tide ebbs, cutting across them. On the opposite shores rise the jet-black smoke-stacks of Llanelly's steel and tin plate works. This is the strange setting for a scene that might be taking place in the dawn of history ... Two civilizations are represented by the cockle-women of Penclawdd and the tin-plate workers of Llanelly, who look at each other over two or three miles of the Llanrhidian Sands. (Morton 1932: 230, 233)

Morton, like many after him, waxed lyrical about the Gower as a 'land of golden gorse, blue butterflies and winds from the sea' (Morton 1932: 233), little realising that the bucolic Gower landscape of the 1930s was relatively recent. Less intensively farmed than in centuries past due to the decline of the rural workforce, it quickly became overgrown, giving the illusion of timeless wilderness. The golden gorse Morton admired would not have grown so profusely on the common lands in the heyday of Gower livestock keeping; gorse was used for animal feed and fuel, and ferns for bedding, and without these there would not have been so many butterflies.

Nonetheless, the symbolic opposition of past and present, industry and nature was deeply felt and pervasive throughout Wales at this time. Just offshore from the worst of the industrial pollution, the Gower became a *tabula rasa* for many imaginaries – the mythic Arthurian and druidical past of nascent Welsh nationalism; the aristocratic Norman imaginary in which names like de Braose and de Mowbray are embedded in the landscape and a feudal sense of stewardship of local heritage sites can be detected; and the imaginary of a romanticised agricultural past similar to that seen in the National History Museum at St Fagan's, which was founded as a reaction to the perceived threat to Welsh identity and culture of industrialisation. Above all, and despite the fact that much of the peninsula was for so long *Anglicana*, the Gower came to be seen as the quintessential embodiment of South Welsh-ness, a symbolic ancestral terrain, so much so that whether or not the 'heritage foods' of South Wales, laver and cockles, are actually gathered on the shores of the Gower, people like to think that they are, as if to consume them is to consume the very place and its perceived past. This was fertile ground for late industrial salvage conservation, profiting from the devaluation of agricultural land. It was in 1933 that the National Trust began to buy land on the Gower, which led to the creation of the AONB, and subsequently the emergence of the local interpretation of 'natural beauty' as ICZM 'protected' zones that go beyond the understandable desire to return to a romanticised pre-industrial era, seeking instead to create a pristine dehumanised past that never was, justified in the language of 'scientific environmental management' (Carrier 2003).

The South Wales Coast Today

Today it is a matter of considerable civic pride in Llanelli that nearly all traces of the industrial past have been excised, replaced by the amenities of renewal, further enhanced by the creation of the award-winning Millennium Coastal Park and ten mile pathway that follows the shore of the cleared industrial land that lies between Llanelli and the sand dunes of Pembrey. The new promenade that fronts the town gives panoramic views of the silver sweep of Carmarthen Bay, the Burry Estuary and the North Gower coast. If you know when and where to look, far out on the Gower headland tiny figures – seemingly walking on water – head out to sea or return just ahead of the incoming tide. These are the cockle pickers of Penclawdd, people in a persistent place; yet many – both visitors to the coast and residents – seem unable to see them. Heritage is process (Harvey 2001) and perception cultural; things must have meaning in order to be 'seen', and meanings change, are re-imagined or are 'forgotten'. Some reasons for the 'invisibility' of shellfish collectors generally, and in South Wales in particular, have been set out above. That the shellfish collectors are less visible in South Wales today than they were to Morton in the 1930s is due in large part to subsequent dynamics of post-industrial Welsh identity. The romanticised peasant folk life celebrated at the Folk Life Museum at St Fagan's as epitomising the 'authentic' Welsh identity were later challenged by miners, factory workers and their descendants who considered that themselves to be as Welsh as anyone else, and whose contribution to Welsh life is now enshrined in the new National Waterfront Museum in Swansea. The tension between farm and smallholding on the one hand, and factory and mine on the other, remains unresolved, but both have become dominant constructs in Welsh nationalism, with those holding to one or other construct at least sharing an identity as inward-looking 'peoples of the valley' whose national dish is lamb. Lamb has a central role in Welsh national identity, and is associated with the inland valleys, even though in antiquity and through to the twentieth century, the most commonly eaten meat in Wales has been not lamb but pork. Moreover as in France, the best lamb in Wales has always been the salt marsh lamb from the coast.

With the rise of Welsh nationalism, expressed through fetishizing the valley landscape and lamb, the older culture of coastal peoples and their emblematic foods have been displaced. In South Wales, among those with coastal backgrounds, cockles and seaweed call up all the fierce feelings typical of national foods, even though they may not eat them frequently. But 'official' Wales turns inwards towards the valleys, which is why tourists arriving in Wales today find it difficult to relate to the coast. Despite the stunning visual beauty of the coast, there is little official promotion or even recognition of Welsh coastal history and culture, no formal representations of the coastal past to enrich the coastal present and safeguard its future, only 'national' museums devoted to agriculture and industry. Dedicated gastro-tourists and celebrity chefs in search of regional foods have also commented on the strange invisibility of Welsh shellfish and seaweed in their native place. Indeed, this echoes the cultural invisibility of the coast itself.

But the Welsh shellfish industry should not to be thought of as an artisanal pursuit in rapid decline. Shellfish collecting in Wales has always moved with the times, expanding its market with the coming of the railways and the expansion of the industrial population (Jenkins 1984), and taking advantage of the latest developments in scientific shellfish culturing and monitoring. Today, the collecting is done from tractors and four-wheel drive vehicles rather than donkey carts, and by men rather than by women, bringing in a highly profitable catch that is mainly sold abroad, where its high quality is better appreciated than at home. Spain, Portugal and the Netherlands are the biggest European customers, with new markets opening up further afield. In addition to being a thriving industry in an otherwise declining marine field, with an unrealised potential to improve nutrition in the UK if the domestic consumption of shellfish and seaweed products were to increase (and a high potential to tap into *umami*, the new 'fifth sense'), the shellfish farmers and seaweed collectors of South Wales represent the latest link in a uniquely long chain of successful local human interaction with the environment that demands incorporation in the new coastal legislation. As Ingold (2000: 76) put it, 'faced with an ecological crisis whose roots lie ... in the separation of human agency and social responsibility from the sphere of our direct involvement with the non-human environment, it surely behoves us to reverse this order of priority'.

Conclusions

Even as the Marine and Coastal Access Bill continued its progress through Parliament, concerns continued to grow that the designation of parts of the coast as Marine Conservation Zones (MCZs) would take too much account of future leisure and recreational factors at the expense of the extractive shellfish industries long established within the zones (Research Paper 09/79, Marine and Coastal Access Bill, Committee Stage Report 2009). Ministerial amendments were made to the Bill that could legally undermine what protection Britain's shellfish farmers have had for over a century, but the Shellfish Association of Great Britain (SAGB), the shellfish industry's national trade association, was not informed of these changes, and the SAGB's legal advisers had to draw up a formal memorandum of protest about lack of due consultation, which was submitted to Parliament along with a list of their own amendments in an attempt to safeguard shellfish farmers and farming (Memorandum Submitted by the Shellfish Association of Great Britain 06, July 2009). The Bill finally passed through Parliament in November 2009, but since then a change in government and economic constraints have prevented full implementation. One thing is certain: whatever the final applications of the Marine and Coastal Access Bill may be, the future of shellfish farming and shellfishers in Wales and Britain, and the life of the coast itself, will be uncertain for years to come.

The lines, then, are drawn – and though they are drawn in sand and water, they go deep. To 'read' the scapes of land, coast and sea, to understand what shellfish and seaweed have meant and still mean in Wales and along the British coast generally (Murphy 2009), is to see history as a long process of interaction between the biophysical and the socio-cultural (Ingold 2001, Cunliffe 2008). As Sahlins (1985: xvii) put it, the difference between culture and history, past and present, static and dynamic, system and event is misleading and analytically debilitating. Imagining landscapes allows us to trace forces and influences going back over many centuries, as outlined here. These continue to influence coastal politics, practices and perception in Wales today. With the full record of the Bill's passage now in the public domain, the extent to which imagined and invisible landscapes figured in the debates is apparent. From imagining landscapes, an integrated historical and biophysical anthropology must proceed to the consequences of these forces, and to the explication and experience of the concrete event. To the longitudinal and *etic* background presented here, my ethnography in Wales will go on to add the *emic* view, the world of shellfishing and seaweed gathering from the inside, embattled on a coast that some would make non-existent, trapped between new law and old custom, confronting contending imaginaries of the past, and contesting visions of the future.

Acknowledgement

The support of the Glamorgan County History Trust in carrying out this research is gratefully acknowledged.

References

Aldhouse-Green, S. and Pettitt, P. 1998. Paviland Cave: Contextualising the 'Red Lady'. *Antiquity*, 72, 756–72.

Borsay, P. 2008. Welsh Seaside Resorts: Historiography, Sources and Themes. *Welsh History Review*, 24(2), 92–119.

Bender, B. 1998. *Stonehenge: Making Space*. Oxford and New York: Berg.

Carrier, J.G. 2003. Biology, Ecology, Political Economy: Seascape and Conflict in Jamaica, in *Landscape, Memory and History: Anthropological Perspectives*, edited by P.J. Stewart and A. Strathern. London and Sterling, VA: Pluto Press, 210–28.

Cobb, H. 2005. Straight Down the Line? A Queer Consideration of Hunter-gatherer Studies in North-west Europe. *World Archaeology*, 37(4), 630–36.

Cristancho S. and Vining, J. 2004. Culturally Defined Keystone Species. *Human Ecology Review*, 11(2), 153–64.

Crossley-Holland, K. (trans. and ed.) 1982. *The Anglo-Saxon World*. Oxford: Oxford University Press.

Cunliffe, B. 2008. *Europe between the Oceans: Themes and Variations 9000BC–1400AD*. New Haven and London: Yale University Press.

Davidson, A. (ed.) 2002. *The Coastal Archaeology of Wales*. York: Council for British Archaeology.

Davies, R.W. 1971. The Roman Military Diet. *Britannia*, 2, 122–42.

Davies, W. 1990. *Patterns of Power in Early Wales*. Oxford: Clarendon Press.

Davies, W. 2004. Looking Backwards to the Early Medieval Past: Wales and England, a Contrast in Approaches. *Welsh History Review*, 24(2), 197–221.

Dillehay, T.D. 1999. The Late Pleistocene Cultures of South America. *Evolutionary Anthropology*, 7(6), 206–15.

Draisey, D. 2002. *A History of Gower.* Herefordshire: Logaston Press.

Emery, F.V. 1956. West Glamorgan Farming, circa 1580–1620. *National Library of Wales Journal*, Part I 1956 Winter Vol. IX/4 and Part II 1957 Summer Vol. X/1.

Erlandson, J.M., Graham, M.H. and Bourque B.J. et al. 2007. The Kelp Highway Hypothesis: Marine Ecology, the Coastal Migration Theory and the Peopling of the Americas. *Journal of Island and Coastal Archaeology*, 2, 161–74.

Erlandson, J.M. and Fitzpatrick, S.M. 2006. Oceans, Islands and Coasts: Current Perspectives on the Role of the Sea in Human Prehistory. *Journal of Island and Coastal Archaeology*, 1(1), 5032.

Fenn, P.T. 1925. Justinian and the Freedom of the Sea. *American Journal of International Law*, 19(4), 716–27.

Fenn, P.T. 1926. Origins of the Theory of Territorial Waters. *American Journal of International Law*, 20(3), 465–82.

Fitzpatrick, S.M., Erlandson, J.M., Anderson A. and Kirch, P.V. 2007. Straw Boats and the Proverbial Sea: A Response to 'Island Archaeology: In Search of a New Horizon'. *Island Studies Journal*, 2(2), 229–38.

Garibaldi, A. and Turner, M. 2004. Cultural Keystone Species: Implications for Ecological Conservation and Restoration. *Ecology and Society*, 9(3), 1. [Online]. Available at: <http://www.ecologyandsociety.org/vol9/iss3/art1/>.

Glassow, M.A. and Wilcoxon. L.R. 1988. Coastal Adaptations Near Point Conception, California, with Particular Regard to Shellfish Exploitation. *American Antiquity*, 53(1), 36–51.

Gower and Carmarthen Bay website. [Online]. Available at: <http://www.gowerandcarmarthenbay.co.uk/index.html> [accessed 8/2009].

Harris, O. 1996. Introduction, in *Inside and Outside the Law: Anthropological Studies of Authority and Ambiguity*, edited by O. Harris. London and New York: Routledge, 1–15.

Harvey, D.C. 2001. Heritage Pasts and Heritage Presents: Temporality, Meaning and the Scope of Heritage Studies. *International Journal of Heritage Studies*, 7(4), 319–38.

Horden, P. and Purcell, N. 2000. *The Corrupting Sea: A Study of Mediterranean History.* Oxford: Blackwell.

Research Paper 09/79, Marine and Coastal Access Bill, Committee Stage Report. 2009. London: House of Commons.

Ingold, T. 1992. Culture and the Perception of the Environment in, *Bush Base, Forest Farm: Culture, Environment and Development*, edited by E. Croll and D. Parkin. London: Routledge, 39–56.

Ingold, T. 2000. *The Perception of the Environment: Essays in Livelihood, Dwelling and Skill.* London and New York: Routledge.

Ingold, T. 2001. Preface, in *Ecologia Della Cultura*, edited and translated by C. Grasseni and F. Ronzon. [Online]. Available at: <http://architectures.home. sapo.pt/Ingold-retrospect.pdf> [accessed 14/02/2010].

Integrated Coastal Zone Management (ICZM). 2009. London: DEFRA. [Online]. Available at: <http://www.defra.gov.uk/environment/marine/iczm/stocktake/ index.htm> [accessed 8/2009].

Jacobi, R.M. and Higham, T.F.G. 2008. The 'Red Lady' Ages Gracefully: New Ultrafiltration AMS Determinations from Paviland. *Journal of Human Evolution*, 55, 898–907.

Jenkins, J.G. 1972. Customs of Welsh Fishermen. *Folklore*, 83(1), 1–19.

Jenkins, J.G. 1984. *Cockles and Mussels: Aspects of Shellfish-gathering in Wales*. Cardiff: Welsh Folk Museum/National Museum of Wales.

Jenkins, J.G. 1991. *The Inshore Fishermen of Wales*. Cardiff: University of Wales Press.

John, A.H. 1995. *The Industrial Development of South Wales, 1750–1850*. Cardiff: Merton Priory Press.

Jones, T.L. 1991. Marine-resource Value and the Priority of Coastal Settlement: A California Perspective. *American Antiquity*, 56(3), 419–43

Lewis, E.A. 1903. The Development of Commerce and Industry in Wales during the Middle Ages. *Transactions of the Royal Historical Society*, New Series, Vol. 17, 121–73.

Macaulay, V., Hill, C. and Achilli, A. et al. 2001. Single Rapid Coastal Settlement of Asia Revealed by Analysis of Complete Mitochondrial Genomes. *Science*, 308(5724), 1034–6.

Mannino, M.A. and Thomas, K.D. 2002. Depletion of a Resource? The Impact of Prehistoric Human Foraging on Intertidal Mollusc Communities and its Significance for Human Settlement, Mobility and Dispersal. *World Archaeology*, 33(3), 452–74.

Marine Programme Plan 2009/2010. London: DEFRA.

Matthews, M.D. 2003. 'Adventurer of Both Ship and Cargo': Sir Thomas Stepney, Businessman and Baronet (1725–72). *Welsh History Review*, 21(3), 455–80.

McGlashan, D.J., Duck, R.W. and Reid, C.T. 2005. Defining the Foreshore: Coastal Geomorphology and British Laws. *Estuarine, Coastal and Shelf Science*, 62, 183–92.

MCZ Project Wales/Countryside Council for Wales 2011. [Online]. Available at: <http://www.ccw.gov.uk/landscape--wildlife/managing-land-and-sea/marine- policies/planning--management/marine-protected-areas/mcz-project-wales. aspx> [accessed 9/2011].

Memorandum Submitted by the Shellfish Association of Great Britain (SAGB), MC 06, for the Attention of Marine and Coastal Access Public Bill Committee, July 2009. [Online]. Available at: <www.parliament.uk> [accessed 14/2/2010].

Milner, N., Craig, O.E. and Bailey, N.E. et al. 2003. Something Fishy in the Neolithic? A Re-evaluation of Staple Isotope Analysis of Mesolithic and Neolithic Coastal Populations. *Antiquity*, 78(229), 9–22.

Morris, B. (ed.) 2000. *Gabriel Powell's Survey of the Lordship of Gower 1764.* Llandybie: Gower Society Publications.

Morton, H.V. 1932. *In Search of Wales.* London: Methuen & Co.

Murphy, P. 2009. *The English Coast: A History and Prospect.* London and New York: Continuum.

Nader, L. 2002. *The Life of the Law: Anthropological Projects.* Berkeley and London: University of California Press.

Neher, P.A., Arnason, R. and Mollet, M. (eds) 1989. *Rights Based Fishing.* ASI series, Series E, Applied Sciences No. 169. Brussels: NATO.

Nicholl, L.D. 1936. *The Normans in Glamorgan, Gower and Kidweli.* William Lewis: Cardiff.

Niven, K. 1978. Beach Access: An Historical Overview. *New York Sea Grant Law and Policy Journal*, 2, 161–99.

O'Connor, K. 2006. *The English Breakfast: The Cultural Biography of a National Meal.* London and New York: Kegan Paul.

O'Connor, K. 2009. The Secret History of the Weed of *Hiraeth*: Laverbread, Identity and Museums in Wales. *Journal of Museum Ethnography*, 22, 2010.

O'Connor, K. 2013. *The English Breakfast, the Cultural Biography of a National Meal.* London: Berg/Bloomsbury. [Revised edition].

Ohnuki-Tierney, E. 1995. Structure, Event and Historical Metaphor: Rice and Identities in Japanese History. *The Journal of the Royal Anthropological Institute*, 1(2), 227–53.

O'Sullivan, A. 2003. Place, Memory and Identity Among Estuarine Fishing Communities: Interpreting the Archaeology of Early Medieval Fish Weirs. *World Archaeology*, 35(3) (Seascapes), 449–68.

Purcell, N. 2001. Eating Fish: The Paradoxes of Seafood, in *Food in Antiquity*, edited by J. Wilkins, D. Harvey and M. Dobson. Exeter: University of Exeter Press.

Renouf, M.A.P. 1984. Northern Coastal Hunter-Fishers: An Archaeological Model. *World Archaeology*, 16(1), 18–27.

Roscoe, T. 1837. *Wanderings and Excursions in South Wales.* London: Bohn.

SAGB – Shellfish Association of Great Britain Newsletter, Winter 2008.

Sahlins, M. 1985. *Islands of History.* Chicago: University of Chicago Press

Schiller, A.A. 1994. Custom in Classical Roman Law, in *Folk Law: Essays in the Theory and Practice of Lex Non Scripta Vol I*, edited by A.D. Renteln and A. Dundes. Madison: University of Wisconsin Press, 33–47.

Schlanger, S.H. 1992. Recognizing Persistent Places in Anasazi Settlement Systems, in *Space, Time and Archaeological Landscapes*, edited by J. Rossignol and L. Wandsnider. New York: Plenum Press, 91–111.

Schulting, R.J. and Richards, M.P. 2002. Finding the Coastal Mesolithic in Southwest Britain: AMS Dates and Stable Isotope Results on Human Remains from Caldey Island, South Wales. *Antiquity*, 76(294), 1011–25.

Simpson, A.W.B. 1994. The Common Law and Legal Theory, in *Folk Law: Essays in the Theory and Practice of Lex Non Scripta Vol I*, edited by A.D. Renteln and A. Dundes. Madison: University of Wisconsin Press, 119–39.

Sobecki, S.I. 2008. *The Sea and Medieval English Literature.* Cambridge: D.S. Brewer.

Sollas, W.J. 1913. Paviland Cave: An Aurignacian Station in Wales. *Journal of the Royal Anthropological Institute of Great Britain and Ireland*, 43 (Jul–Dec), 325–74.

Steane, J.M. and Foreman, M. 1988. Medieval Fishing Tackle, in *Medieval Fish, Fishing and Fishponds in England*, edited by A. Michael. Oxford: British Archaeological Reports, British Series 182.

Stevens, J.S. 1980–81. The Public Trust: A Sovereign's Ancient Prerogative becomes the People's Environmental Right. *University of California at Davis Law Review*, 14, 195–232.

Torben, R.C., Erlandson, J.M. and Vellanoweth. R.L. 2001. Palaeocoastal Marine Fishing on the Pacific Coast of the Americas: Perspectives from Daisy Cave, California. *American Antiquity*, 66(4), 595–613.

Turner, N.J., Davidson-Hunt, I.J. and O'Flaherty, M. 2003. Living on the Edge: Ecological and Cultural Edges as Sources of Diversity of Socio-Ecological Resilience. *Human Ecology*, 31(3), 439–61.

Vinogradoff, Sir P. 1923. The Roman Element's in Bracton's Treatise. *Yale Law Journal*, XXXII(8), 751–6.

Yale Law Journal 1969–70. The Public Trust in Tidal Areas: A Sometimes Submerged Issue. *Yale Law Journal*, 79, 762–73.

Chapter 8

Imagining the Forces of Life and the Cosmos in the Kelabit Highlands, Sarawak

Monica Janowski

In this chapter I want to pose questions about how we should imagine the relationship between humans and the cosmos in which they live, drawing on data which I have gathered on indigenous ideas and beliefs about life and the meaning of being human during fieldwork over more than 20 years in the Kelabit Highlands in Borneo; and on Tim Ingold's processual approach to the nature of life. I suggest that, building on Ingold's work, we can use Kelabit ideas to encourage us to think further about the nature of individuation within a continuous flow of power and life through the cosmos.

The Kelabit Highlands

Pa' Dalih is a longhouse-based settlement of about 120 people at the headwaters of the Baram river (see Figure 8.1). The Kelabit Highlands, in which it is situated, lies at between 3,000 and 4,000 feet above sea level, abutting the border with East Kalimantan, and forms part of a large plateau in the centre of Borneo, surrounded by mountains, which is mainly over the border in East Kalimantan, Indonesia. The plateau is a fertile and relatively populated area compared to many other parts of interior Borneo. The whole of the plateau is notable for the fact that its linguistically related inhabitants[1] practise wet cultivation of rice (Janowski 2004) as well as dry shifting cultivation; and for the presence of many megalithic monuments, some erected up to the 1950s (Banks 1937, Harrisson 1958, Schneeberger 1979). Both rice and megalithic monuments relate closely to the way in which the Kelabit 'imagine' the workings of the cosmos and their role in this, as I will show.

Until the 1960s, when an air service was set up to the highlands, it took many weeks by boat and then on foot to reach the area from the coast. Although there were always contacts between the highland area and the coast, these were rare. The point at which the Kelabit Highlands entered the outside world, symbolically,

---

1 Speaking languages belonging to the Apo Duat (more properly called Apad Uat, or 'Root Range', after the range of mountains running down the middle of the area) group of languages (Hudson 1992).

**Figure 8.1 The longhouse community of Pa' Dalih, with, in the distance,
a mountain ridge said to be a longhouse turned to stone
(*ruma batu*)**

Source: Image courtesy of Kaz Janowski.

may be said to be 25 March 1945, when Tom Harrisson[2] was parachuted into
the Kelabit Highlands as a Special Operations Executive operative, to organise
resistance against the Japanese among the interior peoples. The impact of
involvement in this campaign was very significant in creating a strong impetus
towards the outside world and in particular towards the belief system perceived
to be that of Harrisson and his European colleagues – Christianity. After the war
ended, Borneo Evangelical Mission missionaries established bases and short
airstrips throughout the highlands and the Kelabit showed themselves to be very
willing converts to Christianity.

Little is known about the environmental or human history of the Kelabit
Highlands or indeed of the interior of Borneo. Very limited written records extend
back to the beginning of the twentieth century, when administrative officers of
the Sarawak government made their first visits to the interior. In this context, the

---

2   Harrisson, who in the 1930s had led an Oxford University expedition to Borneo and
participated in setting up the Mass Observation archive, went on to become an important
figure in Sarawak and in relation to the Kelabit as a people after the Second World War. He
became Curator of the Sarawak Museum and published a number of articles and a book on
the Kelabit (Harrisson 1959).

Cultured Rainforest project,[3] which worked in the Kelabit Highlands between 2007 and 2011, brought together anthropology, archaeology and environmental history to begin to develop a picture of past and present relations between people and landscape in the highlands. The project, for which I led the anthropological work, included excavation at old settlement sites and interviews about settlement history and genealogies; excavation at megalithic cemetery sites and interviews about pre-Christian disposal of the dead; the taking of earth cores leading to the analysis of pollen and phytoliths, and interviews about the history of rice cultivation and attitudes to alternative starch sources such as sago palms; and the gathering of myths and stories relating to the landscape.

Metaphysical Speculation among the Kelabit

I have found that metaphysical speculation – what one might describe as 'imagining' the nature of reality and the role of human beings in it – is inherent in the way my friends and neighbours in Pa' Dalih think. Although individuals vary, it is generally not difficult to engage 'ordinary'[4] Kelabit in discussions about the way the world works, and they often spontaneously offer speculation. This contrasts with the response of most 'ordinary' Europeans to being asked big questions about how the cosmos works; most feel that this is not something about which it is appropriate for them to speculate. In the main, 'ordinary' Europeans see such speculation as the business of specialists, whether priests or scientists. The Kelabit, on the other hand, see speculation about the workings of the cosmos, and – linked to such speculation – intervention on their part in these workings, as something to which all humans can and should aspire.

For the Kelabit, intervention in the workings of the cosmos is seen as an achievement, and is the basis of status. Their interest in metaphysical speculation seems to be part of a wider interest in trying out new ways of thinking and doing, and a belief that this is important in achieving their capabilities as humans (*lemulun*) rather than animals (*poong*). The Kelabit are often talked of in Sarawak, and talk of themselves, as particularly capable innovators; and they are very proud of this. They point to their rapid adoption of new techniques of rice cultivation, their success in education, and their early and eager adoption of Christianity as proof of their innovatory ability. Other tribal groups in Sarawak appear to admire and respect the Kelabit for this ability, although they sometimes criticise them for their arrogance!

---

3 Funded by the UK Arts and Humanities Research Council. See <http://www.arch.cam.ac.uk/cultured-rainforest/>.

4 By 'ordinary' Kelabit and 'ordinary' Europeans I refer here, loosely, to people who are not educated above secondary level and who may not pretend to have specialised scientific knowledge about any aspect of the dynamics of the cosmos.

Christianity was not forced upon the Kelabit. Following the Second World War, they invited missionaries to come and convert them. During the 1950s and 1960s, the Borneo Evangelical Mission built short airstrips throughout the Kelabit Highlands, including at Pa' Dalih, and visited regularly in that period. By the early 1970s its successor the Sidang Injil Borneo or SIB (the Borneo Evangelical Church) was formed, and the foreign missionaries who led the BEM were able to leave.[5] Before they were converted the Kelabit prayed to a variety of spirits or deities for success in agriculture and hunting; now the Kelabit have switched to praying to Jesus Christ. They have almost completely abandoned any interest in pre-Christian practices, believing that the new religion, and in particular Jesus Christ, provides an immensely powerful new platform from which to link directly to the Creator Deity and to manage and manipulate the cosmos. In this, they contrast with most other tribal groups in Borneo, who have also converted to Christianity or Islam but who are generally more syncretic in their approach to the new religion.

Despite the 'break with the past' which the Kelabit themselves see in their lives with the coming of Christianity,[6] there are some parallels between pre-Christian and Christian belief and practice in relation to ideas about *lalud*. The relationship with potent entities, including both pre-Christian spirits and Jesus, is set up through prayer, now called *sembahyang* (using the Malay term). This is still, as it was before Christianity arrived, forest- and mountain-oriented. Although each community has a church, the Kelabit regularly pray on forested hills and mountains, and there is an annual pilgrimage to a nearby mountain which is attended by both Kelabit and related Lun Dayeh and Lun Bawang. It seems that the main difference between the two systems, in Kelabit eyes, lies in the much greater effectiveness of Christianity in terms of the ability it bestows upon them to manipulate the cosmos.

In addition, Christianity appears to have provided the Kelabit with a new platform from which to launch their thoughts about the meaning and direction of the cosmos. While linked to practice, this is also purely philosophical. Each Kelabit person has his or her own take on the workings of the cosmos and how he or she can interact with them, and most are willing to talk these through with anyone interested. Sidang Injil Borneo church orthodoxy is malleable and shifting, reflecting constant discussion among individuals. It is a charismatic and evangelical church which encourages everyone to interpret the meaning of the Bible, and this encourages high levels of philosophical speculation. The Bible can be interpreted in many ways, and is particularly mysterious in its import for peoples living in such a different cultural and environmental context from those who wrote it. There is a palpable sense of exploration and excitement among the congregation in church during sermons, which may be delivered by any member.

---

5   See Lees (1979) for a description of the conversion of the Kelabit.

6   This is quite explicit; for example, one of the chapters in the BA thesis written by a young Kelabit in 1976, Robert Lian-Saging, is entitled 'Break with the Past' (Lian-Saging 1976/77).

The Bible is seen as giving important clues about how the cosmos works and how people can intervene in its workings successfully; but these are mysteriously worded, and there to be questioned and explored by all.

Lalud: The Flow of Life in the Kelabit Highlands

Although each man and woman engages in his or her own speculations, certain strong threads are common to all of my Kelabit friends. The most central of these is the concept of *lalud*. *Lalud* is akin to concepts in other parts of Southeast Asia and the Pacific, including Polynesian *mana* and Javanese *kasekten* (Anderson 1972), Balinese *sakti* (Geertz 1980) and Polynesian *mana*. It is manifest power. *Lalud* drives volcanoes, rivers, the rain, the sun – and, most importantly, life itself. Life is, in fact, the manifestation of *lalud*. Through *lalud*, people, plants and animals are able to live, *mulun*. As our friend and next door neighbour in the longhouse, Balang Pelaba[7] – 'Very Much a Tiger'– said to me in 2008: 'If it weren't for *lalud*, you wouldn't be alive'. Where there is movement and activity, there is believed to be life and *lalud*.

Lalud is fundamental to the cosmos. Without it the cosmos would not exist. The Kelabit view of the cosmos is close to that which, according to Ingold, is held by peoples in many parts of the world, including Southeast Asia, for whom 'the animacy of the lifeworld … is not the result of an infusion of spirit into substance, or of agency into materiality, but is rather ontologically prior to their differentiation' (Ingold 2006: 10). The Kelabit see *lalud* as concentrated in and deriving from a parallel part of the cosmos, associated with spirits (*ada'*) and God – and nowadays with Jesus. God, Tuan Allah in Christianity, is seen as the same Creator Deity as the pre-Christian Creator Deity, known by various names. The parallel spirit part of the cosmos is invisible or only partially visible. It appears to be co-present with the material world, and *ada'* are in it when they are sometimes perceived (*kelit* – see below) by humans. *Lalud* associated with the spirit world can only be expressed through the material cosmos. Thus, the material world and the force of *lalud* are inextricably linked. The material world is essentially a fully perceptible manifestation of the spirit world. Through the playing out of *lalud* the material world itself is played out.

Humans and *Lalud*

The parallel reality of the spirits, and of God, is only partially perceptible by humans. While it is encountered by all at some level when they are in the forest, and particularly at cemetery sites, only certain people can interact with it directly. Women, in the past, were particularly associated with one major spirit, Deraya,

---

7   Sadly deceased on 6 October 2009.

associated with rice, but this appears not to have been a close personal relationship but a sense that Deraya was favourably inclined towards them. It was men who, as shamans (*dayong*), journeyed in trances to bring back people's spirits which had wandered into the spirit world, and certain men were sought out by and had personal dealings with the Great Spirit (*Ada' Raya*) of the forest, known also as Pun Tumid, 'Grandfather Heel' – thus called because, having originally been a member of a pre-human race called the *Lun Rabada*, he became a spirit when his feet were reversed after a rockfall damaged them (inversion is associated with the spirit world). Balang Pelaba, who lived at the next-door hearth to us in the longhouse, used to be such a shaman, and before that, when he was a young man, he had a relationship with Pun Tumid. He told me how Pun Tumid had approached him when he was a bachelor with the suggestion that they be friends, and had given him glass phials of *lalud*-laden liquid with which he could heal or kill. Other men also told me that they had met Pun Tumid. Balang Pelaba and the others who had met him said that they 'perceived' (*kelit*) the Great Spirit but did not 'see' (*ne'ar*) him with their eyes. They were aware of a presence and they partially knew what Pun Tumid 'looked' like; but when asked why he could not 'see' (*ne'ar*) him, Balang Pelaba exclaimed that he is a spirit; how could one see him? Many people have told me that they have heard Pun Tumid hunting with dogs at night; only a spirit would do this, they say, as normal people cannot see at night to hunt with dogs. He is drawn to young men, and wants to be friends with them – and give them *lalud*. Now, Balang Pelaba told me, he is 'lonely', since his previous friends have abandoned him, and he wanders alone through the forest.

Jesus, too, seeks humans out to give them *lalud*, although humans themselves have to be open to this and to seek him out too. Through Jesus, individuals are able to access high levels of *lalud* – much higher, they say, than they could ever hope for from spirits, even from Pun Tumid. The Kelabit believe that Jesus has bestowed on them the ability to excel in the modern world.

Lalud flows. The way in which life-force or power flows is described in the essays in the collection of articles edited by James Fox (Fox 1980). Water, and liquid in general (one term, *pa'*, is used for both liquid and water), is associated with *lalud*. *Lalud* flows through liquid and like liquid. Deep pools of water are believed to contain powerful spirits known as *menegag*, related to the wider beliefs throughout the region in the powerful spirit water serpent, *naga*. Blood, the liquid which flows through the body, was used until the 1950s as a means of transmitting *lalud*: pigs were killed and their blood smeared on those who were in transition between the spirit world and the material world, such as children being initiated into human life and men who had taken dead bodies to the cemetery. Another powerful liquid, *borak* (rice beer), was a vital part of all human gatherings beyond the immediate family and underlined and activated the role of rice in generating human kinship (Janowski 2011).

As *lalud* flows, it is also seen to saturate the inhabited landscape. To an extent which has only gradually become clear to me, the Kelabit live in a landscape which is dynamically animated. People move through the landscape on the basis of assumptions of the presence of *lalud* everywhere, albeit in greater or lesser degree. This presence is to be interpreted as it manifests itself. When I walk through the landscape with a Kelabit friend, I know that I am not experiencing it in the same way as he or she is. Not only am I not aware of the history of each tree, plant and stone we pass; I am also not on the lookout for signs of *lalud* in those trees, plants and stones. For my Kelabit companion, on the other hand, the landscape is a field of flow for *lalud*, although its actual flow cannot be predicted with certainty; it must constantly be tracked and signs of the flow sought.

In flowing, *lalud* coalesces in certain sites. The concentration of *lalud* at a site expresses itself through the presence of *ada'* – 'spirits' or 'souls'. The bigger and stronger the *ada'* of an entity, the more *lalud* it has. The highest concentrations of *lalud* are pure *ada'*, which cannot be 'seen' (*ne'ar*) with the normal eye – they can only be 'perceived' (*kelit*). Visibility dissipates, as it were, as *lalud* rises.

Lalud does not only coalesce in humans and animals; it also coalesces in entities and substances which are – in Western terms – non-living. While *lalud* flows through water, hardness, and especially stoniness, is associated with the coalescence of *lalud*. Living things, as they become older and develop stronger *ada'*, become more stone-like and have more *lalud*. Big, old trees have stronger

**Figure 8.2 The twin stone peaks of Batu Lawi mountain,
said to be male and female**

Source: Image courtesy of the author.

**Figure 8.3 Melkey, Roger and Lian of Pa' Dalih at the megalithic cemetery
    at Long Diit**
Source: Image courtesy of Kaz Janowski.

ada' than young saplings. Big mountains, especially if they are made of stone like
Batu Lawi (see Figure 8.2), have powerful *ada'*. Batu Lawi is said to be a married
couple who moved around the landscape – burning places where they stopped off,
which can still be identified because they are overgrown with a certain fern-laden
ecology – before eventually being turned to stone. Married couples, as I have
discussed elsewhere (Janowski 2007), are particularly strongly associated with
lalud, being a source of it for their dependants through their focal role in the rice
meal (Janowski 1995).

The transformation of Batu Lawi from human married couple to mountain is
an instance of the process of *balio*. *Balio* is the transformation of a living entity
from one form to another. Animals may become human or humans may become
animals; and animals or humans may become spirits (*ada'*). People and animals
may also become stone. The most common reason for petrification is when people
have laughed at animals. This leads to thunder, lightning and the descent of 'stone
rain', *udan batu* (hail) and eventually the transformation (*balio*) of the person and
(usually) the whole house in which he or she lives into stone. Many large stone
features of the landscape are said to be houses which have been transformed into
stone (see Figure 8.1). *Balio* is said to spread across the landscape as though it
were water flowing, turning everything in its path to stone.

Bones are strongly associated with stone: this is underlined by the fact that in the past human bones were placed in stone burial jars or within stone cists (see Figure 8.3). Bones are considered to be repositories of *lalud* deriving from the living entity for which they once provided a structure. The bones of ancestors carry those ancestors' *lalud*. The *lalud* of groups of ancestors should be together; thus, their bones are placed together in the same cemetery and, until the 1950s when people stopped using megalithic cemeteries, often in the same stone jar or under the same stone cist.

The jars and cists in megalithic cemeteries are believed to have been made by ancestors living in the origin time of *getoman lalud*, 'joining with *lalud*'. The Kelabit say that in the past there was much more *lalud* in the world, and living beings could do things they cannot do now. The culture heroes living in *getoman lalud*, like Tukad Rini (Janowski, forthcoming), are said to have been giants (see Figure 8.4). Tukad Rini left marks on stone with his hands and feet (see Figure 8.5), and is said to have been able to fly; he is said to have flown to the moon.

Figure 8.4 Baye Ribuh of Pa' Dalih by the giant 'sharpening stone' of the culture hero Tukad Rini

Source: Image courtesy of the author.

**Figure 8.5 A 'footprint' said to have been made by the culture hero
Tukad Rini on a stone in the Kelapang river**
Source: Image courtesy of Kaz Janowski.

Lalud settles in hard objects, and these are believed to be 'alive' and to be repositories of life which is accessible to humans. This is expressed in the pre-Christian practice of collecting, keeping, feeding and regarding as a source of power any strange hard objects which are found in the landscape. Many people, particularly men, used to have collections of hard objects which they had found in the landscape, such as strange-shaped stones, deer's antlers or crystals, which were considered to be repositories of *lalud* which could be accessed and used by their owners. Such objects had to be fed blood or else they would consume their owner; thus they were regarded as both living and dangerous. Some men still maintain collections of these objects, although they say that they no longer feed them or use them to access *lalud* (see Figure 8.6). One of the most common kinds of objects kept in this way comprised what are called 'thunderstones' – *batu pera'it*. These objects are believed by both the Kelabit and by their neighbours, the hunter-gatherer Penan, to represent the coalesced and petrified form which the *lalud* of thunder and lightning takes upon reaching the earth (see Figure

**Figure 8.6 A collection of hard objects from the forest collected by
Telona Bala of Pa' Dalih**

Source: Image courtesy of the author.

**Figure 8.7 A 'thunderstone' (*batu pera'it*), once kept in a rice barn
in Pa' Dalih**

Source: © Trustees of the British Museum.

8.7).[8] They were kept by the Kelabit in rice barns in pre-Christian times, until the 1950s, because they were believed to increase the amount of rice stored there.

Marking the Landscape

I have discussed elsewhere (Janowski 2007) how Kelabit married couples harness *lalud* through bringing wild plants and meat together with rice to generate a way of living life which is distinctive to human beings, which they call *ulun*. Through the rice meal, *lalud* from wild animals and plants is harnessed with the structuring capacity of rice, and transmitted to those dependent on the couple providing the meal (see Janowski 1995). I have also argued that this is the foundation for a form of social hierarchy founded in inter-generational kin relations. Hierarchy is, in fact, basic to *ulun*.

The achievement of harnessing and transmitting *lalud* is marked on the physical landscape. One way of doing this is through the creation of rice fields themselves, both dry fields and wet fields but particularly wet fields. Kelabit dry rice fields are described as *late luun*, or 'field for growing rice on the surface'. They are used not only for growing rice but for a wide variety of other plants, including fruit trees, plants which are eaten as accompaniments to rice at the rice meal, and grains or roots which are eaten as snacks or, before the Kelabit became Christian, used to make beer. Although they are normally only used for one year for growing rice, they are used over many years for other crops, and therefore have a long-term impact on the environment and on ties between people and the environment. Wet rice fields are known as *late baa*, or 'wet field for growing rice'. Nowadays, these are very similar to the *sawah* of the lowland areas of Java and other Indonesian islands, but they appear until the 1960s to have been quite variable in their structure and use. Some seem to have been used over long periods of time, while others were used for a few years and then moved. Some were made in extended stream beds and palaeo-channels of the river, others in flooded marshy areas. The *Cultured Rainforest* project has found evidence of a very long history for growing rice in palaeo-channels of the river Kelapang near Pa' Dalih, possibly going back several thousand years. However, the largest and most highly developed *late baa* in recent times appear not to have been in the Kelabit Highlands but in the part of the plateau across the border in East Kalimantan, in the Kerayan river area (Schneeberger 1979, Padoch 1983). Here, terracing was carried out and very extensive permanent *late baa* existed when Schneeberger visited the area in the 1930s. In the Kelabit Highlands it is only in recent years, since the 1960s, that large-scale earthworks were carried out to create large and permanent *late baa*. However, even before this, earthworks were carried out to create irrigation and

---

8   We now know that such stones were once sago-pounders; one of the investigators on the *Cultured Rainforest* project, Huw Barton, has found traces of starch from a variety of local sago-bearing palms on them (see Barton and Janowski, forthcoming).

drainage ditches, and, according to a number of my informants, also to create *late baa* through the encouragement of oxbow lakes.

An earthwork built to make or extend *late baa* is described as a form of 'mark' or *etuu*. Other marks were made by setting up standing stones, carving stones (see Figure 8.8), digging ditches on ridges (often to create a new path) and removing trees at a point on a ridge. Such marks were made, until the 1960s, at *irau ate*

Figure 8.8 A carved stone (*batu narit*) near the abandoned Kelabit settlement of Pa' Bengar, said to have been made at an *irau* feast in the past

Source: Image courtesy of Kaz Janowski.

('death *irau*'), which were occasions for broadcasting the ability of the dead person and his or her heirs – who provide the *irau* – to feed many people. Those who are fed are presented at the *irau* as his or her descendants as well as dependants. This is so because kinship, as I have shown elsewhere, is constructed through the rice meal, of which an *irau* is an expanded version (Janowski 1995).

The ability to feed others is proclaimed through the making of *etuu* marks. In the case of earthworks to facilitate rice-growing, this would contribute directly to that continuing ability. In the case of marks made at *irau* feasts, a lasting record of the ability to feed others is created. The size and scale of the mark reflects the number of guests at the feast; the aim is to make a statement about the ability to feed as many people as possible.

Interrupting and Channelling *Lalud*

Making earthworks and erecting and working stone involve taking a hand in the creation of the animated landscape. They are expressions of the ability to interrupt and channel *lalud*, proven through the ability to feed others. Doing these things is an expression of the way of life described as *ulun*, a way of life which is distinctively human. There is a distinction between just being alive – *mulun* – and having *ulun*; while all living entities live, *mulun*, only humans are described as having *ulun*.

The ability to interrupt and channel *lalud* is something which those with stronger ties to the spirit world and to ancestors are believed to have in greater measure than others. Higher status people are at the centre of centripetal genealogies into which all others tie themselves. These link back to powerful ancestors (Janowski 2007). The even more powerful ancestors who lived at the time of 'joining with great power' (*getoman lalud*) are believed to have taken an even greater hand in this creative process.

It is the Kelabit view that in order to establish rights over a landscape it is essential to show evidence, through making *etuu* marks, of having been instrumental in this creative process of interrupting and channelling *lalud*; they argue that the lack of such evidence of *etuu* marks on the part of the hunter-gatherer Penan who are their neighbours is grounds for arguing that the Penan should not have rights over that landscape (Janowski and Langub 2011). A successful human, of high status, should demonstrate the ability to manage and manipulate *lalud* effectively, and this should be visible through the *etuu* marks he or she makes on the landscape. This remains as true now as it was before the Kelabit became Christian, and is expressed in the large numbers of new wet rice fields which have been constructed since the 1960s in Pa' Dalih (Janowski 1988, 2004). With the coming of logging to the highlands, debates about the significance of *etuu* have taken on a particular significance, since they bear on questions of whether Kelabit or Penan have the right to receive compensation.

Individuation in a Holistic Field of Flow

The Kelabit notion of the cosmos is a holistic one. For my Kelabit friends, all forces in the universe are reducible to one: *lalud*. *Lalud* drives life; and it is the fundamental cosmic force. In their view it is because of the western world's early adoption of Christianity that scientists, raised in this world and with a consequently enhanced ability to manipulate this fundamental force, have been able to perform such marvels as harnessing of the power of the atom. It was Christianity, they say, that granted science the ability to harness the *lalud* of the cosmos to a heightened degree. Likewise, the Kelabit attribute their own success in the modern world to their adoption of Christianity. Thus modern science, from their perspective, has not introduced a move away from a holistic notion of the workings of the cosmos. It has rather underlined this holism. Life for them is what *lalud* is all about; they say that the power which is harnessed through science is the same as that which makes life tick.

This contrasts with the approach taken by the majority of western-trained physicists and cosmologists, for whom understanding the cosmos does not depend on understanding life. Arguably, however, life should not be treated as an extraneous force which intervened at some unknown point in the development of the cosmos, but should rather be seen as inherent in it (Ingold 2008). The physicist David Bohm has suggested that both inanimate matter and life can be comprehended on the common ground of what he calls the 'implicate order' (Bohm 1980: 193–213). Most physicists, however, have tended to ignore life in their quest to understand the universe in a unified way.

Ingold has demonstrated the importance of taking seriously the cosmologies and philosophical musings of non-Western peoples. He has also argued for the need to reconsider the nature of life itself, focusing in his recent work (Ingold 2011) on its processual and interactive nature. Building on the writings of such philosophers as Bergson (1911), Heidegger (1971) and more recently Deleuze and Guattari (1983, 2004), Ingold has argued that life should not be seen as a fixed, internal property of mobile entities but that it is rather defined by movement (Ingold 2008, 2010). The centrality of movement to understanding the nature of living entities and of consciousness within the cosmos has also been stressed by the philosopher Sheets-Johnstone (1998). The implication of an approach to life which sees living entities not as inserted into the world, but rather as continually coming into being within it, is that the boundaries between entities are in some sense illusory; life is a continuous 'meshwork', in which materials are woven together.

This analysis fits well with Kelabit ideas about the flow of *lalud*. It also fits with the holistic nature of the Kelabit contention that the material world and *lalud* itself are one and the same: two sides of the same coin; neither able to exist without the other. For the Kelabit, all matter contains *lalud*; indeed, perhaps, *is lalud*. In some senses, this echoes the equivalence of mass and energy proposed by modern physics – except for the exclusion of life.

Kelabit imagine that people – and other living entities – live within the flow of *lalud*. They are certainly part of it. However, they do not simply float along, acquiescing in a flow which takes place around them and through them. As we have seen, they both participate in the creation of this flow and actively divert it. This involves interaction and engagement with other living entities within the field of flow in which they live, including other humans, animals, trees and stones; all of them considered to be living. In some sense, then, the continuous field of flow of life is made up of distinct entities.

Kelabit conceive of humans interacting with other entities in two ways (Janowski and Langub 2011). One is through the trails or footprints which they leave. The hunter-gatherer Penan, who leave such trails, call them *oban. Oban* may be seen as a record of the ways in which living entities bump into, alter and divert each other – 'entangle' with each other, to use Ingold's term – in their journeyings through the cosmos. Another way in which the Kelabit – but not the Penan – relate to other entities within the animated cosmos is through the making of *etuu* marks, discussed above. It is these that most clearly express the Kelabit belief that it is possible to deliberately channel and manipulate the flow of life. *Etuu* are deliberate inscriptions. Parallels with this kind of deliberate inscription on the cosmos can be found in many societies across the globe. Ingold and Vergunst have discussed how, in the history of colonialism, humans have aimed to place their 'stamps' on the world as an index of possession (Ingold and Vergunst 2008); the impetus to create *etuu* might be seen as carrying something of the same force.

Distinctness and Directionality within a Field of Flow

The differentiation between those who are successful manipulators of *lalud* and those who are less successful, marked through *etuu*-making, implies the distinctness of the individual entities making the marks. Indeed, for the Kelabit distinctness is – by implication, if not explicitly – a function of life. All beings considered to be alive, to have *lalud* – including stones and mountains – have their own distinct trajectories. They interact and affect each other as distinct entities. It is the distinctness of living things that draws together and organises matter.

If distinctness is what organises matter into living entities, consciousness and direction on the part of living entities are, for the Kelabit, what drives the world forward. The interactions of living entities are not random; they are the result of myriad decisions and micro-decisions. Consciousness and direction, then, are also functions of life. The clearest example of this is the making of *etuu*, which broadcast the distinctness and differentiation both between different humans and between humans and other living entities which do not make *etuu*.

Thus the Kelabit not only see the entire cosmos as a field of flow for *lalud*; they also see themselves as part of a world that is continually in formation. At the same time they assert that life is conscious and individuated. It is through the existence of individuated conscious entities that life, for the Kelabit, has 'direction'. They see living entities as constantly forming and dissipating, as life coheres and accumulates at sites. As living entities become more powerful accumulations of *lalud*, they develop greater power to consciously 'direct' the *lalud* which they possess. Humans, as powerful centres at which *lalud* accumulates, are particularly able to manipulate and direct *lalud*. They remain, at the same time, part of a continual field of flow of life.

Modern biology, too, seeks to identify distinct living entities: individual members of a species. As Ingold has pointed out, modern science sees such organisms as 'discrete, pre-specified entit[ies]' (Ingold 2004: 219), entering into the world with an underlying script for their development already written before their lives begin. He criticises this approach, pointing out that it is only through their interaction with the world that living entities come into being, and that each living entity should rather be seen as 'a particular locus of growth and development within a continuous field of relationships'. This is indeed much closer to the way in which the Kelabit see things.

The Kelabit approach to the flow of life and the nature of individuation raises philosophical questions about the role of individuation and of distinct living entities or organisms within the field of flow of life. These questions are also raised, for me, by Ingold's emphasis on life as a continuous meshwork without boundaries between entities (Ingold 2006; 2008) and at the same time as concentrated in distinct organism-persons within that meshwork (Ingold 2009). What is the role of individuation within the meshwork of life? For my friends in Pa' Dalih, the 'meshwork' or flow of life could not, in fact, exist unless it were directed by the individual accumulations of *lalud* which are living entities. It is through these that life has existence. Living entities, for the Kelabit, are by their very essence conscious, have mind; as they become more powerful cohesions of *lalud* this becomes more and more evident. Because all matter contains *lalud*, it follows that it has the rudiments of mind and consciousness; entities which are greater accretions of *lalud* simply have more mind, more consciousness. Spirits have the highest levels of *lalud*; but humans can also be very powerful, very *lalud*-laden. This is expressed and proven through altering the landscape, through making *etuu* marks.

Conclusion

The Kelabit of Sarawak, probably in common with all other peoples not living (at least until recently) within broader political, institutional and religious structures which present them with orthodoxies ready-made, have a strong inclination towards philosophical speculation. This is a function both of practicality (they need to interact effectively with the world around them and for this they need a philosophical basis) and, arguably, of a quite general desire to comprehend the world in which they live. There is a good deal of variation in the ways in which individual Kelabit see the workings of the cosmos, but they are agreed in viewing these in a holistic way, and as driven by a unitary force which they call *lalud*. *Lalud* links the material and the unseen (or only partially perceptible) elements of the cosmos, which are two sides of the same coin. It flows through the material and the veiled parts of the cosmos. It coheres in certain sites, which are living entities. The presence of *lalud* is expressed through life; indeed, *lalud* and life cannot be disentangled. Living entities – cohesions of *lalud* – include humans, animals and plants; but they also include mountains and stones.

The Kelabit understanding of the nature of life and its relationship to the material world accords well with a focus on life as processual and in constant movement, as recently underlined by Ingold. However, the Kelabit also lay great emphasis on the way in which life coheres into distinct individuated entities, which have consciousness and directionality within the broader field of flow. Consciousness is an integral part of life; and living entities take a conscious hand in manipulating and managing the flow of life through them and other living entities. For the Kelabit, it is important to manipulate and manage the flow of *lalud*. The more a living entity is able to focus, manipulate and manage *lalud*, the more it shows itself to be a cohesion of *lalud*. This is expressed, at a human level, through the growing of rice and the feeding of rice meals from senior to junior kin, who are related as persons of higher and lower status. The Kelabit attitude to the Penan (Janowski 1997) emphasises the need for them to settle and grow rice. This expresses what they consider to be a benevolent desire to enable the Penan to become greater managers and manipulators of *lalud*, and to develop higher status.

Deleuze and Guattari (1983) have used the image of the rhizome, and Ingold (2003) that of the fungal mycelium – 'an ever-ramifying bundle of lines of growth' (Ingold 2008: 1807) – as ways of thinking about the nature of living entities in the context of an understanding of life and the cosmos as processual, flowing and constantly coming into being. Perhaps, building on this, Kelabit philosophical musings may help us, since they raise the question of directionality and encourage us to think further about this. For the Kelabit, living entities are part of a field of flow; within this, however, they are not only individuated but their individuation is inseparable from their role as direction-makers for the broader flow. The straightening of crooked rivers by leading Kelabit in the past is a metaphor for a broader cosmological role. The Kelabit view is that humans, like all living entities, are able to direct the flow of life of which they are part. By contrast to the Penan hunter-gatherers who live adjacent to them, the Kelabit add a further contention: that humans *ought* to take on a leading role in directing the flow of life if they are to fulfil their destiny. Why this should be regarded – not only by the Kelabit, but arguably by humans in a wide range of societies – as human destiny is another important question, which I cannot begin to address here.

Acknowledgements

I would like to thank the people of the Kelabit Highlands, particularly of the community of Pa' Dalih. I would also like to thank the UK Economic and Social Research Council, which funded my initial PhD fieldwork in 1986–88, and the British Academy and the UK Arts and Humanities Research Council, which have funded subsequent periods of fieldwork.

References

Anderson, B. 1972. Power, in *Culture and Politics in Indonesia*, edited by R. Benedict, C. Holt, O.G. Anderson and J. Siegel. Ithaca: Cornell University Press, 17–77.

Banks, E. 1937. Some Megalithic Remains from the Kelabit Country in Sarawak with Some Notes on the Kelabits themselves. *Sarawak Museum Journal*, 4, 411–37.

Barton, H. and Janowski, M. forthcoming. Reading Human Activity in the Landscape: Stone and Thunderstones in the Kelabit Highlands. *Indonesia and the Malay World*.

Bergson, H. 1911. *Creative Evolution*. London: Macmillan.

Bohm, D. 1980. *Wholeness and the Implicate Order*. London: Routledge and Kegan Paul.

Deleuze, G. and Guattari, F. 1983. *On the Line*. New York: Semiotext(e).

Deleuze, G. and Guattari, F. 2004. *A Thousand Plateaus: Capitalism and Schizophrenia*, trans. B. Massumi. London: Continuum [originally published as *Mille Plateaux*, vol. 2 of *Capitalisme et Schizophrénie*, Paris: Minuit, 1980].

Fox, J.J. (ed.) 1980. *The Flow of Life: Essays on Eastern Indonesia*. Harvard Studies in Cultural Anthropology. Cambridge, MA and London: Harvard University Press.

Geertz, C. 1980. *Negara*. Princeton: Princeton University Press.

Harrisson, T. 1958. A living Megalithic in upland Borneo. *Sarawak Museum Journal*, VIII, 694–702.

Harrisson, T. 1959. *World Within*. London: The Cresset Press.

Heidegger, M. 1971. *Poetry, Language, Thought*. New York: Harper and Row.

Hudson, A.B. 1992. Linguistic Relations among Bornean Peoples with Special Reference to Sarawak: An Interim Report, in *Shifting Patterns of Language Use in Borneo. Papers from the Second Bi-Ennial International Conference, Kota Kinabalu, Sabah, July 1992*, edited by P.W. Martin. Williamsburg: Borneo Research Council.

Ingold, T. 2003. Two Reflections on Ecological Knowledge, in *Nature Knowledge: Ethnoscience, Cognition, Identity*, edited by G. Sanga and G. Ortalli. New York: Berghahn, 301–11.

162 *Imagining Landscapes*

Ingold, T. 2004. Beyond Biology and Culture. The Meaning of Evolution in a Relational World. *Social Anthropology*, 12(2), 209–21.

Ingold, T. 2006. Rethinking the Animate, Re-animating Thought. *Ethnos*, 71(1), 9–20.

Ingold, T. 2007. Earth, Sky, Wind, and Weather. *Journal of the Royal Anthropological Institute*, 13(1), 19–38.

Ingold, T. 2008. Bindings against Boundaries: Entanglements of Life in an Open World. *Environment and Planning A*, 40, 1796–810.

Ingold, T. 2009. The Trouble with 'Evolutionary Biology'. *Anthropology Today*, 23(2), 13–17.

Ingold, T. 2010. Footprints through the Weather-World: Walking, Breathing, Knowing. *Journal of the Royal Anthropological Institute*, 16, 121–39.

Ingold, T. 2011. *Being Alive: Essays on Movement, Knowledge and Description*. London: Routledge.

Ingold, T. and Vergunst, J.L. 2008. Introduction, in *Ways of Walking*, edited by T. Ingold and J.L. Vergunst. London: Ashgate, 1–19.

Janowski, M. 1988. The Motivating Forces behind Changes in the Wet Rice Agricultural System in the Kelabit Highlands. *Sarawak Gazette*, CXIV(1504), 9–20.

Janowski, M. 1997. The Kelabit Attitude to the Penan: Forever children. *La Ricerca Folklorica*, 34, 55–8.

Janowski, M. 2004. The Wet and the Dry: The Development of Rice Growing in the Kelabit Highlands, Sarawak, in *Smallholders and Stockbreeders. Histories of Foodcrop and Livestock Farming in Southeast Asia*, edited by P. Boomgard and D. Henley. Leiden: KITLV, 139–62.

Janowski, M. 1995. The Hearth-Group, the Conjugal Couple and the Symbolism of the Rice Meal among the Kelabit of Sarawak, in *About the House: Levi-Strauss and Beyond. J. Carsten and S. Hugh-Jones*. Cambridge: Cambridge University Press, 84–104.

Janowski, M. 2007. Being 'Big', Being 'Good': Feeding, Kinship, Potency and Status among the Kelabit of Sarawak, in *Kinship and Food in Southeast Asia*, edited by M. Janowski and F. Kerlogue. Copenhagen: NIAS Press, 93–120.

Janowski, M. 2011. Rice Beer and Social Cohesion in the Kelabit Highlands, Sarawak, in *Liquid Bread: Beer and Brewing in Cross-Cultural Perspective*, edited by W. Schiefenhovel and H. Macbeth. Oxford and New York: Berghahn, 183–95.

Janowski, M. forthcoming. *Tukad Rini: Cosmic Traveller from the Heart of Borneo*. Kuching: Sarawak Museum.

Janowski, M. and Langub, L. 2011. Marks and Footprints in the Forest: The Kelabit and the Penan of Borneo, in *Why Cultivate? Anthropological and Archaeological Approaches to Foraging-Farming Transitions in Southeast Asia*, edited by G. Barker and M. Janowski. Cambridge: McDonald Institute for Archaeological Research, 121–32.

Lees, S. 1979. *Drunk before Dawn*. Sevenoaks, Kent: Overseas Missionary Fellowship.

Lian-Saging, R. 1976/77. *An Ethno-History of the Kelabit Tribe of Sarawak. A Brief Look at the Kelabit Tribe before World War II and after*. Graduation Exercise Submitted in Partial Fulfilment of the Requirements for the Degree of Bachelor of Arts, Hons., Jabatan Sejarah, University of Malaya, Kuala Lumpur.

Padoch, C. 1983. Agricultural Practices of the Kerayan Lun Dayeh. *Borneo Research Bulletin*, 15(1), 33–8.

Schneeberger, W.F. 1979. *Contributions to the Ethnology of Central Northeast Borneo*. Berne: Institute of Ethnology, University of Berne.

Sheets-Johnstone, M. 1998. *The Primacy of Movement*. Amsterdam: John Benjamins Publishing Company.

Index

Aberdeenshire 21, 22–4
ada' (Kelabit term for spirits) 147–50
Africa 68, 81
Al Awaynat 82, 84, 90
anaerobic digester 9, 68–9, 72
archaeology 24–6, 28, 36, 40–41, 44–7,
    51, 55, 80–82, 91, 101, 121, 124,
    126–7, 129, 145
    archaeological survey 54, 91
architecture 28, 39, 41, 45, 50, 53, 102
    vernacular architecture 39–40, 45, 50, 53
Area of Outstanding Natural Beauty
    (AONB) 123, 130, 134
aridity 13, 78–81, 83, 91–2
Arnol 42–3, 44–5, 52
art 4–5, 14, 16, 29, 33, 77
atmosphere 13

Bachelard, Gaston 20–21, 32
Bailies of Bennachie 21, 23–4, 26, 30–31,
    33
balio (Kelabit term for 'to transform from
    one form to another') 150
Bateson, Gregory 20
batu pera'it, see thunderstone, *under* stone
Belize 13, 97, 99–101, 103–04, 107, 110,
    114, 116
Bennachie (North-west Scotland) 6–8,
    21–6, 29–33, 36
Bergson, Henri 29, 157
Biagetti, Stefano 12
Bible 146–7
blackhouse(s) 7–8, 39–55
blood 103, 148, 152
Bohm, David 157
Borneo Evangelical Mission 144, 146
Brodgar, Ring of 9, 59, 63–4

Callanish, Isle of Lewis 41–2, 45
care 43, 69, 71–2, 109

cartography, mapping 28, 47–8, 86, 113
Chalcraft, Jasper Morgan 12
Childe, Gordon 41
Christianity 105n13, 144–7, 157
Clark, Andy 16–17
climate 12–13, 80, 83, 107, 131
coast 14, 35, 42, 48, 59, 100–01
coastal resources 127
cockles (*Cardium edule*) 123, 129, 131–2,
    135–6
cognition 2, 16, 19–20, 36
collaboration 55, 60, 61, 72–3
    between archaeologists and
        anthropologists 55, 145
commonty 23
community
    community-based archaeology 6, 19,
        21, 23–4, 36, 40
    community leaders 100
    communities' relationship with the
        landscape 67, 72–3, 108, 112–14
    communities' relationship with the past
        41, 47, 51–4
    imagined communities 101, 112
    nature of community 112–13
Comunn Eachdraidh Nis 47
consciousness 6, 20, 157–60
conservation 22–3, 109, 115, 121–3,
    126–7, 129, 135
correspondence 14–15
cosmology 157–9
croft, crofting 6, 8, 21, 23–4, 31–3, 39,
    42–3, 45–6, 48, 52–3
'cultural keystone species' 128–30
'culture heroes' 151
Cultured Rainforest project 145, 154
Curwen, Cecil 41, 49

Deleuze, Gilles 10–12, 157, 160–61
'demo' 66, 69, 73

development (as 'progress') 10, 13, 63, 68, 77, 81, 97–101, 104, 109, 111, 113, 115, 122
devolution 122
digestion 13–14
drawing 6–8, 19–21, 24–36
dwelling
 dwelling perspective 40, 47, 54
 (as noun) 7, 21, 35, 45, 103,
 (as verb) 21, 23, 36, 40, 46–7, 54–5, 77, 90

earth 39, 48, 53, 108, 145, 158
 earth cores (for palynology) 145
 earthworks 154–6
Edensor, Tim 35
environment (natural) 2–4, 6–8, 10, 12, 13, 14, 19–20, 31, 33, 42, 43, 61, 66–8, 77–80, 91–2, 97–9, 103, 105–06, 111–12, 115, 121, 122, 128, 129, 130, 137, 154
 agricultural environment 109
 coastal environment 124, 129
 sensory environment 12
ethnoarchaeology 80–81, 91
ethnography 12, 21, 74, 121, 124, 138
etuu (Kelabit term for mark on the landscape) 156
European Marine Energy Centre 60, 71
European marine sites 129

farming
 in Belize 105–06
 rice farming in Kelabit Highlands, Sarawak 143, 145, 154, 156
Fenton, Alexander 42–3, 53
Fermtouns 22–3
Fezzan 77, 82, 84
foresight 10–13
forest 13, 19, 23, 33–4, 103, 108–09, 112, 114, 146, 147–8
forestry 21, 23, 33–4, 113
Forestry Commission (UK) 23–4, 33
futures 9, 13, 59–60, 62, 64–8, 71–4, 98, 101

Gaelic 53
gathering/foraging 82, 105–06, 123, 125, 127, 133, 138

gender 31, 113, 127, 147–8
genealogies 156
Geographical Information/Positioning Systems (GIS/GPS) 47–8, 113
gestures 6–7, 9, 19–21, 24, 27–32, 34–6
Ghat 82, 84, 90
Gibson, James 2–3, 4, 5–7
Gombrich, Ernst 5
Gower, South Wales 14, 121–38
Gregory, Richard 5, 10
Guattari, Félix 10–12, 157, 160
guelta (rock pool in the Sahara) 84–6, 88, 91–92

Haines, Sophie 13
Harrisson, Tom 144
hearing 11–12
Hebrides, Hebridean 7, 40–42, 45–6, 53
Heidegger, Martin 21, 157
heritage 8, 23, 42, 45, 59, 61, 77, 99, 102, 103n8, 112, 121–2, 124, 129–30, 134–6
 heritage centre 47, 54
 heritage coast 14
 heritage foods 128
hierarchy 154
Historic Scotland 43
holism 116, 157, 160
houses 6–8, 13, 19–21, 23, 26, 28–33, 36, 74, 85, 107, 110, 114 (*see also* blackhouses and longhouses)
human-environment interaction 77, 80, 82, 92
hunting 11–12, 106, 125, 146, 148
Huntly 24

identity 89, 91, 99, 105, 107, 115–16, 128
 community identity 41–2, 53
 national identity 42, 72, 132, 134–6
 as a scholar 12
illusion 1, 4–5, 20, 135
image 1, 3–4, 6–8, 14, 16, 20–21, 23, 29–31, 36, 41, 45, 47, 51–2, 55, 160
imagination 1, 3–7, 10–14, 16, 19–21, 24, 26, 29, 32, 36, 39, 41, 99, 101, 115
infrastructure 69, 101, 114

Ingold, Tim 19, 20, 40, 47, 74, 137, 143, 147, 157, 158, 159, 160
innovation 13, 63, 66, 69, 145
Integrated Coastal Zone Management (ICZM) 122
island life 60, 60–63, 66–7, 69, 72
Italian Libyan Archaeological Mission in the Acacus and Messak 77

Janowski, Monica 15

kasekten (Javanese term for power) 147
Kelabit, of Sarawak 15–16, 143–60
kelit (Kelabit term for 'to perceive') 149
Kelapang river 154
Kerayan river 154
kinship 107, 148, 156
Klee, Paul 7

lalud (Kelabit term for life/cosmological power), *see* life
landscape 1–4, 8, 9, 10, 12, 13, 14, 15, 16–17, 19–21, 22, 23, 24, 28–9, 30, 31, 32, 33, 34, 35, 36, 39–40, 44–7, 49–55, 59–60, 63, 66–70, 72–4, 77–8, 84, 98, 121–2, 130, 132, 135, 136, 138, 145, 152
    animated landscapes 148–50, 156
    as apparatus 67
    future landscapes 9–10
    imagining landscape 2, 4, 6, 10, 13–14
    as laboratory 66, 67, 69, 70–73
    marking the landscape 154–6, 159
    melodic landscapes 10–11
    painting landscapes 1, 12
late baa (Kelabit term for wet rice field), *see* farming *under* rice farming in Kelabit Highlands
late luun (Kelabit term for dry rice field), *see* farming *under* rice farming in Kelabit Highlands
laver seaweed (*Porphyra umbicalis*) 14, 129, 132, 135
law 101
    coastal 123–26
learning 21, 24–5, 31, 35
Lefebvre, Henri 20, 113
lemulun (Kelabit term for humans) 145

Lewis, Scotland 7, 40–55
Lian-Saging, Bob 146n6
Libya 12, 77–92
life 7, 8, 14, 15
    flow/currents of life 11, 15, 143, 147, 148, 152, 156–58
    human life 20, 23–4, 32, 39–40, 42, 45, 52–4, 60, 62, 66, 67, 86, 89–90, 101, 107, 122, 124, 127–28, 136, 143, 154, 156–58
    individuation of life 143, 157–60
    lalud (life/cosmological power) 15, 147–61
    lines of life 1, 9, 15, 16, 157–60
    ulun (human way of life) 154, 156
lintels (of houses) 21–3
Llanelli, Wales 12, 133–36
logging 109n16, 112n19, 156
Long, Richard 16
longhouses 143, 147, 148
Lun Bawang 146
Lun Dayeh 146

Magritte, René 1–4
mana 147
Marine and Coastal Access Bill 126, 137
Marine Conservation Zone (MCZ) 123, 126, 127
marine renewable energy 60, 61, 64, 70, 72
Mass Observation 144n2
Massey, Doreen 14, 32
material culture 8, 42–3, 51, 54–5, 92, 129
material world (as opposed to spirit world) 147
materials 10–11, 15, 19, 26, 34, 39, 40, 50–53, 105, 110, 128, 130, 157
McLean, Stuart 14
memory 2, 4, 8, 16, 19, 21, 35, 52, 54, 89, 91, 98, 105, 108
menegag (Kelabit term for spirit water serpent) 148
Merleau-Ponty, Maurice 10–11, 14, 98
metaphysics 14, 128, 130
    metaphysical speculation 145–6
mind 2–7, 13, 16, 19–20, 31, 78, 103, 159
Mitchell, Sir Arthur 40
'mobile, mutable/immutable' 68
Morton, H.B. 134–6

monks, of mediaeval Europe 13–14
mountains 14, 15, 16, 21, 78, 91, 103, 105,
        107, 146, 150
    mountains as animate beings 150, 158,
        160
    prayer on mountains 146
movement 7–9, 13, 15–16, 20, 22, 32, 147,
        157, 160
mulun (Kelabit term for 'to live') 147, 156
musical composition 11

naga (SE Asian spirit water serpent) 148
narrative 9, 33, 74, 98, 121
National Museum of Scotland 42
National Trust 135
    for Scotland 41–2, 45
ne'ar (Kelabit term for 'to see') 149
Ness 40–55
Ness Archaeological Landscape Survey
        46–8, 54

O'Connor, Kaori 14
Ohnuki-Tierney, Emiko 121
oral history 21, 23
origin story 63–4, 148, 151
Orkney Islands 9–10, 14, 15, 22, 59–74

Pa' Dalih (Sarawak, Malaysia) 143–6, 154,
        156, 159
painting 1, 4–5, 10, 12
palaeo-channels, of river 154
pastoralism 81–2, 91
Penan 152, 156, 158, 160
perception 1–7, 12–14, 16, 19, 46, 78, 80,
        92, 98, 108, 115, 124, 133, 136,
        138, 148–9
'persistent places' 129–30, 136
phenomenology 35, 99
    of imagination 20
picture 1–2, 5, 8, 16, 19, 20, 22–3, 54, 130,
        145
pigs 148
pilgrimage 20, 146
place 2, 19, 21, 22, 26, 60, 62–4, 69, 72–3,
        77, 80, 82, 89, 102–03, 107, 121,
        125–6, 130, 133, 135–6
Poller, Tessa 7–8
poong (Kelabit term for animal) 145

Popper, Karl 5
power, cosmological 147–71
practice, material 16, 24, 49, 59, 62, 69, 72,
        98–9, 146
    anthropological/ethnographic practice
        12
    archaeological practice 24, 26, 35, 40,
        45–7, 51, 54–5, 59
    drawing practice 31
prayer 146

Rapaport, Herman 16
representation 1, 3–5, 7–8, 10, 14–16, 20,
        29, 33, 97–8, 115, 136
rice 105, 148 (*see also* farming)
    rice beer 148, 154
    rice and cosmological power 154, 160
    rice and human kinship 148
    rice meal and feasting 150, 154, 155–6,
        160
rock art 12, 73, 77, 80, 92

Sahara 77, 79–82, 84, 86, 90–92
Sahlins, Marshall 137
sakti (Balinese term for power) 147
Sarawak Museum 144n2
scale 20, 23, 25, 28, 47, 64, 71, 123, 154
Schama, Simon 1–3, 16
science, modern 157, 159
Scotland 6, 19, 21, 22, 23, 24, 33, 53, 59,
        60, 66, 122, 126
Scottish Highlands and Islands 39, 43
seaweed 121, 123, 127, 129–30, 132,
        136–8
Second World War 42, 47, 50, 144n2, 146
settlement 6, 23, 45, 49–53, 89–92, 100,
        103, 107–09, 127, 143, 145
shamans 148
Sheets-Johnstone, Maxine 157
shellfish 121–3, 125, 127, 130–31, 133,
        136–7
Skye, Isle of 53
Special Operations Executive 144
spirits and the spirit world 103–04,
        105n13, 108, 146–50, 156, 159
symbiosis 72
stone 6, 9, 15, 25–34, 36, 39, 48, 51, 53,
        59, 59–61, 63–5, 149–60

megaliths 143, 145, 151
  'stone rain' (*udan batu*) (hail) 150
  thunderstone 152
Sweden 33

Tadrart Acacus 77, 78, 82–5, 90–92
terroir 14, 128
thatch 13, 45, 53, 110
thunder and lightning 150, 152
Tilley, Christopher 33, 35–6
touch 11–12
transformation 14, 121, 150
Tuareg, Tel-Adrart 12–13, 77–92
turf 28, 35, 39, 53
Turner, Nancy 127–8

Uexküll, Jakob von 10
ulun (Kelabit term for human way of life),
  see life

Vergunst, Jo 6–8
vision
  of future/other reality 5, 9, 11, 13, 15,
    28, 62–3, 72, 98, 122, 138
  as sight 2, 4, 6, 11, 12, 149

wadi Teshuinat 84, 89, 90–91
walking 16, 22–3, 26, 35–6, 47, 51, 62–3,
  67, 72–4, 103, 136, 149
water 9, 13, 14–15, 31, 63, 65–6, 71,
  80–84, 86, 88, 90, 92, 108, 112,
  125, 137, 148–50
Watts, Laura 9
Willerslev, Rane 11–12
World Heritage Site 59
Wylie, John 35